F I N A L

C R I S I S

FINAL CRISIS
ROGUES'
REVENGE

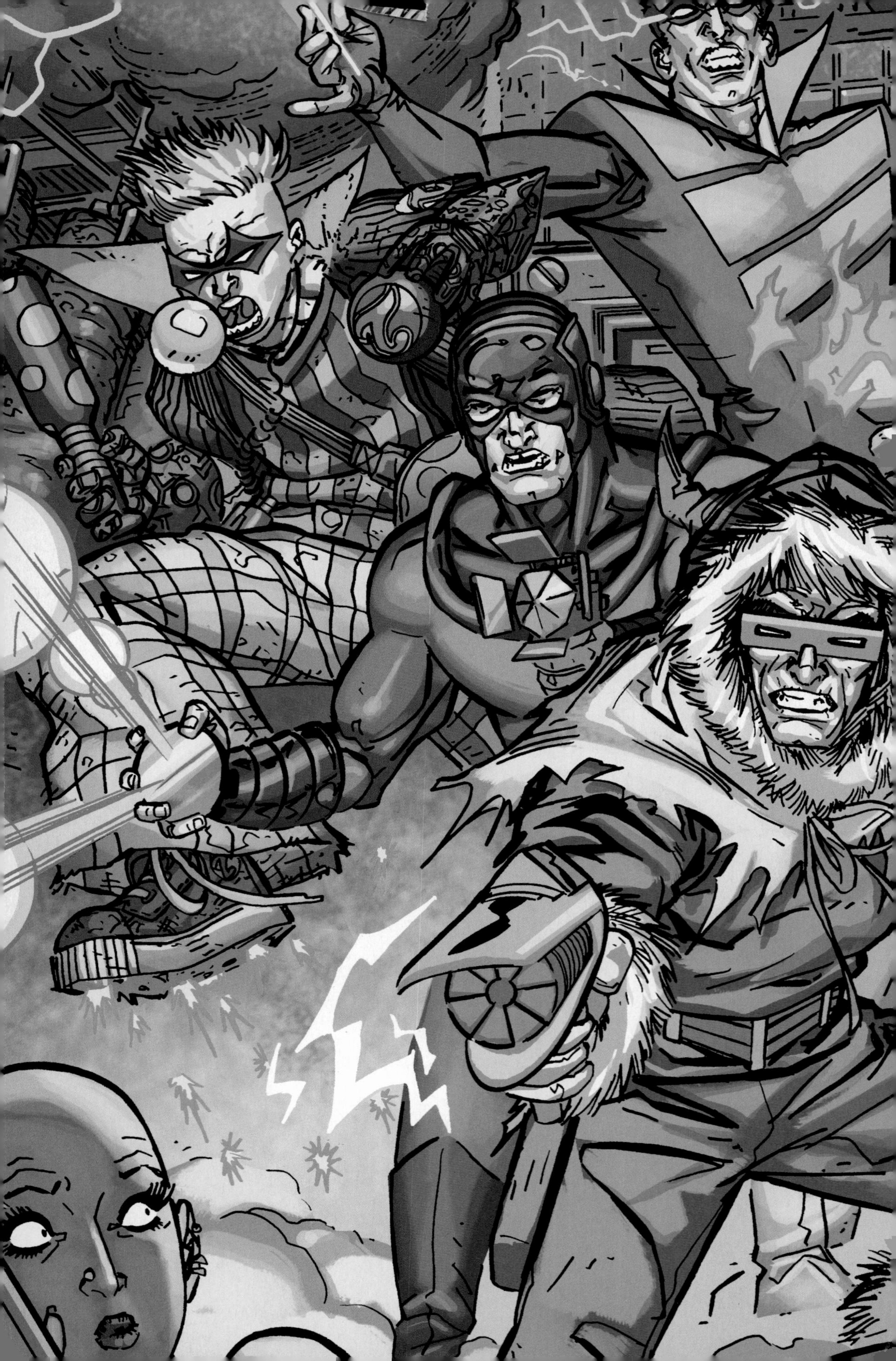

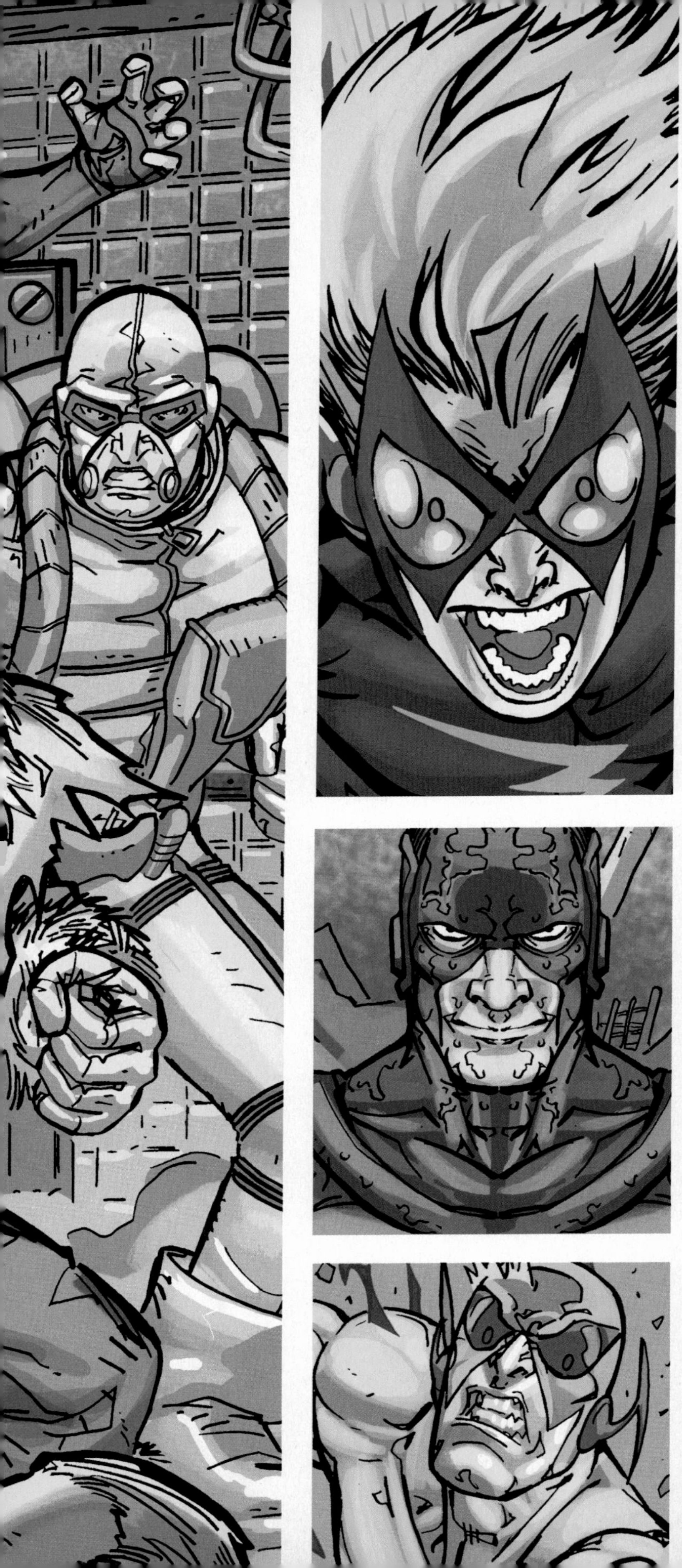

FINAL CRISIS ROGUES' REVENGE

Geoff Johns
Writer

ROGUES' REVENGE

Scott Kolins
Artist and Covers

Dave McCaig
Colorist

Nick J. Napolitano
Letterer

ABSOLUTE ZERO

Scott Kolins
Penciller

Dan Panosian
Inker

James Sinclair
Colorist

Digtal Chameleon
Separator

Gaspar
Letterer

ROGUE PROFILE: ZOOM

Scott Kolins
Penciller

Doug Hazlewood
Inker

James Sinclair
Colorist & Separator

Kurt Hathaway
Letterer

Dan DiDio   Senior VP-Executive Editor
Joey Cavalieri   Editor-original series
Chris Conroy   Assistant Editor-original series
Sean Mackiewicz   Editor-collected edition
Robbin Brosterman   Senior Art Director
Paul Levitz   President & Publisher
Georg Brewer   VP-Design & DC Direct Creative
Richard Bruning   Senior VP-Creative Director
Patrick Caldon   Executive VP-Finance & Operations
Chris Caramalis   VP-Finance
John Cunningham   VP-Marketing
Terri Cunningham   VP-Managing Editor
Amy Genkins   Senior VP-Business & Legal Affairs
Alison Gill   VP-Manufacturing
David Hyde   VP-Publicity
Hank Kanalz   VP-General Manager, WildStorm
Jim Lee   Editorial Director-WildStorm
Gregory Noveck   Senior VP-Creative Affairs
Sue Pohja   VP-Book Trade Sales
Steve Rotterdam   Senior VP-Sales & Marketing
Cheryl Rubin   Senior VP-Brand Management
Alysse Soll   VP-Advertising & Custom Publishing
Jeff Trojan   VP-Business Development, DC Direct
Bob Wayne   VP-Sales

Cover by Scott Kolins

FINAL CRISIS: ROGUES' REVENGE

DC Comics, 1700 Broadway, New York, NY 10019
A Warner Bros. Entertainment Company
Printed in the USA. First Printing.

ISBN: 978-1-4012-2333-5
SC ISBN: 978-1-4012-2334-2

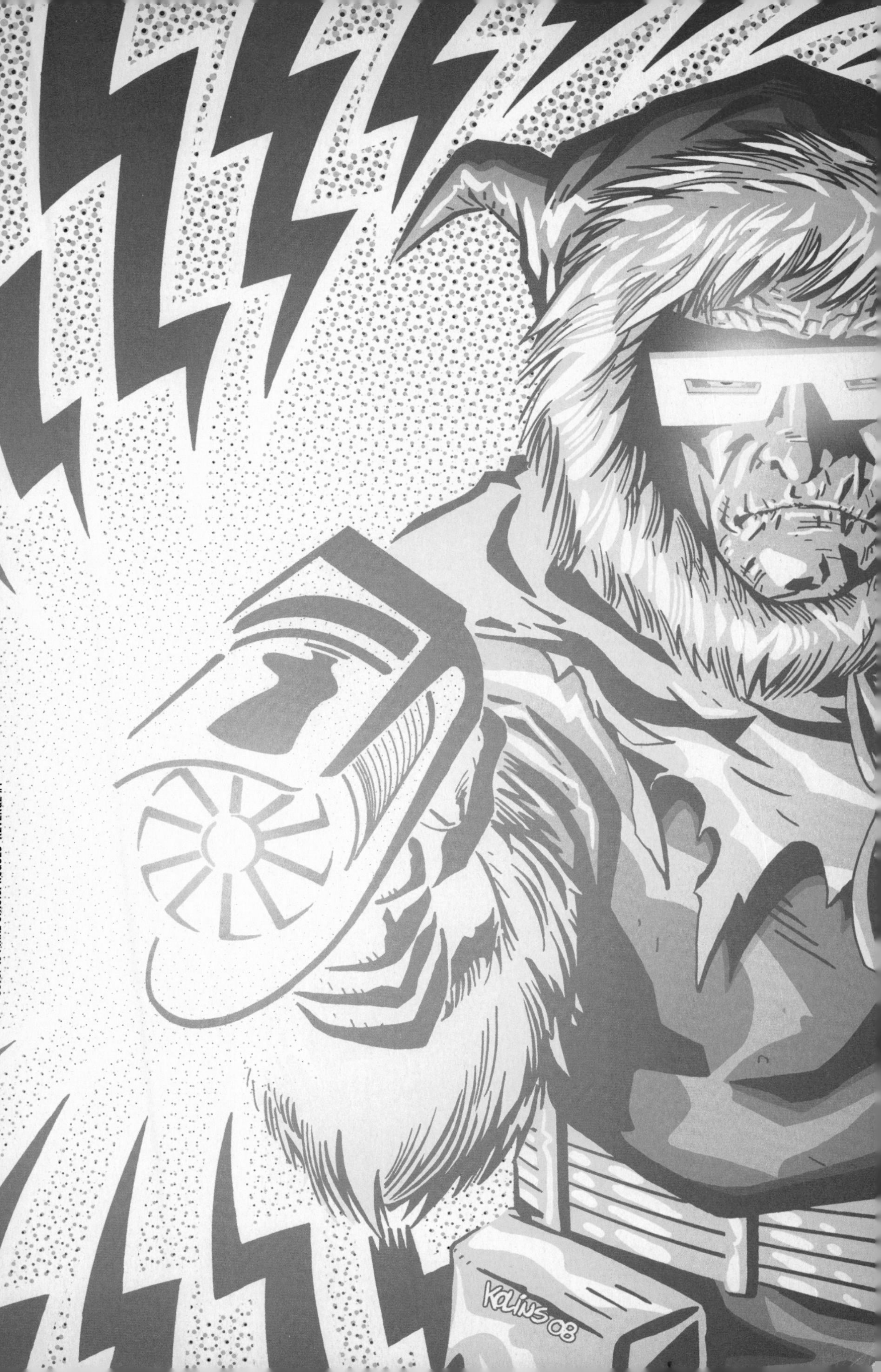
KOLINS 08

Cover to FINAL CRISIS: ROGUES' REVENGE #1

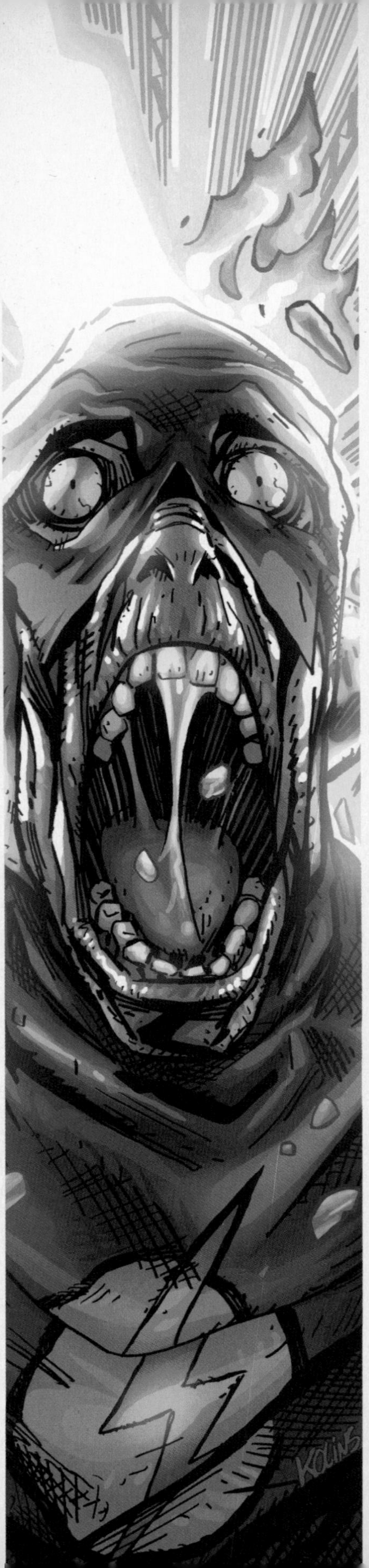
KOLINS

Sliver cover to FINAL CRISIS: ROGUES' REVENGE #1

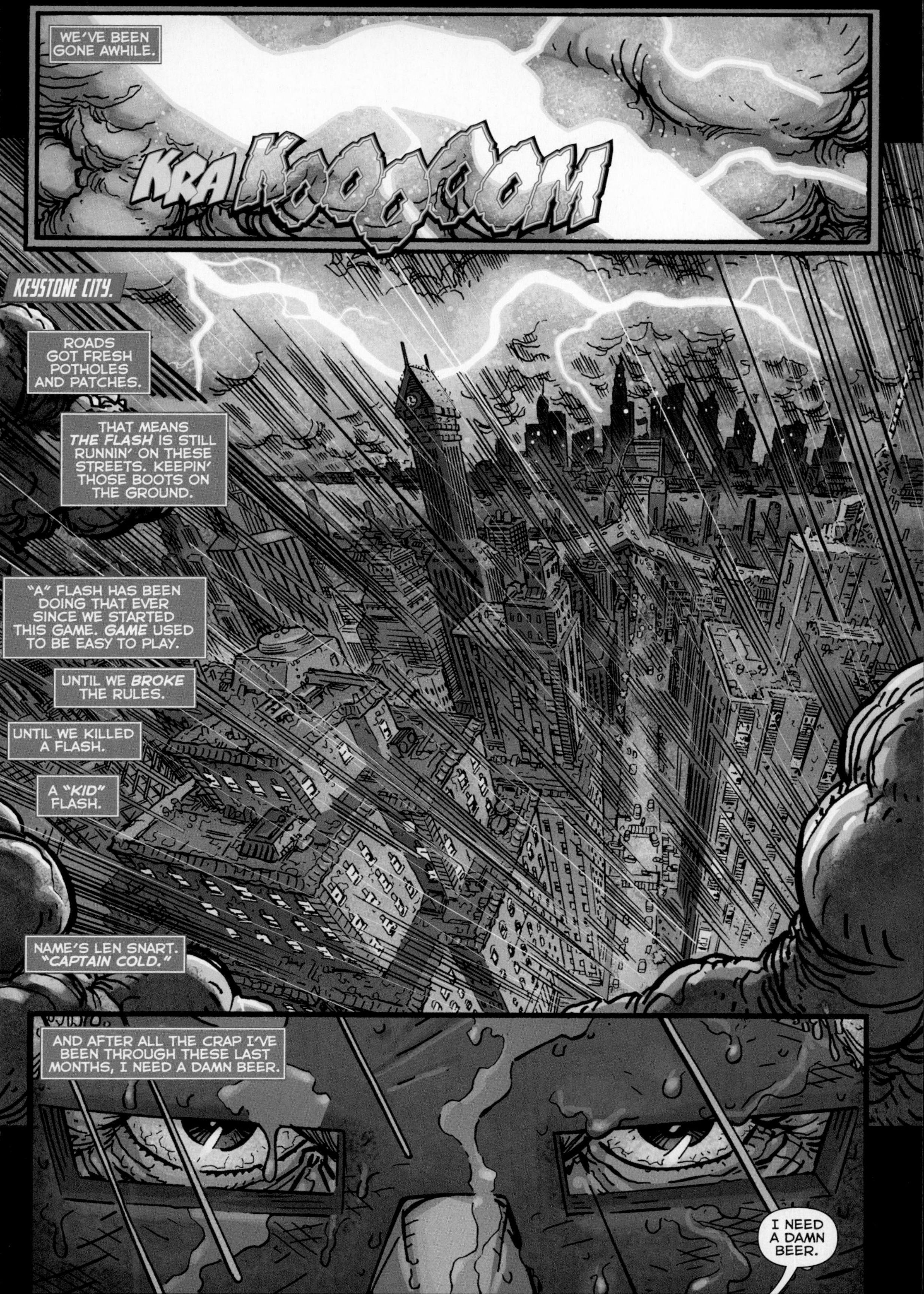
WE'VE BEEN GONE AWHILE.
KRAKOOOOOM
KEYSTONE CITY.
ROADS GOT FRESH POTHOLES AND PATCHES.
THAT MEANS THE FLASH IS STILL RUNNIN' ON THESE STREETS. KEEPIN' THOSE BOOTS ON THE GROUND.
"A" FLASH HAS BEEN DOING THAT EVER SINCE WE STARTED THIS GAME. GAME USED TO BE EASY TO PLAY.
UNTIL WE BROKE THE RULES.
UNTIL WE KILLED A FLASH.
A "KID" FLASH.
NAME'S LEN SNART. "CAPTAIN COLD."
AND AFTER ALL THE CRAP I'VE BEEN THROUGH THESE LAST MONTHS, I NEED A DAMN BEER.
I NEED A DAMN BEER.

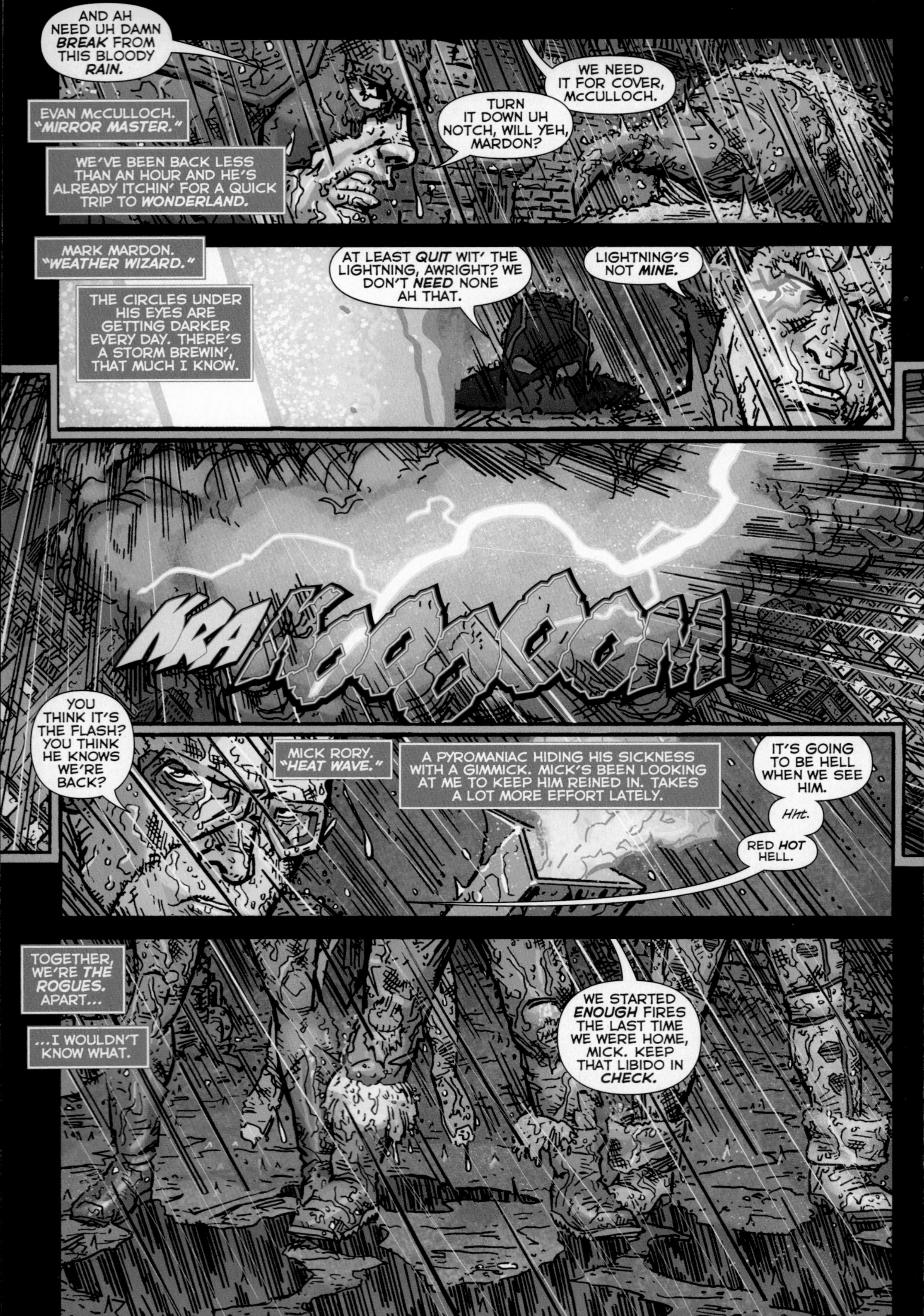

AND AH NEED UH DAMN *BREAK* FROM THIS BLOODY *RAIN.*
EVAN McCULLOCH. *"MIRROR MASTER."*
WE'VE BEEN BACK LESS THAN AN HOUR AND HE'S ALREADY ITCHIN' FOR A QUICK TRIP TO *WONDERLAND.*
TURN IT DOWN UH NOTCH, WILL YEH, MARDON?
WE NEED IT FOR COVER, McCULLOCH.
MARK MARDON. *"WEATHER WIZARD."*
THE CIRCLES UNDER HIS EYES ARE GETTING DARKER EVERY DAY. THERE'S A STORM BREWIN', THAT MUCH I KNOW.
AT LEAST *QUIT* WIT' THE LIGHTNING, AWRIGHT? WE DON'T *NEED* NONE AH THAT.
LIGHTNING'S NOT *MINE.*
KRAKOOSHOOM
YOU THINK IT'S THE FLASH? YOU THINK HE KNOWS WE'RE BACK?
MICK RORY. *"HEAT WAVE."*
A PYROMANIAC HIDING HIS SICKNESS WITH A GIMMICK. MICK'S BEEN LOOKING AT ME TO KEEP HIM REINED IN. TAKES A LOT MORE EFFORT LATELY.
IT'S GOING TO BE HELL WHEN WE SEE HIM.
Hht.
RED *HOT* HELL.
TOGETHER, WE'RE *THE ROGUES.* APART...
...I WOULDN'T KNOW WHAT.
WE STARTED *ENOUGH* FIRES THE LAST TIME WE WERE HOME, MICK. KEEP THAT LIBIDO IN *CHECK.*

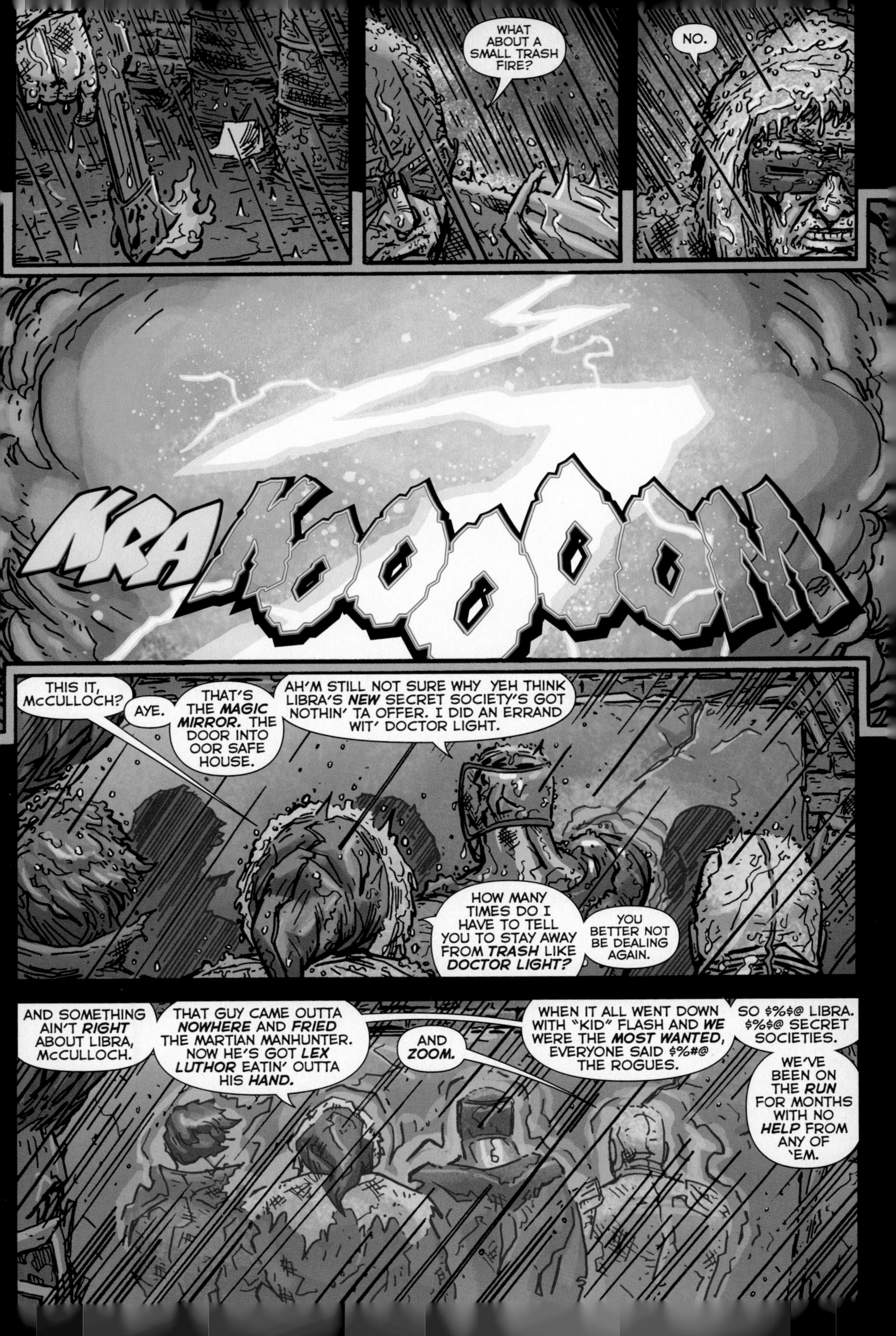
WHAT ABOUT A SMALL TRASH FIRE?
NO.
KRAKOOOOOM
THIS IT, McCULLOCH?
AYE.
THAT'S THE MAGIC MIRROR. THE DOOR INTO OOR SAFE HOUSE.
AH'M STILL NOT SURE WHY YEH THINK LIBRA'S NEW SECRET SOCIETY'S GOT NOTHIN' TA OFFER. I DID AN ERRAND WIT' DOCTOR LIGHT.
HOW MANY TIMES DO I HAVE TO TELL YOU TO STAY AWAY FROM TRASH LIKE DOCTOR LIGHT?
YOU BETTER NOT BE DEALING AGAIN.
AND SOMETHING AIN'T RIGHT ABOUT LIBRA, McCULLOCH.
THAT GUY CAME OUTTA NOWHERE AND FRIED THE MARTIAN MANHUNTER. NOW HE'S GOT LEX LUTHOR EATIN' OUTTA HIS HAND.
AND ZOOM.
WHEN IT ALL WENT DOWN WITH "KID" FLASH AND WE WERE THE MOST WANTED, EVERYONE SAID $%#@ THE ROGUES.
SO $%$@ LIBRA. $%$@ SECRET SOCIETIES.
WE'VE BEEN ON THE RUN FOR MONTHS WITH NO HELP FROM ANY OF 'EM.

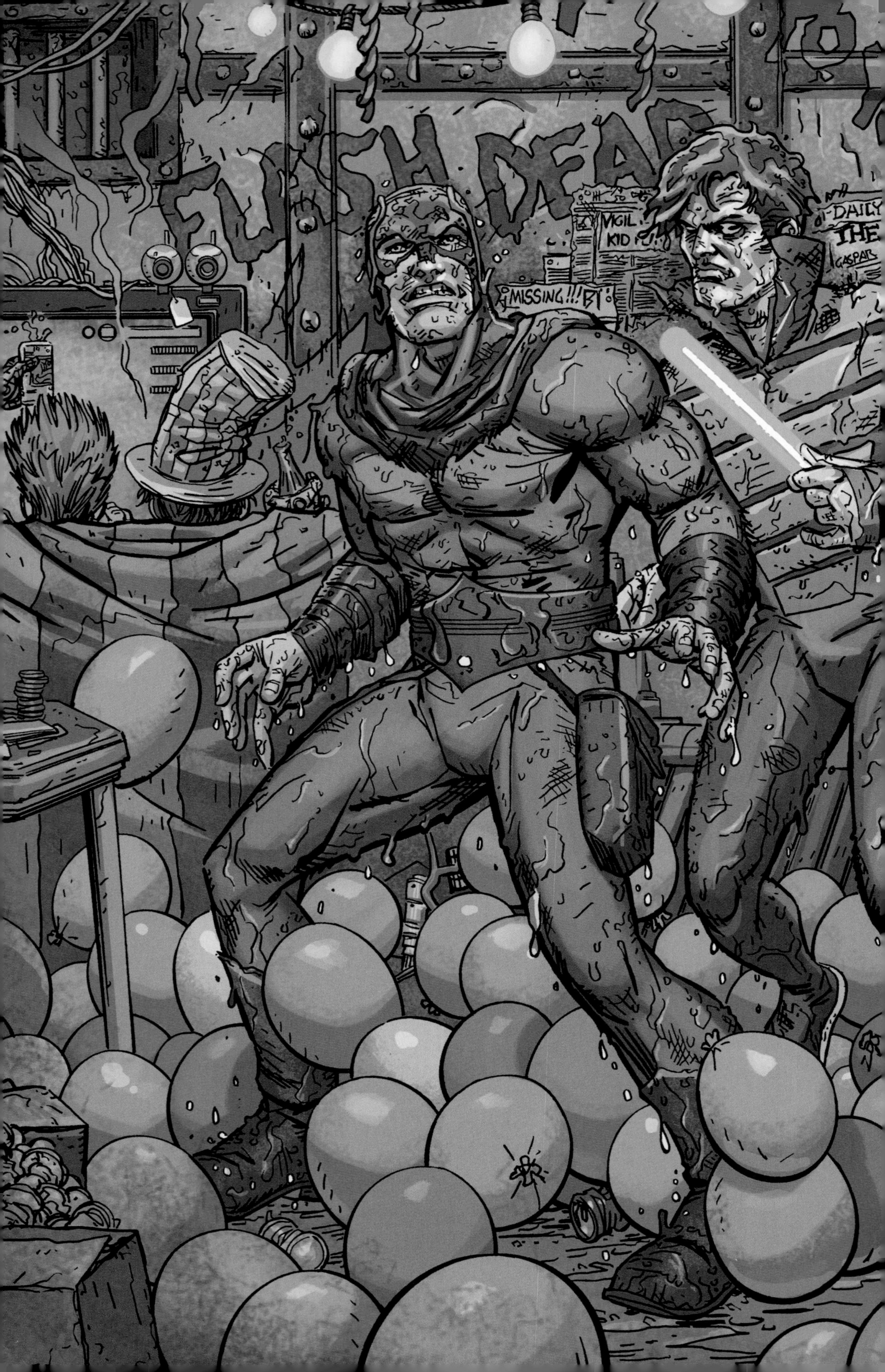
VIGIL
KID
MISSING!!!
DAILY
THE

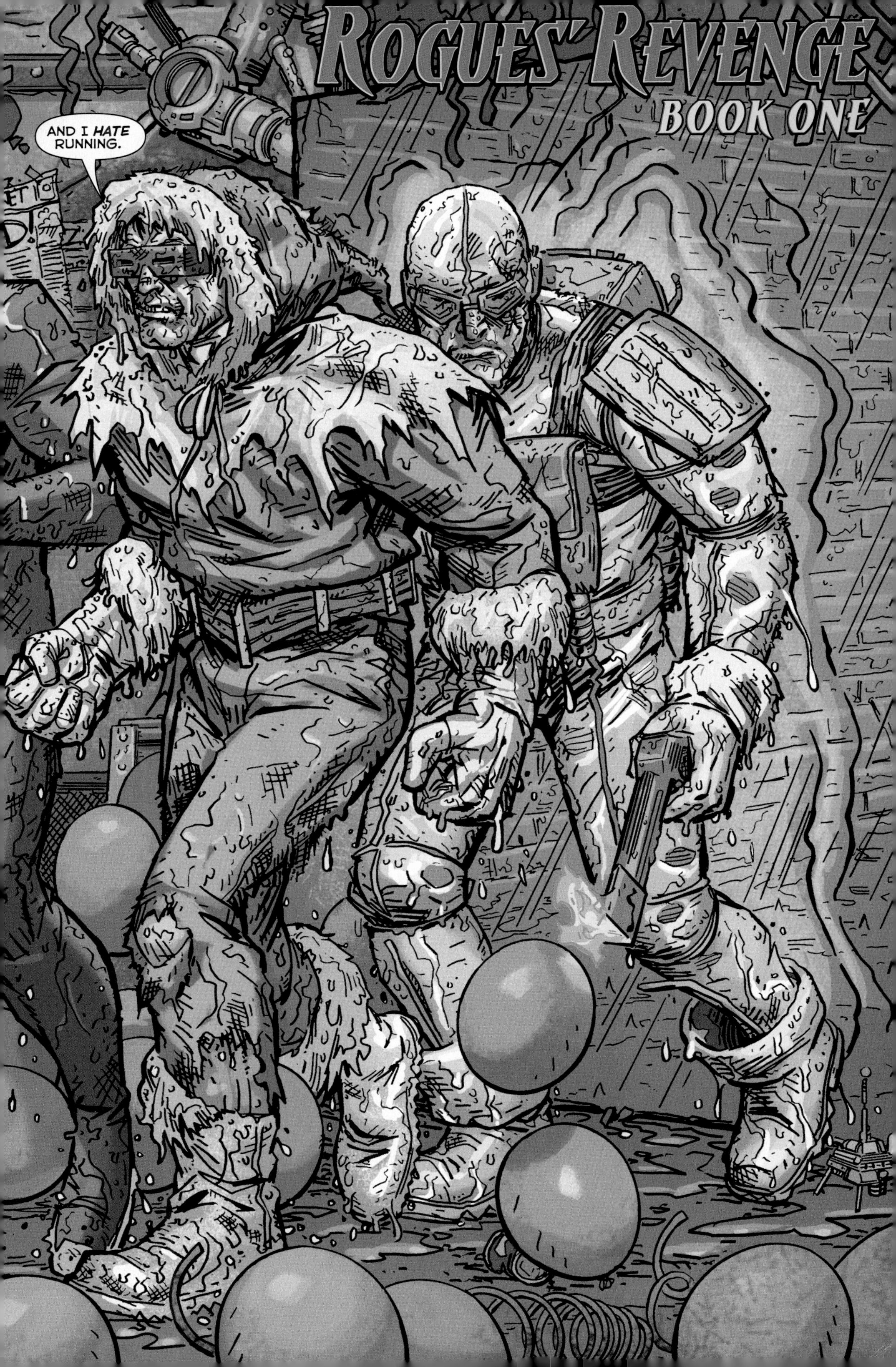
ROGUES' REVENGE
BOOK ONE
AND I HATE RUNNING.

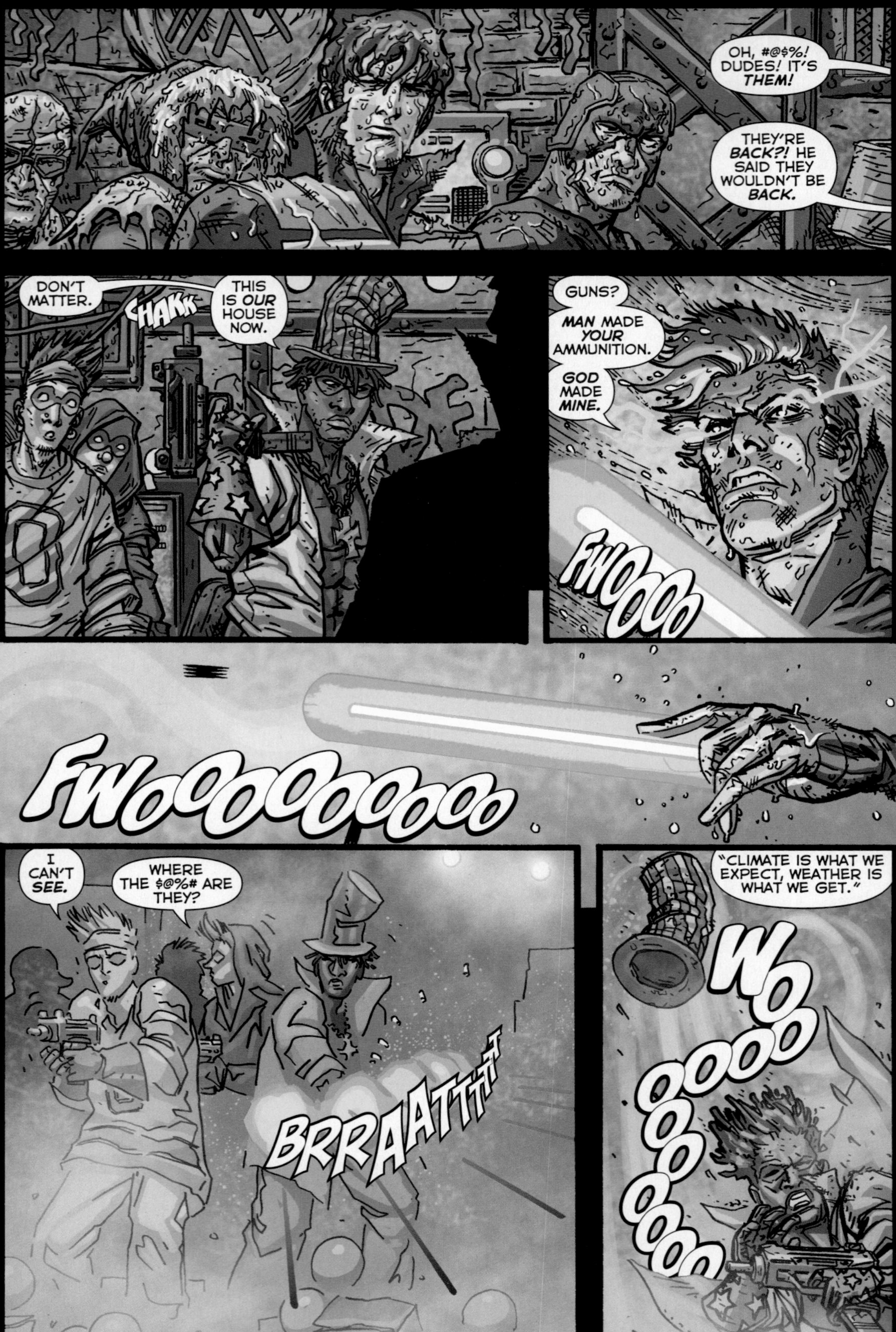
OH, #@$%! DUDES! IT'S THEM!
THEY'RE BACK?! HE SAID THEY WOULDN'T BE BACK.
DON'T MATTER.
THIS IS OUR HOUSE NOW.
CHAKK
GUNS?
MAN MADE YOUR AMMUNITION.
GOD MADE MINE.
FWOOOOO
FWOOOOOOOOOOO
I CAN'T SEE.
WHERE THE $@%# ARE THEY?
BRRAATTTTT
"CLIMATE IS WHAT WE EXPECT, WEATHER IS WHAT WE GET."
WOOOOOOOOOOOO

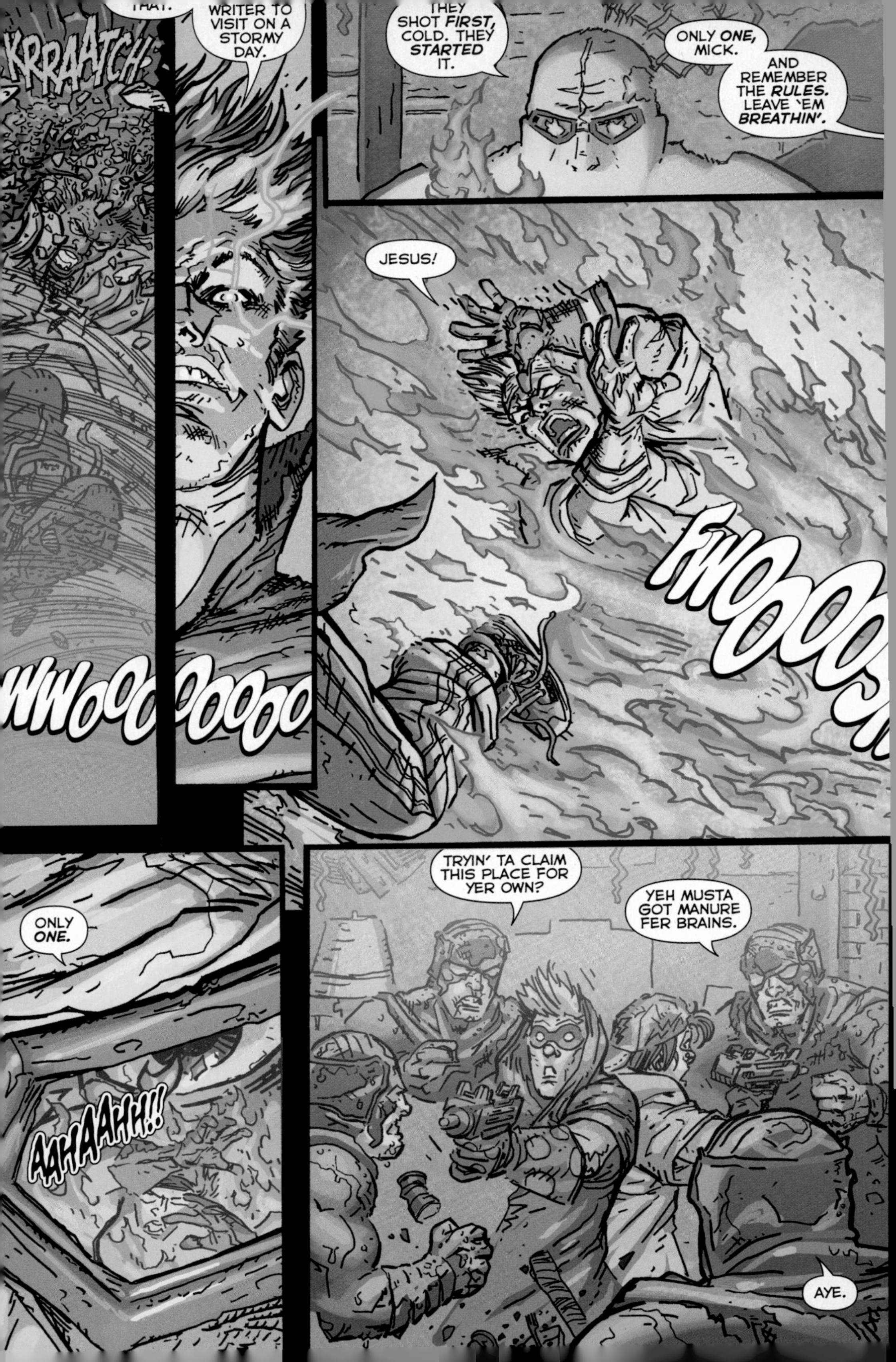
KRRAATCH
THAT.
WRITER TO VISIT ON A STORMY DAY.
THEY SHOT FIRST, COLD. THEY STARTED IT.
ONLY ONE, MICK.
AND REMEMBER THE RULES. LEAVE 'EM BREATHIN'.
JESUS!
WWOOOOOOOOOO
FWOOOOOOSH
ONLY ONE.
AAHAAAHH!!
TRYIN' TA CLAIM THIS PLACE FOR YER OWN?
YEH MUSTA GOT MANURE FER BRAINS.
AYE.

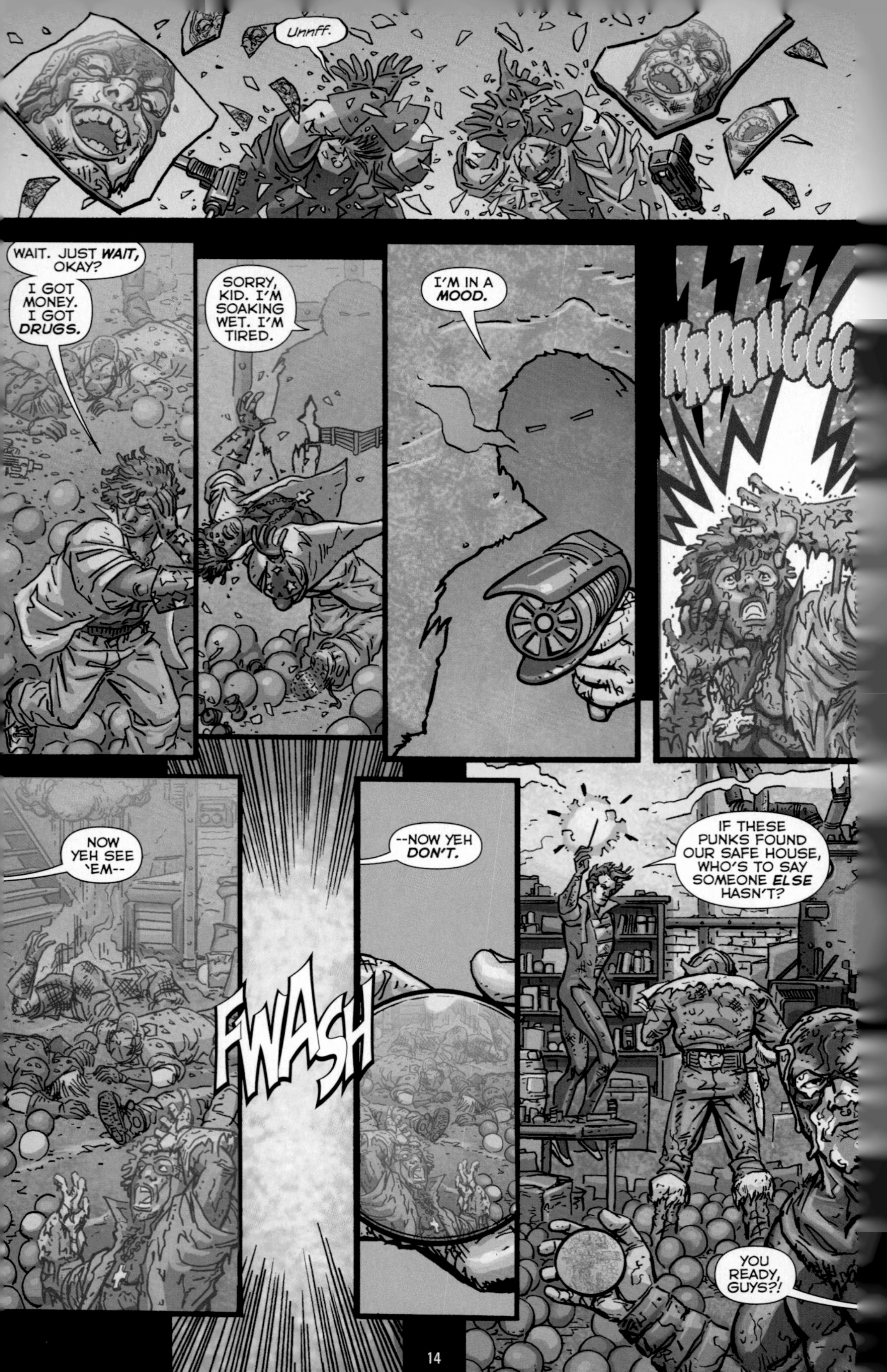
Unnff.
WAIT. JUST WAIT, OKAY?
I GOT MONEY. I GOT DRUGS.
SORRY, KID. I'M SOAKING WET. I'M TIRED.
I'M IN A MOOD.
KRRRNGGG
NOW YEH SEE 'EM--
FWASH
--NOW YEH DON'T.
IF THESE PUNKS FOUND OUR SAFE HOUSE, WHO'S TO SAY SOMEONE ELSE HASN'T?
YOU READY, GUYS?!

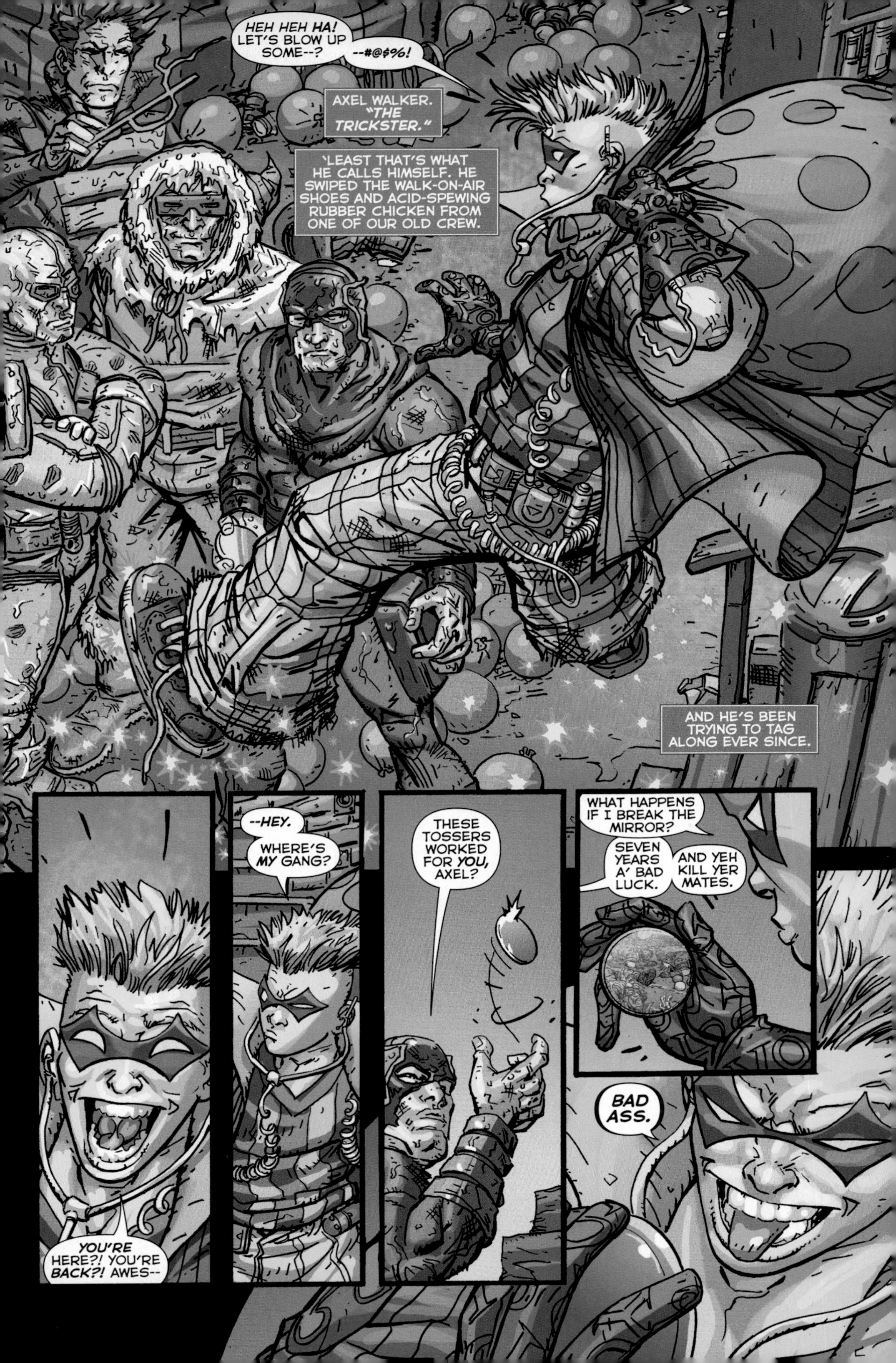
HEH HEH HA! LET'S BLOW UP SOME--?
--#@$%!
AXEL WALKER. "THE TRICKSTER."
'LEAST THAT'S WHAT HE CALLS HIMSELF. HE SWIPED THE WALK-ON-AIR SHOES AND ACID-SPEWING RUBBER CHICKEN FROM ONE OF OUR OLD CREW.
AND HE'S BEEN TRYING TO TAG ALONG EVER SINCE.
YOU'RE HERE?! YOU'RE BACK?! AWES--
--HEY.
WHERE'S MY GANG?
THESE TOSSERS WORKED FOR YOU, AXEL?
WHAT HAPPENS IF I BREAK THE MIRROR?
SEVEN YEARS A' BAD LUCK.
AND YEH KILL YER MATES.
BAD ASS.

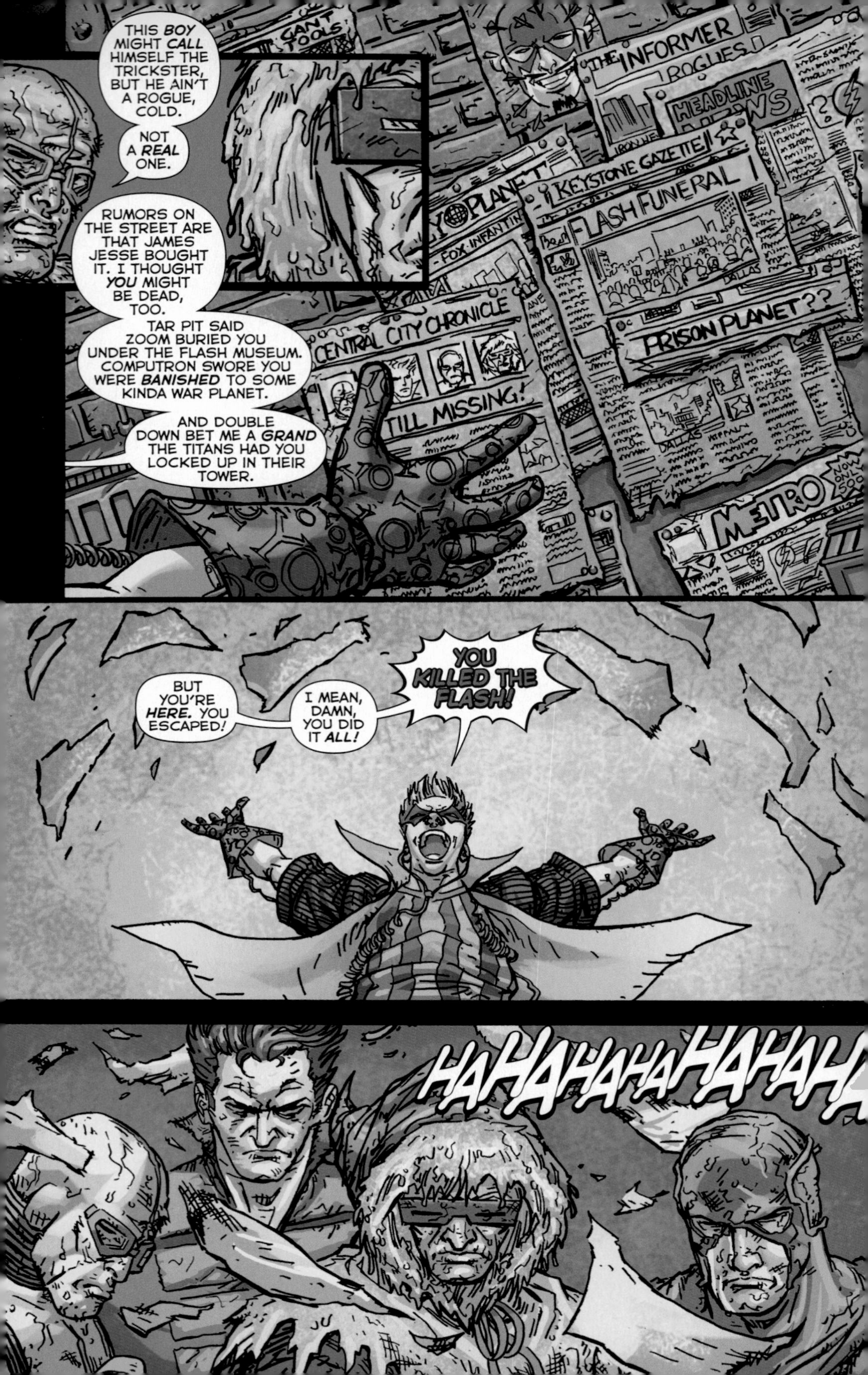
THIS BOY MIGHT CALL HIMSELF THE TRICKSTER, BUT HE AIN'T A ROGUE, COLD.
NOT A REAL ONE.
RUMORS ON THE STREET ARE THAT JAMES JESSE BOUGHT IT. I THOUGHT YOU MIGHT BE DEAD, TOO.
TAR PIT SAID ZOOM BURIED YOU UNDER THE FLASH MUSEUM. COMPUTRON SWORE YOU WERE BANISHED TO SOME KINDA WAR PLANET.
AND DOUBLE DOWN BET ME A GRAND THE TITANS HAD YOU LOCKED UP IN THEIR TOWER.
THE INFORMER
ROGUES
HEADLINE NEWS
KEYSTONE GAZETTE
FLASH FUNERAL
CENTRAL CITY CHRONICLE
PRISON PLANET??
METRO
BUT YOU'RE HERE. YOU ESCAPED!
I MEAN, DAMN, YOU DID IT ALL!
YOU KILLED THE FLASH!
HAHAHAHAHAHAHAH

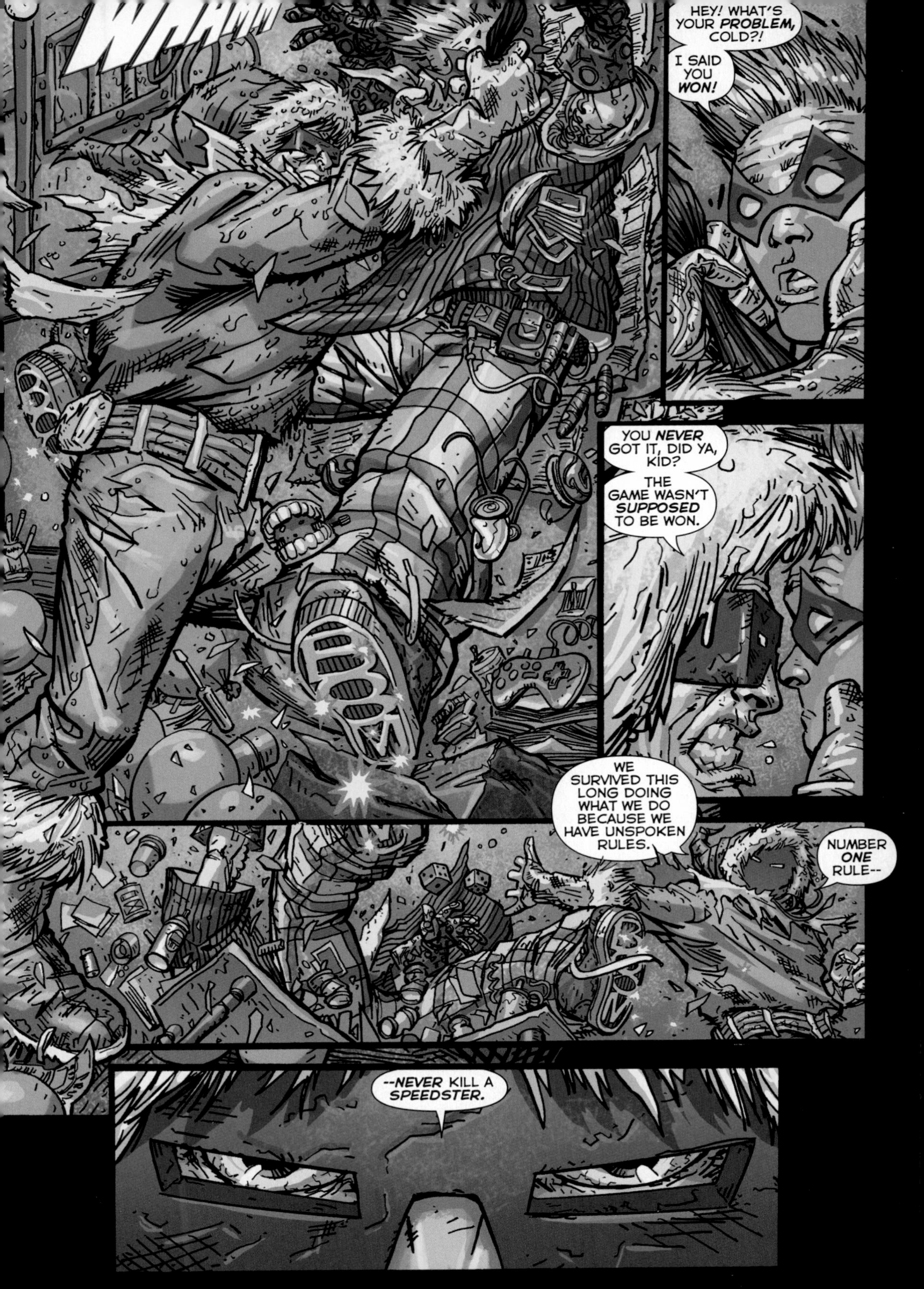
WHAMM
HEY! WHAT'S YOUR PROBLEM, COLD?!
I SAID YOU WON!
YOU NEVER GOT IT, DID YA, KID?
THE GAME WASN'T SUPPOSED TO BE WON.
WE SURVIVED THIS LONG DOING WHAT WE DO BECAUSE WE HAVE UNSPOKEN RULES.
NUMBER ONE RULE--
--NEVER KILL A SPEEDSTER.

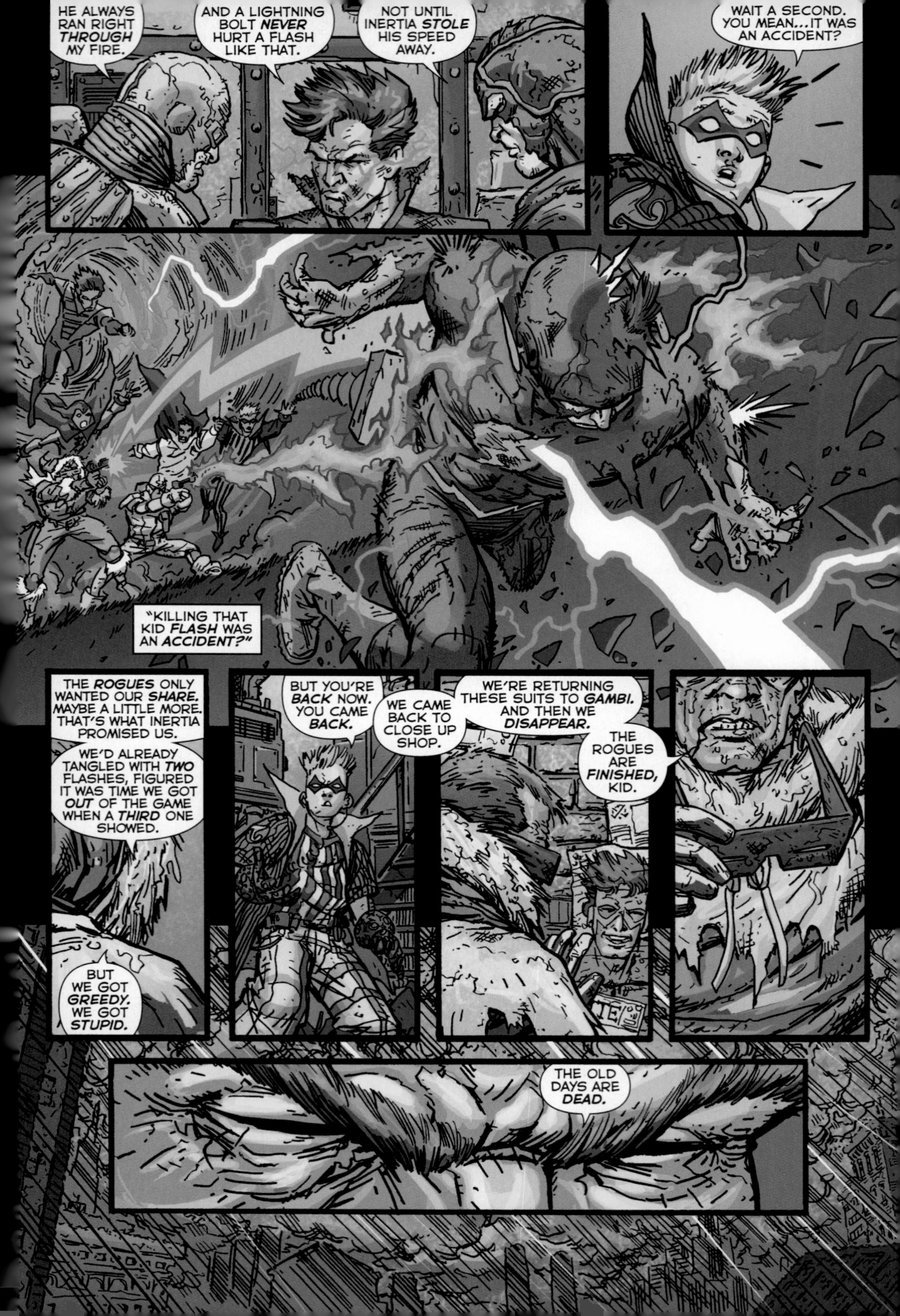
HE ALWAYS RAN RIGHT THROUGH MY FIRE.
AND A LIGHTNING BOLT NEVER HURT A FLASH LIKE THAT.
NOT UNTIL INERTIA STOLE HIS SPEED AWAY.
WAIT A SECOND. YOU MEAN...IT WAS AN ACCIDENT?
"KILLING THAT KID FLASH WAS AN ACCIDENT?"
THE ROGUES ONLY WANTED OUR SHARE. MAYBE A LITTLE MORE. THAT'S WHAT INERTIA PROMISED US.
WE'D ALREADY TANGLED WITH TWO FLASHES, FIGURED IT WAS TIME WE GOT OUT OF THE GAME WHEN A THIRD ONE SHOWED.
BUT WE GOT GREEDY. WE GOT STUPID.
BUT YOU'RE BACK NOW. YOU CAME BACK.
WE CAME BACK TO CLOSE UP SHOP.
WE'RE RETURNING THESE SUITS TO GAMBI. AND THEN WE DISAPPEAR.
THE ROGUES ARE FINISHED, KID.
THE OLD DAYS ARE DEAD.

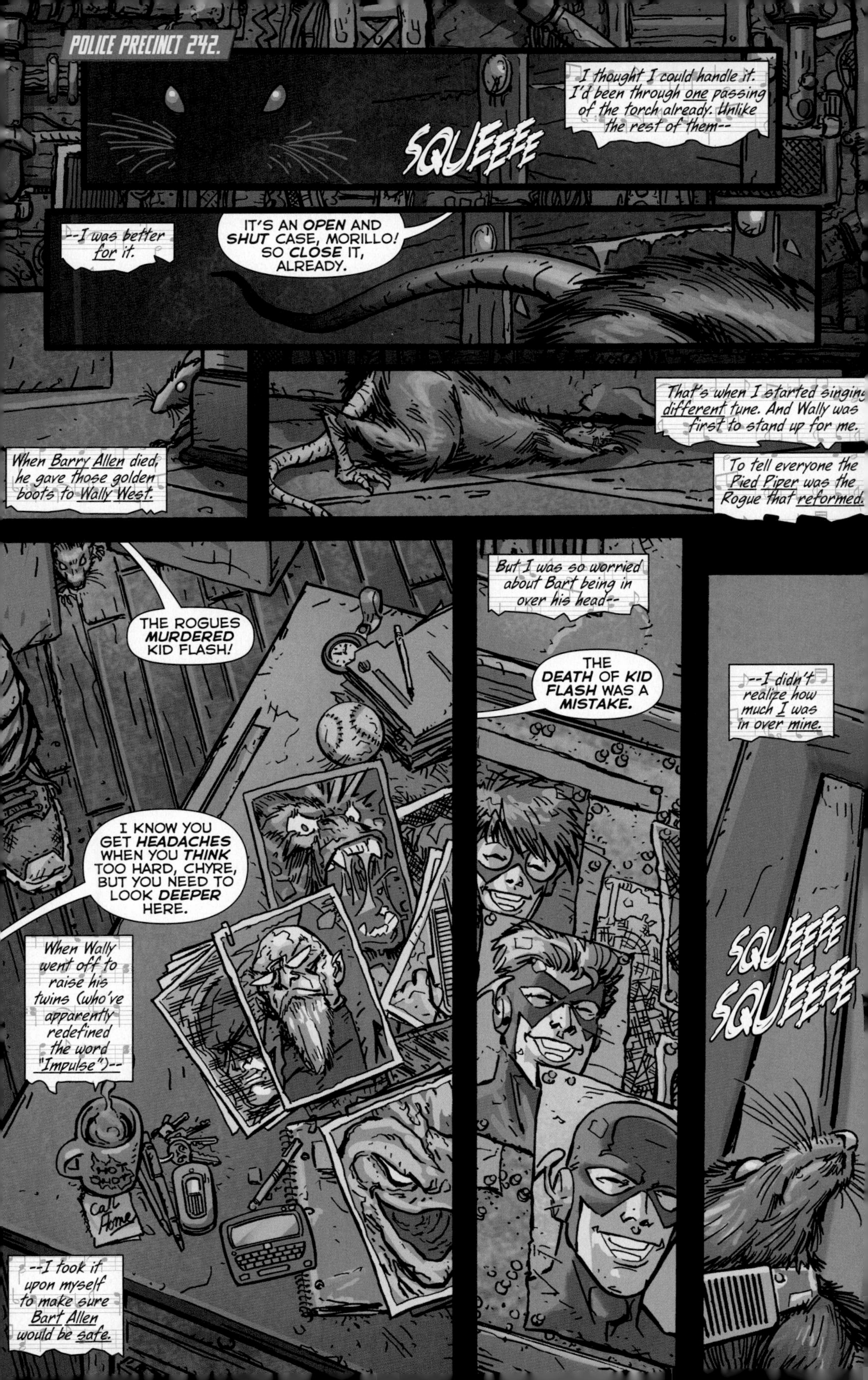
POLICE PRECINCT 242.
I thought I could handle it. I'd been through one passing of the torch already. Unlike the rest of them--
SQUEEEE
--I was better for it.
IT'S AN OPEN AND SHUT CASE, MORILLO! SO CLOSE IT, ALREADY.
When Barry Allen died, he gave those golden boots to Wally West.
That's when I started singing different tune. And Wally was first to stand up for me.
To tell everyone the Pied Piper was the Rogue that reformed.
THE ROGUES MURDERED KID FLASH!
I KNOW YOU GET HEADACHES WHEN YOU THINK TOO HARD, CHYRE, BUT YOU NEED TO LOOK DEEPER HERE.
When Wally went off to raise his twins (who've apparently redefined the word "Impulse")--
--I took it upon myself to make sure Bart Allen would be safe.
But I was so worried about Bart being in over his head--
THE DEATH OF KID FLASH WAS A MISTAKE.
--I didn't realize how much I was in over mine.
SQUEEEE SQUEEEE

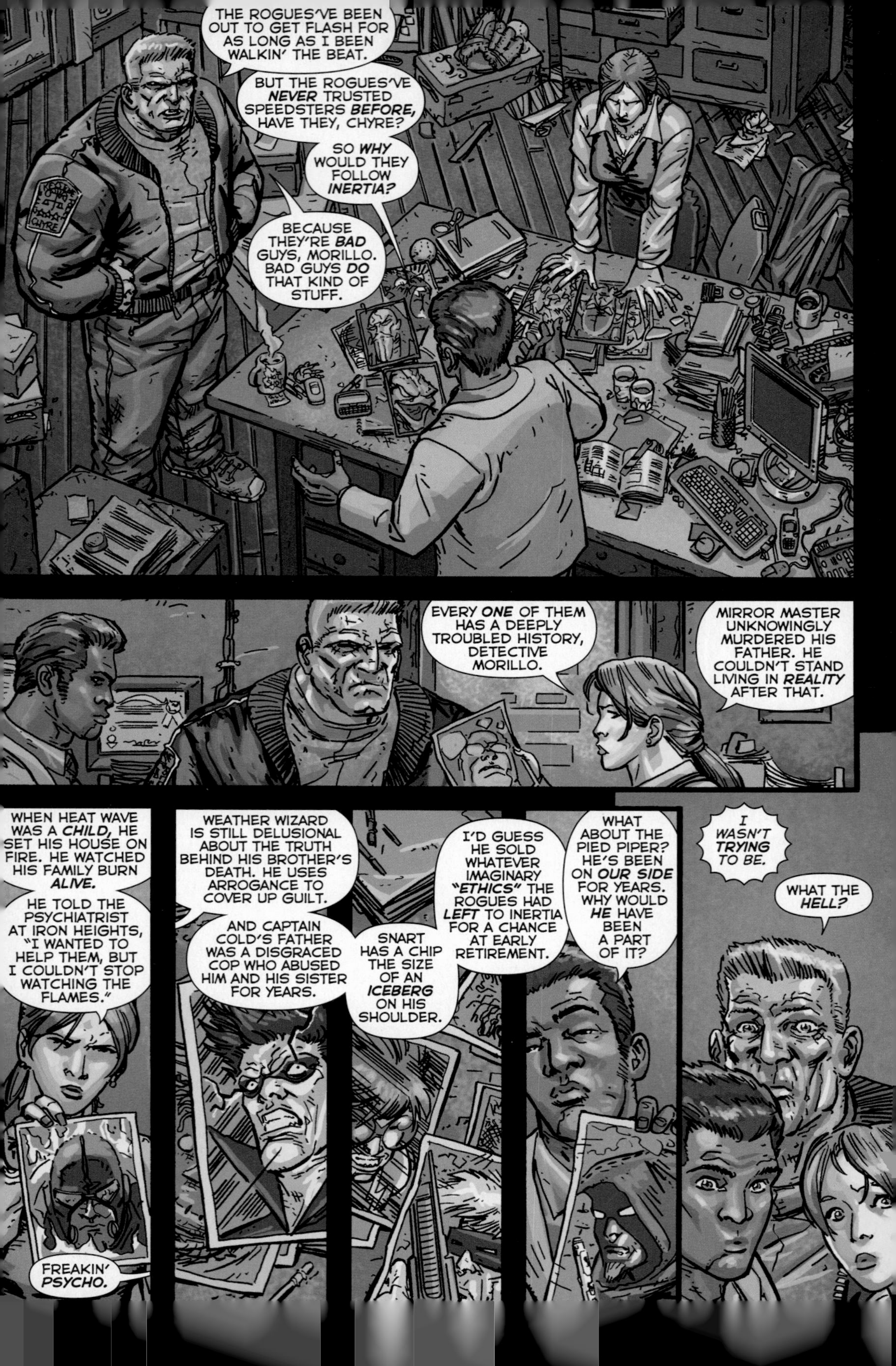
THE ROGUES'VE BEEN OUT TO GET FLASH FOR AS LONG AS I BEEN WALKIN' THE BEAT.
BUT THE ROGUES'VE *NEVER* TRUSTED SPEEDSTERS *BEFORE,* HAVE THEY, CHYRE?
SO *WHY* WOULD THEY FOLLOW *INERTIA?*
BECAUSE THEY'RE *BAD* GUYS, MORILLO. BAD GUYS *DO* THAT KIND OF STUFF.
EVERY *ONE* OF THEM HAS A DEEPLY TROUBLED HISTORY, DETECTIVE MORILLO.
MIRROR MASTER UNKNOWINGLY MURDERED HIS FATHER. HE COULDN'T STAND LIVING IN *REALITY* AFTER THAT.
WHEN HEAT WAVE WAS A *CHILD,* HE SET HIS HOUSE ON FIRE. HE WATCHED HIS FAMILY BURN *ALIVE.*
HE TOLD THE PSYCHIATRIST AT IRON HEIGHTS, "I WANTED TO HELP THEM, BUT I COULDN'T STOP WATCHING THE FLAMES."
FREAKIN' *PSYCHO.*
WEATHER WIZARD IS STILL DELUSIONAL ABOUT THE TRUTH BEHIND HIS BROTHER'S DEATH. HE USES ARROGANCE TO COVER UP GUILT.
AND CAPTAIN COLD'S FATHER WAS A DISGRACED COP WHO ABUSED HIM AND HIS SISTER FOR YEARS.
SNART HAS A CHIP THE SIZE OF AN *ICEBERG* ON HIS SHOULDER.
I'D GUESS HE SOLD WHATEVER IMAGINARY *"ETHICS"* THE ROGUES HAD *LEFT* TO INERTIA FOR A CHANCE AT EARLY RETIREMENT.
WHAT ABOUT THE PIED PIPER? HE'S BEEN ON *OUR SIDE* FOR YEARS. WHY WOULD *HE* HAVE BEEN A PART OF IT?
I WASN'T TRYING TO BE.
WHAT THE *HELL?*

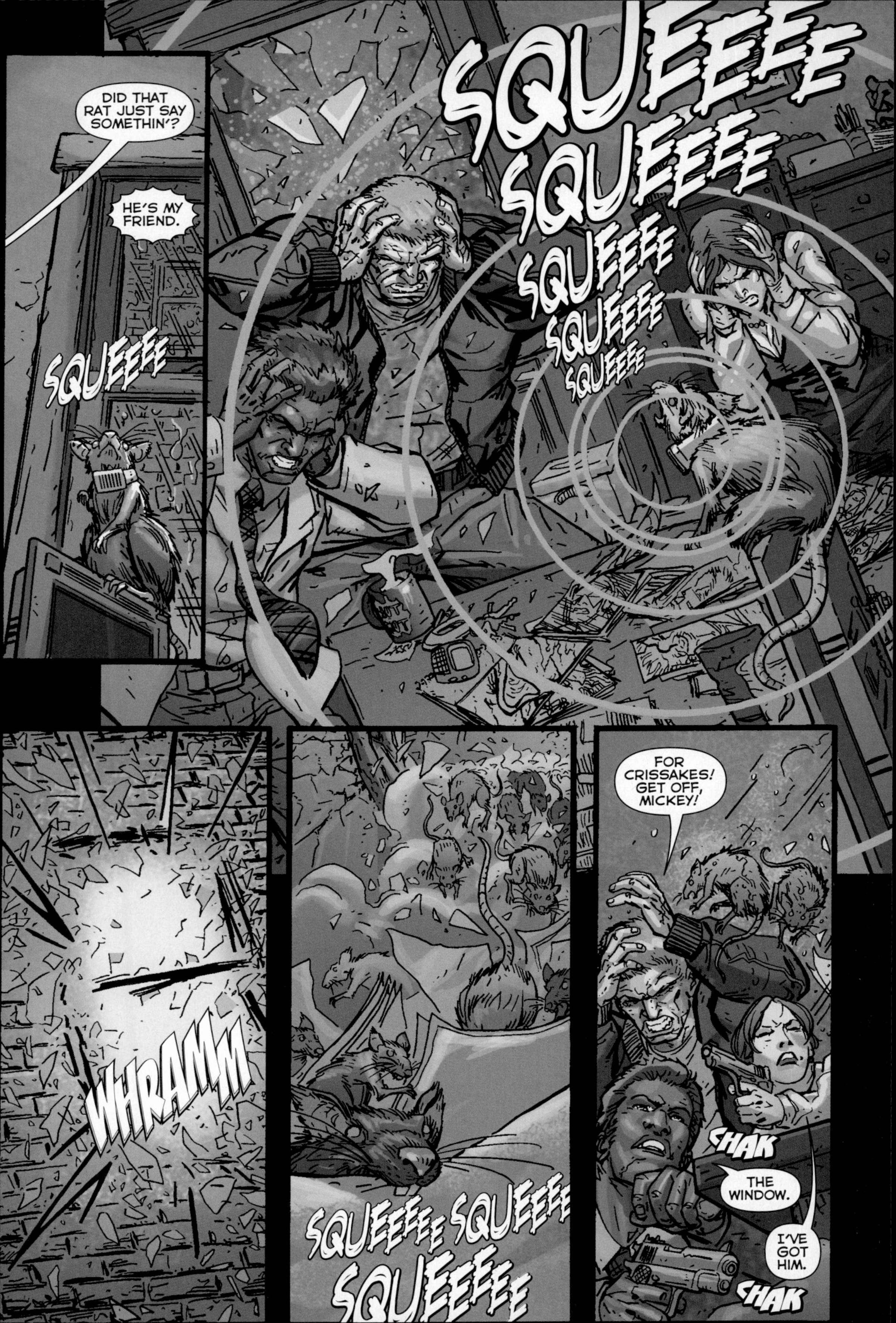
DID THAT RAT JUST SAY SOMETHIN'?
HE'S MY FRIEND.
SQUEEEE
SQUEEEEE
SQUEEEEE
SQUEEEEE
SQUEEEEE
SQUEEEE
WHRAMM
SQUEEEEE SQUEEEE
SQUEEEEE
FOR CRISSAKES! GET OFF, MICKEY!
CHAK
THE WINDOW.
I'VE GOT HIM.
CHAK

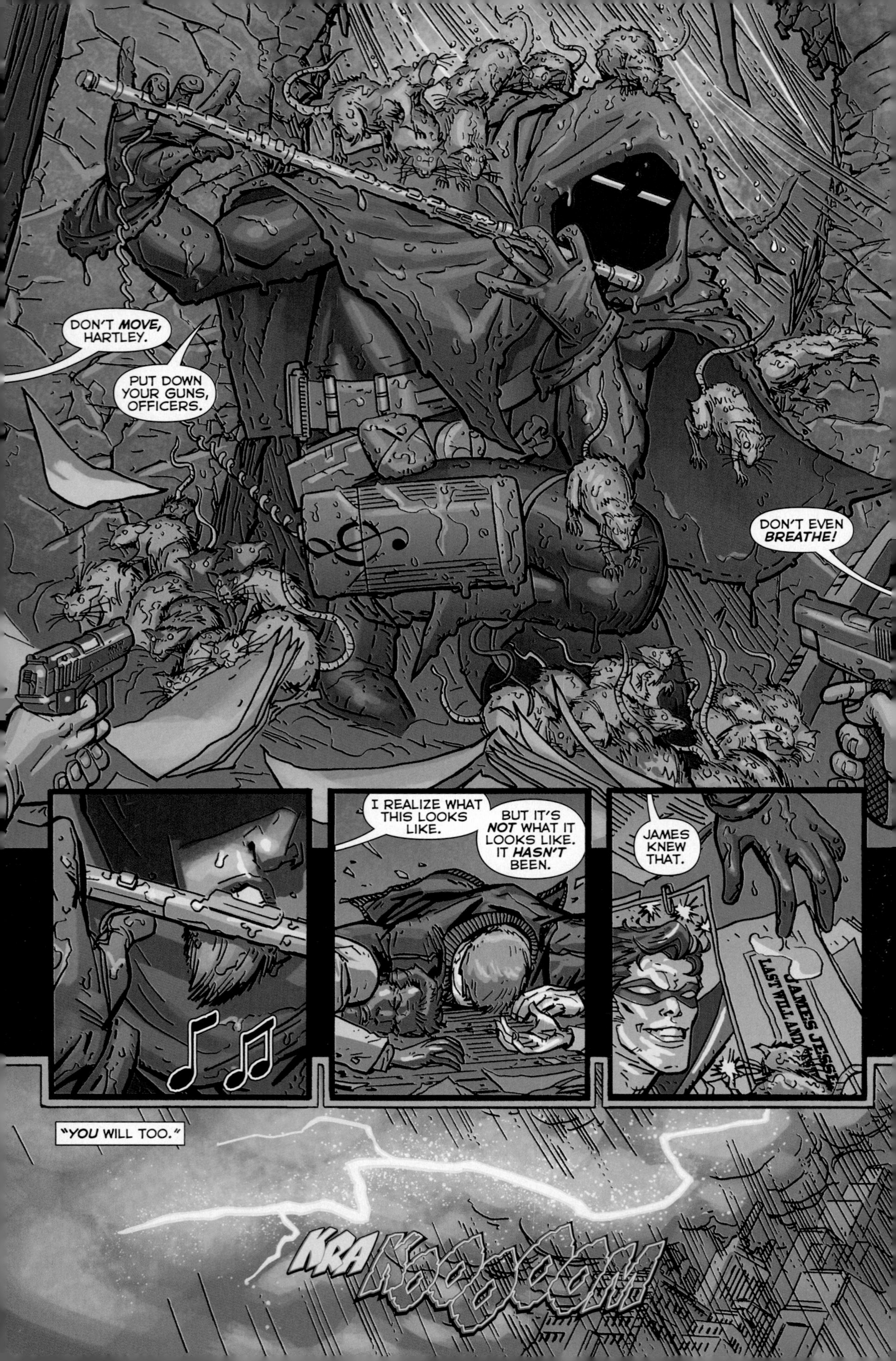
DON'T *MOVE,* HARTLEY.
PUT DOWN YOUR GUNS, OFFICERS.
DON'T EVEN *BREATHE!*
I REALIZE WHAT THIS LOOKS LIKE.
BUT IT'S *NOT* WHAT IT LOOKS LIKE. IT *HASN'T* BEEN.
JAMES KNEW THAT.
JAMES JESSE
LAST WILL AND
"*YOU* WILL TOO."
KRA

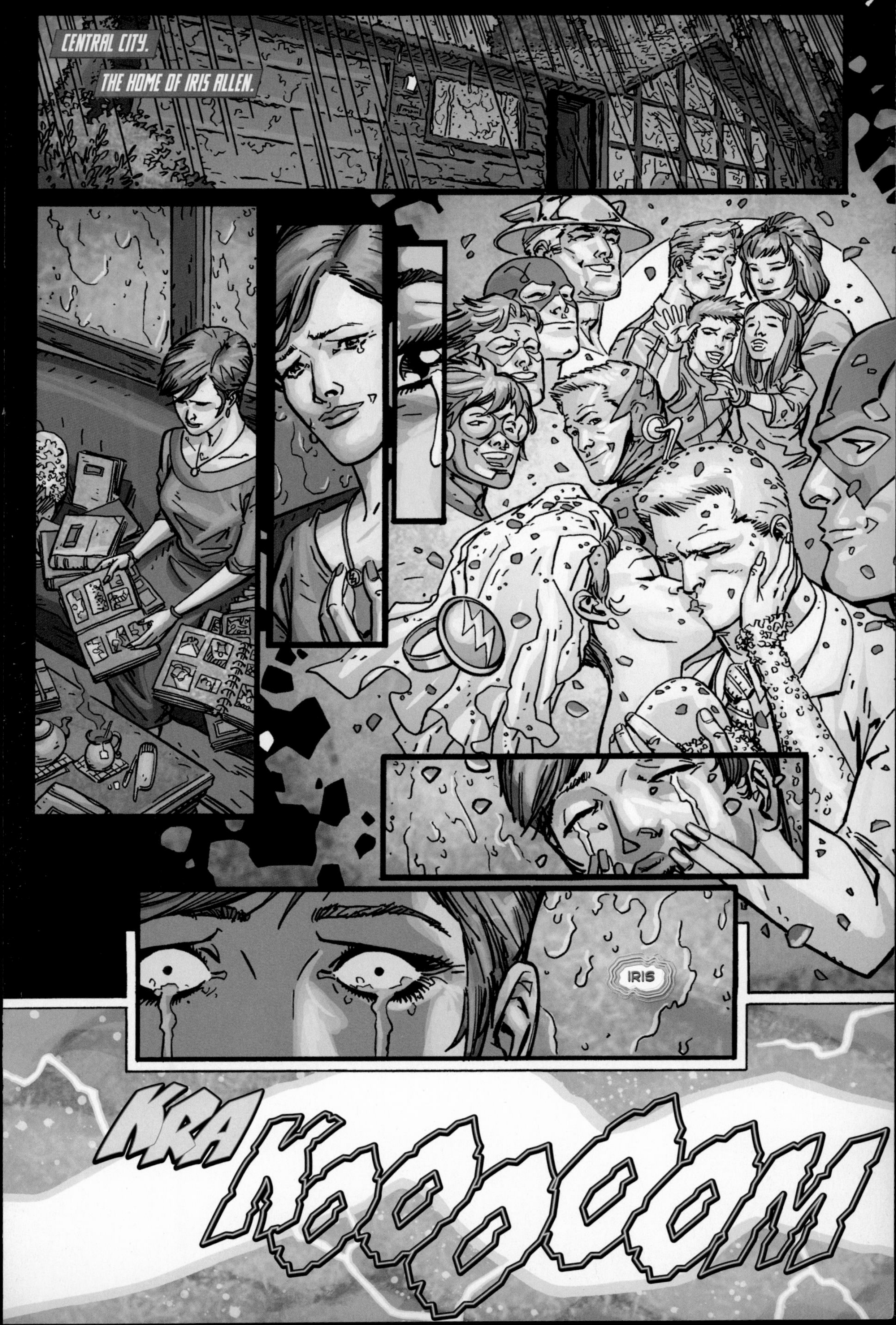
CENTRAL CITY.
THE HOME OF IRIS ALLEN.
IRIS
KRA
KOOOOOM

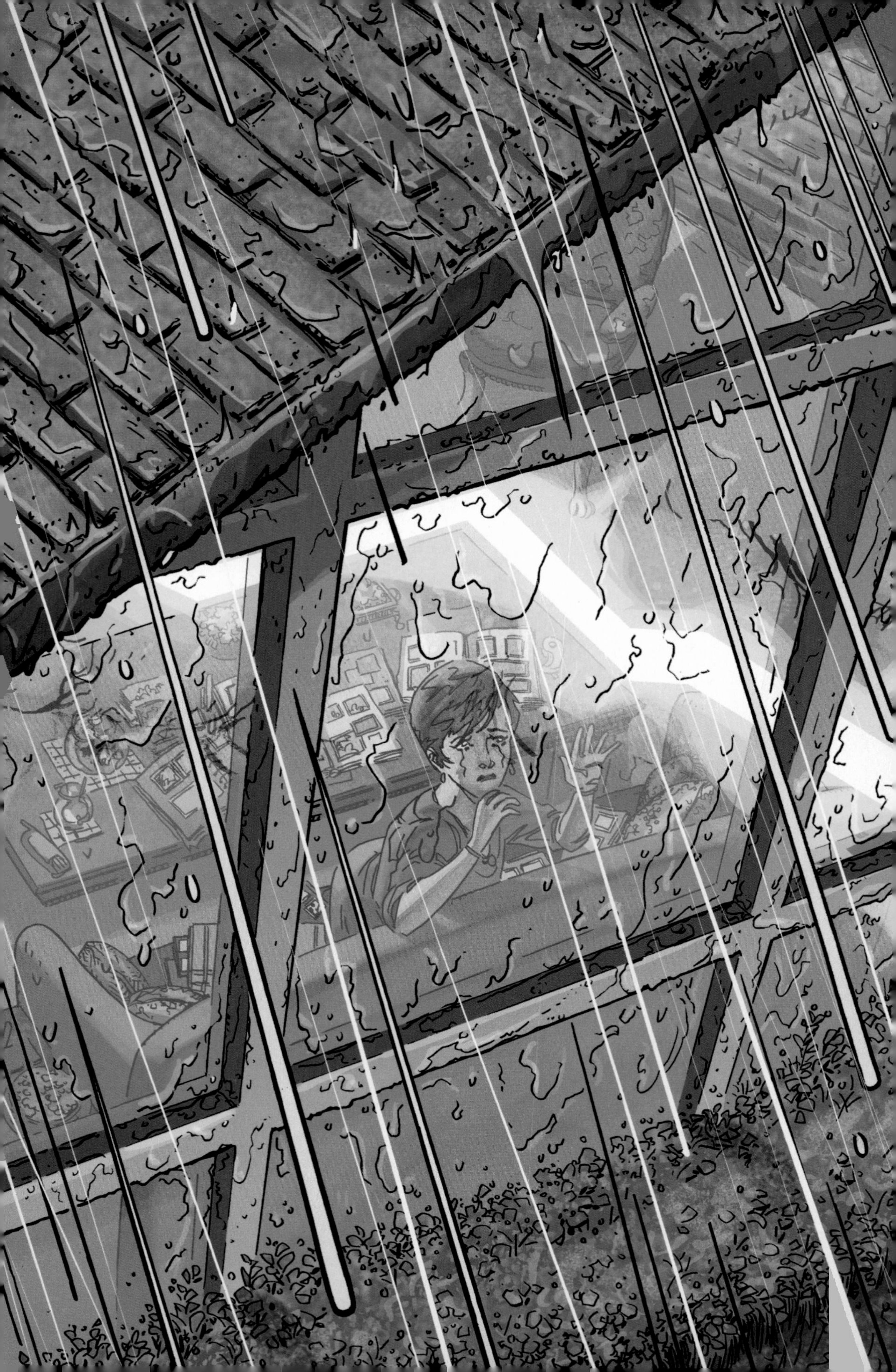

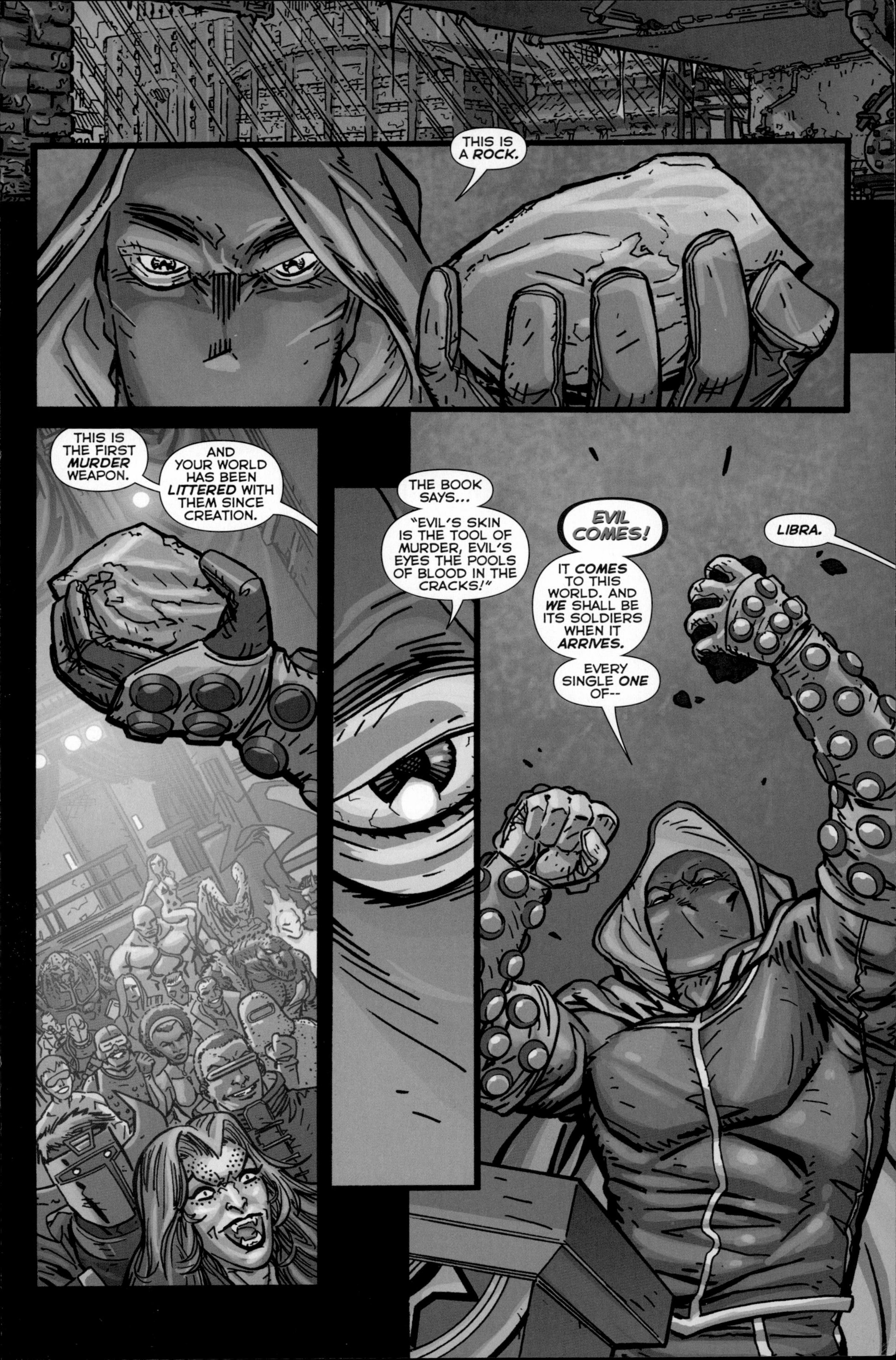
THIS IS A ROCK.
THIS IS THE FIRST MURDER WEAPON.
AND YOUR WORLD HAS BEEN LITTERED WITH THEM SINCE CREATION.
THE BOOK SAYS...
"EVIL'S SKIN IS THE TOOL OF MURDER, EVIL'S EYES THE POOLS OF BLOOD IN THE CRACKS!"
EVIL COMES!
IT COMES TO THIS WORLD. AND WE SHALL BE ITS SOLDIERS WHEN IT ARRIVES.
EVERY SINGLE ONE OF--
LIBRA.

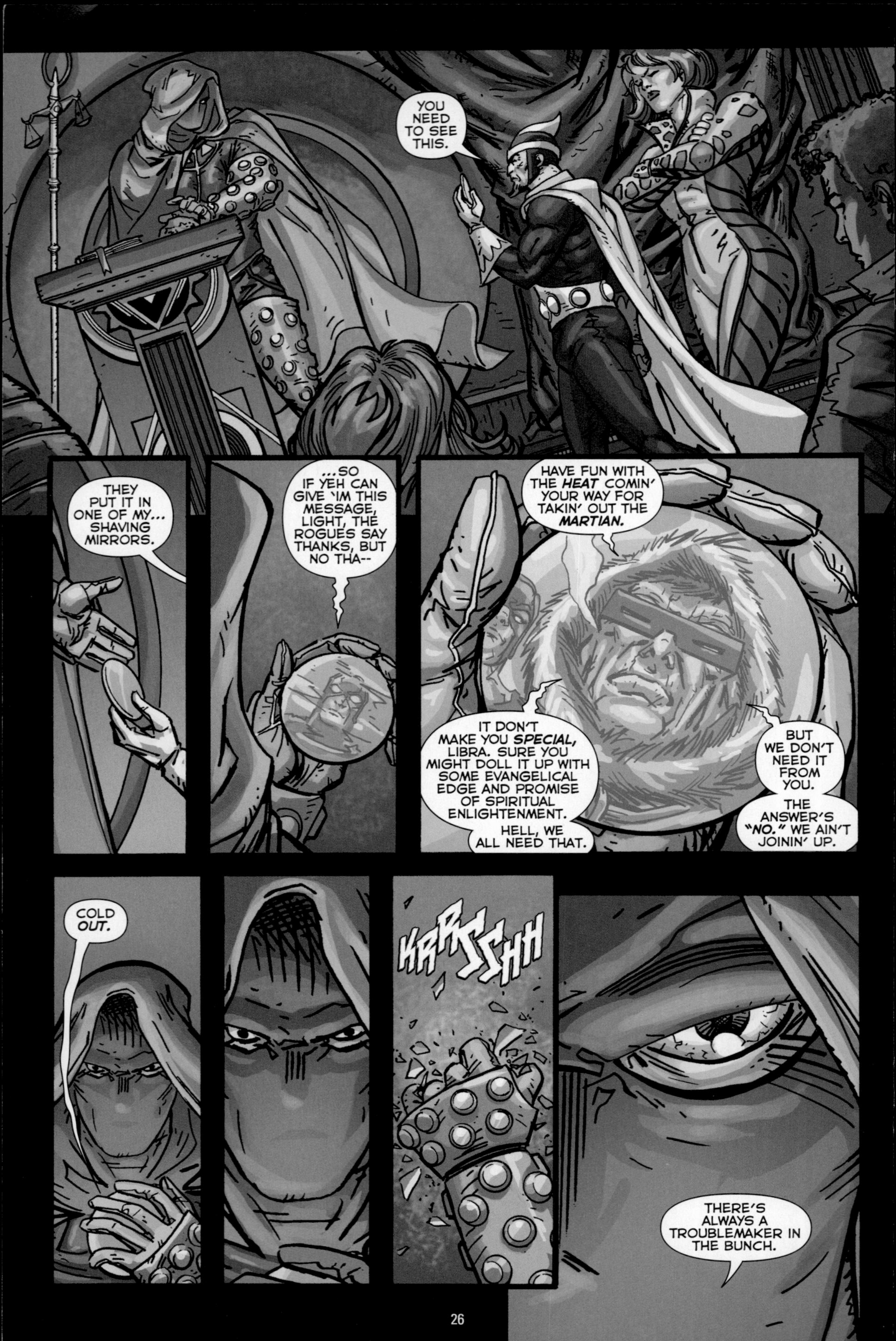
YOU NEED TO SEE THIS.
THEY PUT IT IN ONE OF MY... SHAVING MIRRORS.
...SO IF YEH CAN GIVE 'IM THIS MESSAGE, LIGHT, THE ROGUES SAY THANKS, BUT NO THA--
HAVE FUN WITH THE HEAT COMIN' YOUR WAY FOR TAKIN' OUT THE MARTIAN.
IT DON'T MAKE YOU SPECIAL, LIBRA. SURE YOU MIGHT DOLL IT UP WITH SOME EVANGELICAL EDGE AND PROMISE OF SPIRITUAL ENLIGHTENMENT.
HELL, WE ALL NEED THAT.
BUT WE DON'T NEED IT FROM YOU.
THE ANSWER'S "NO." WE AIN'T JOININ' UP.
COLD OUT.
KRRSSHH
THERE'S ALWAYS A TROUBLEMAKER IN THE BUNCH.

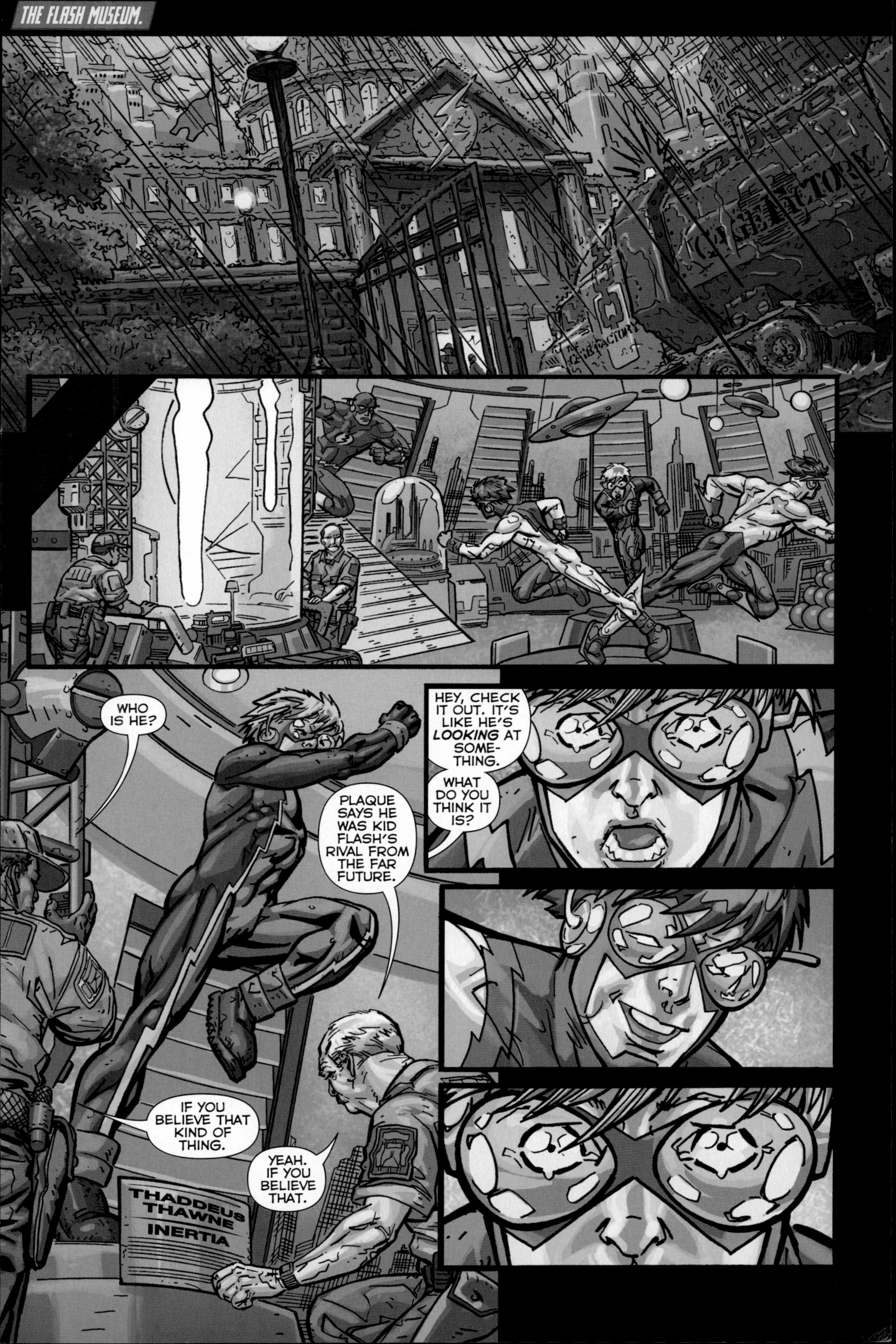
THE FLASH MUSEUM.
WHO IS HE?
PLAQUE SAYS HE WAS KID FLASH'S RIVAL FROM THE FAR FUTURE.
IF YOU BELIEVE THAT KIND OF THING.
YEAH. IF YOU BELIEVE THAT.
THADDEUS THAWNE
INERTIA
HEY, CHECK IT OUT. IT'S LIKE HE'S LOOKING AT SOME-THING.
WHAT DO YOU THINK IT IS?

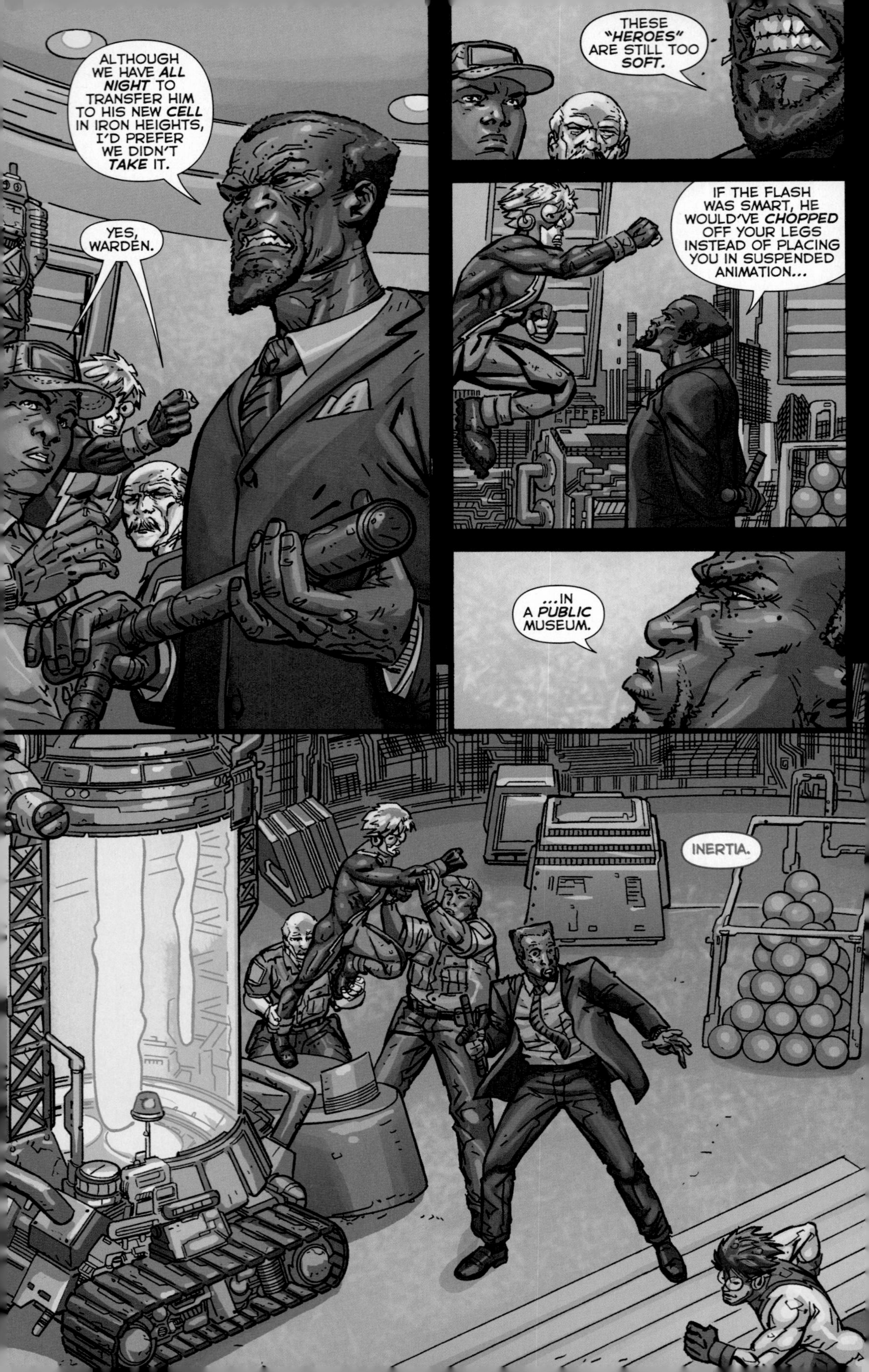
ALTHOUGH WE HAVE ALL NIGHT TO TRANSFER HIM TO HIS NEW CELL IN IRON HEIGHTS, I'D PREFER WE DIDN'T TAKE IT.
YES, WARDEN.
THESE "HEROES" ARE STILL TOO SOFT.
IF THE FLASH WAS SMART, HE WOULD'VE CHOPPED OFF YOUR LEGS INSTEAD OF PLACING YOU IN SUSPENDED ANIMATION...
...IN A PUBLIC MUSEUM.
INERTIA.

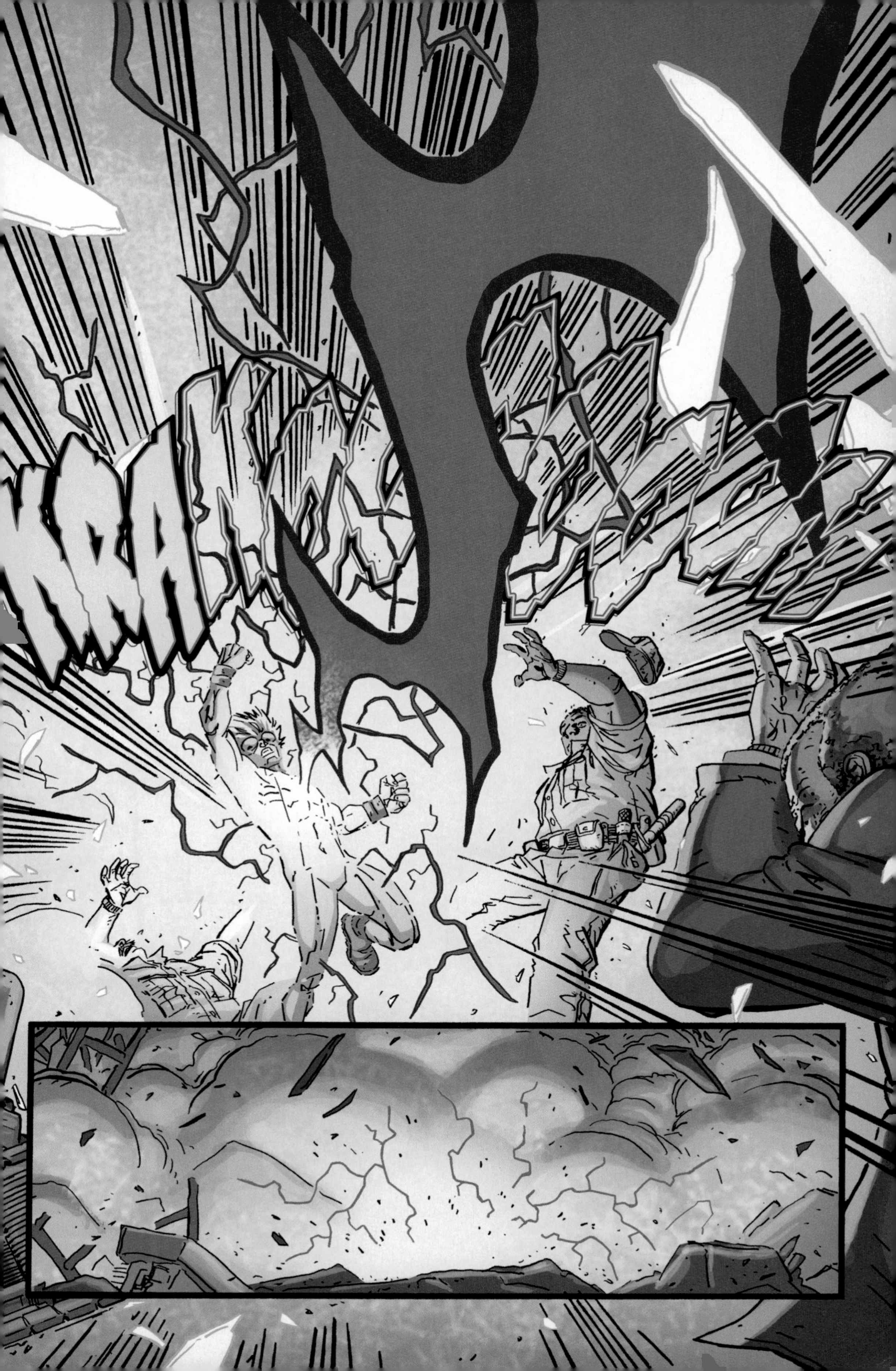
KRA

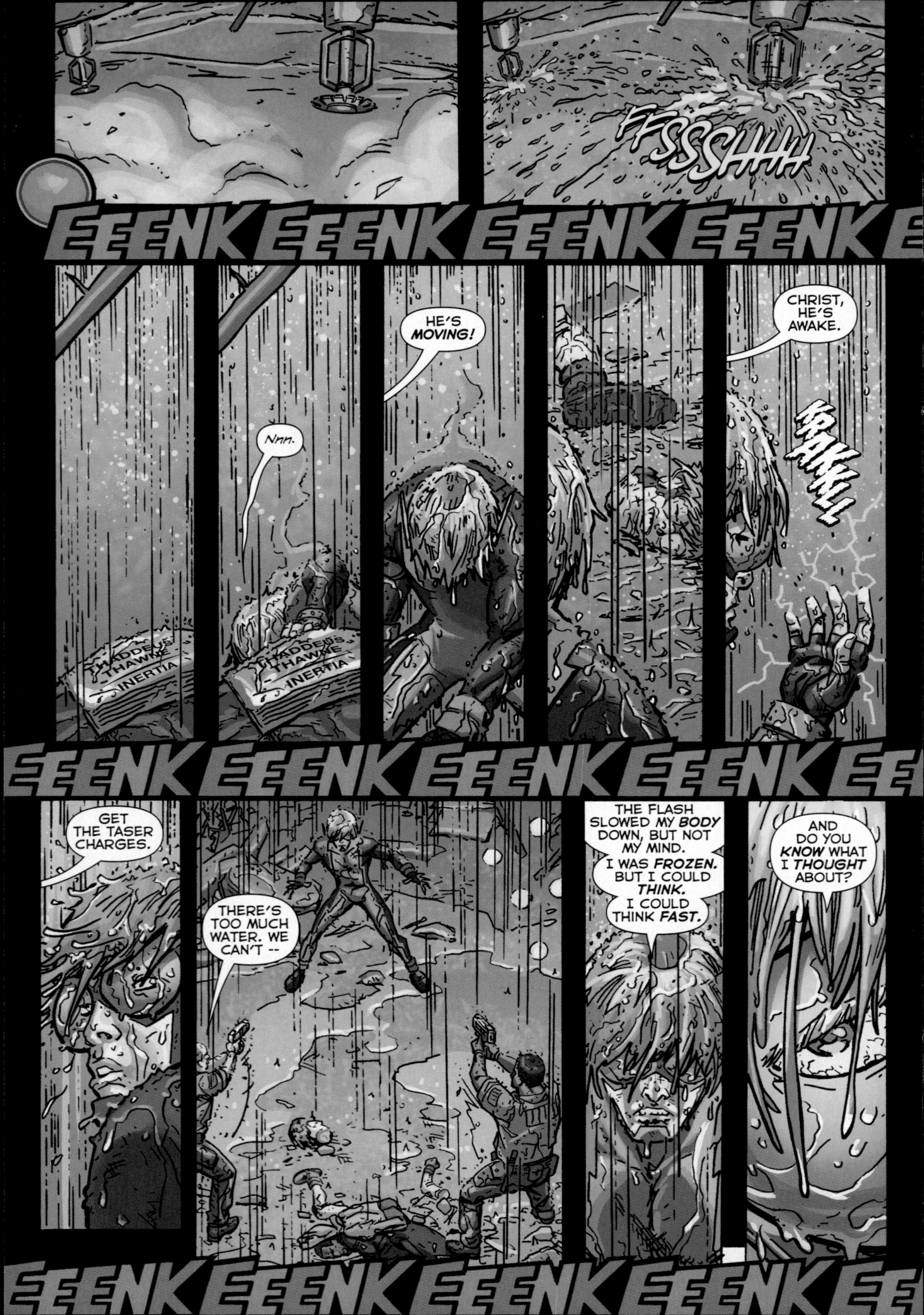
FFSSSHHH
EEENK EEENK EEENK EEENK E
THADDEUS THAWNE INERTIA
Nnn.
THADDEUS THAWNE INERTIA
HE'S *MOVING!*
CHRIST, HE'S AWAKE.
KRAKK!!
EEENK EEENK EEENK EEENK EE
GET THE TASER CHARGES.
THERE'S TOO MUCH WATER. WE CAN'T --
THE FLASH SLOWED MY *BODY* DOWN, BUT NOT MY MIND.
I WAS *FROZEN.* BUT I COULD *THINK.*
I COULD THINK *FAST.*
AND DO YOU *KNOW* WHAT I *THOUGHT* ABOUT?
EEENK EEENK EEENK EEENK EEENK EE

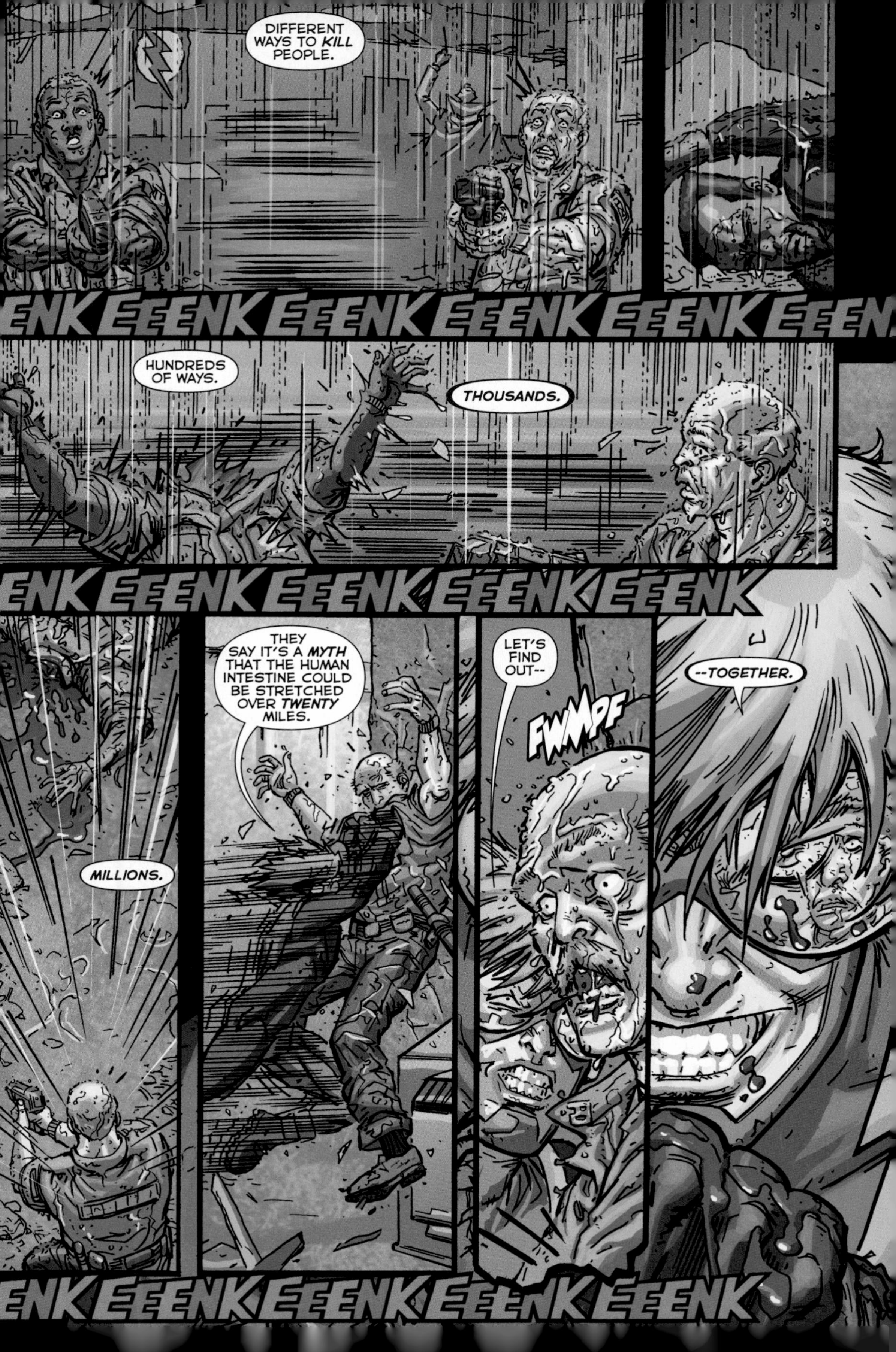

DIFFERENT WAYS TO KILL PEOPLE.
EEENK EEENK EEENK EEENK EEENK
HUNDREDS OF WAYS.
THOUSANDS.
EEENK EEENK EEENK EEENK EEENK
MILLIONS.
THEY SAY IT'S A MYTH THAT THE HUMAN INTESTINE COULD BE STRETCHED OVER TWENTY MILES.
LET'S FIND OUT--
FWMPF
--TOGETHER.
EEENK EEENK EEENK EEENK EEENK

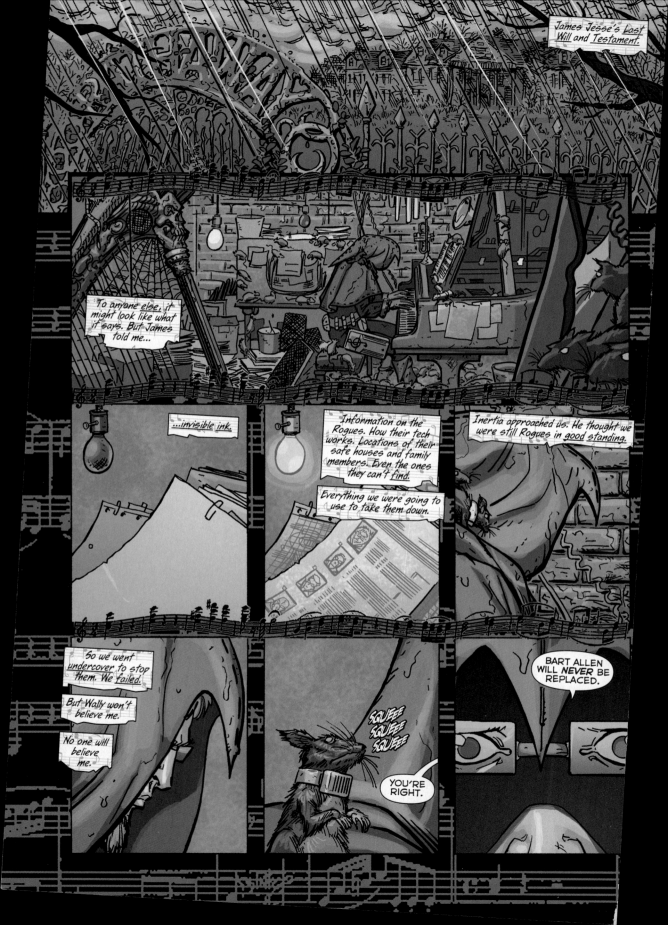

James Jesse's Last Will and Testament.

To anyone else, it might look like what it says. But James told me...

...invisible ink.

Information on the Rogues. How their tech works. Locations of their safe houses and family members. Even the ones they can't find.

Everything we were going to use to take them down.

Inertia approached us. He thought we were still Rogues in good standing.

So we went undercover to stop them. We failed.

But Wally won't believe me.

No one will believe me.

SQUEEE SQUEEE SQUEEE

YOU'RE RIGHT.

BART ALLEN WILL NEVER BE REPLACED.

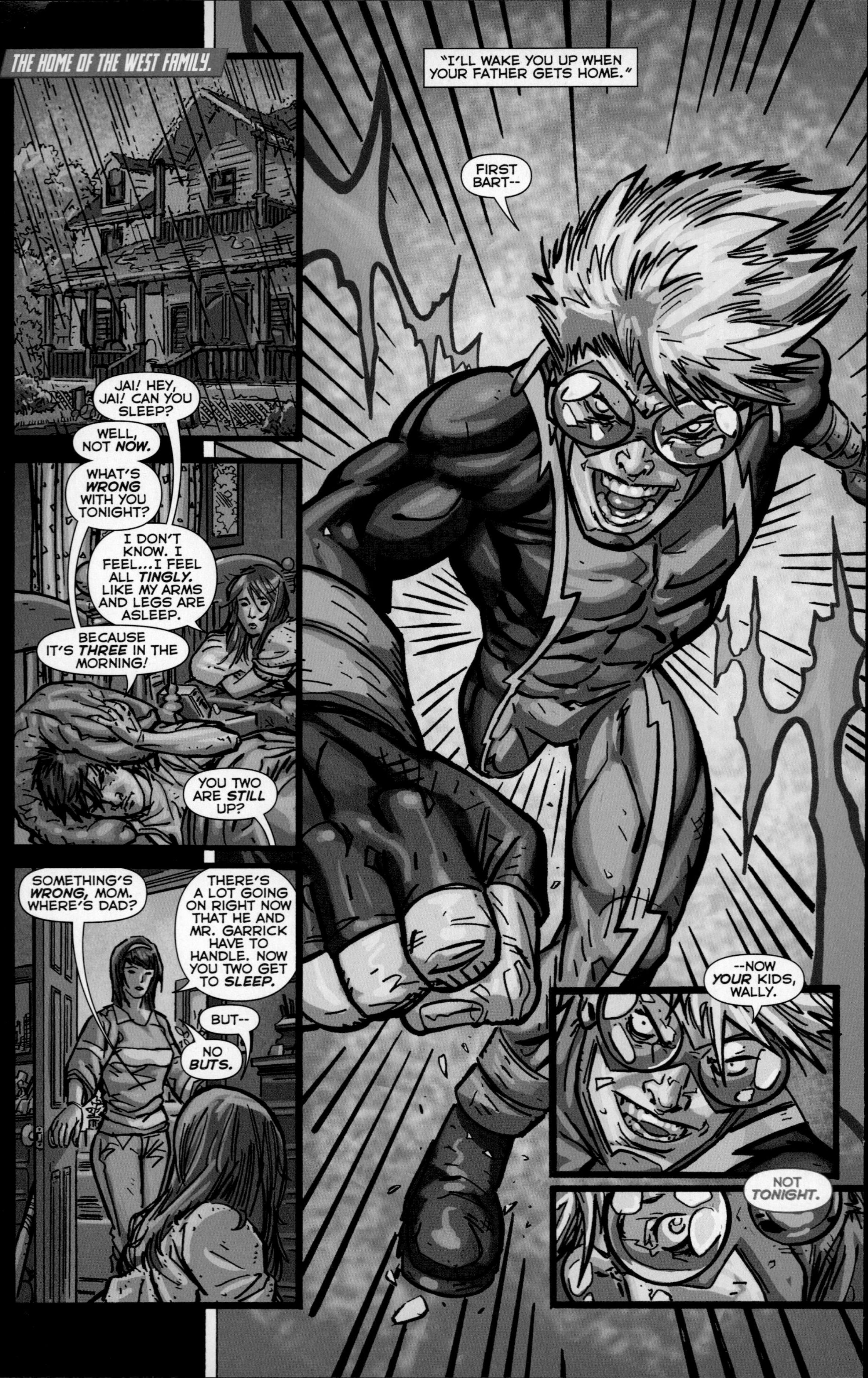
THE HOME OF THE WEST FAMILY.
"I'LL WAKE YOU UP WHEN YOUR FATHER GETS HOME."
FIRST BART--
JAI! HEY, JAI! CAN YOU SLEEP?
WELL, NOT NOW.
WHAT'S WRONG WITH YOU TONIGHT?
I DON'T KNOW. I FEEL...I FEEL ALL TINGLY. LIKE MY ARMS AND LEGS ARE ASLEEP.
BECAUSE IT'S THREE IN THE MORNING!
YOU TWO ARE STILL UP?
SOMETHING'S WRONG, MOM. WHERE'S DAD?
THERE'S A LOT GOING ON RIGHT NOW THAT HE AND MR. GARRICK HAVE TO HANDLE. NOW YOU TWO GET TO SLEEP.
BUT--
NO BUTS.
--NOW YOUR KIDS, WALLY.
NOT TONIGHT.

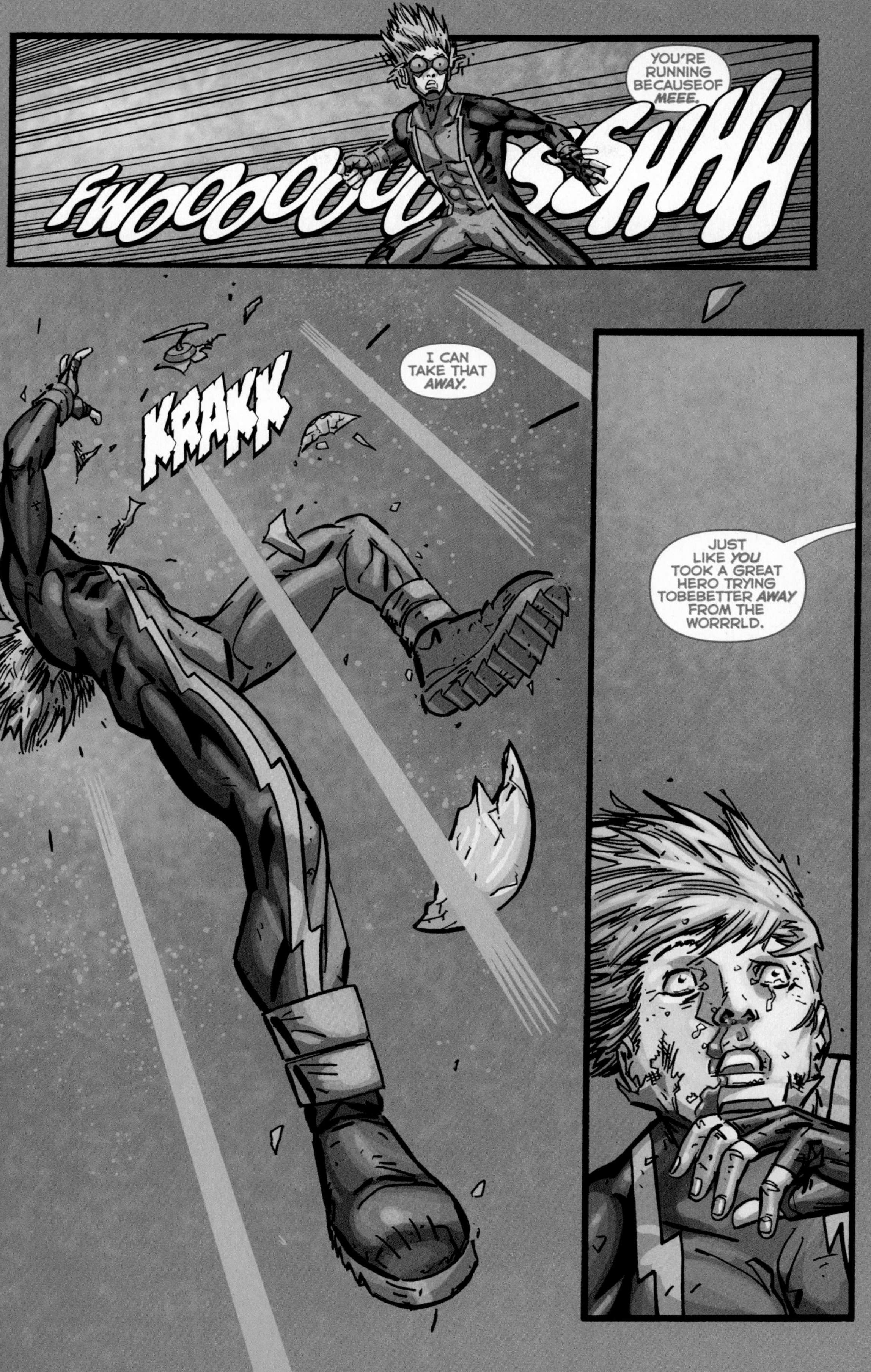
YOU'RE RUNNING BECAUSEOF *MEEE.*
KRAKK
I CAN TAKE THAT *AWAY.*
JUST LIKE *YOU* TOOK A GREAT HERO TRYING TOBEBETTER *AWAY* FROM THE WORRRLD.

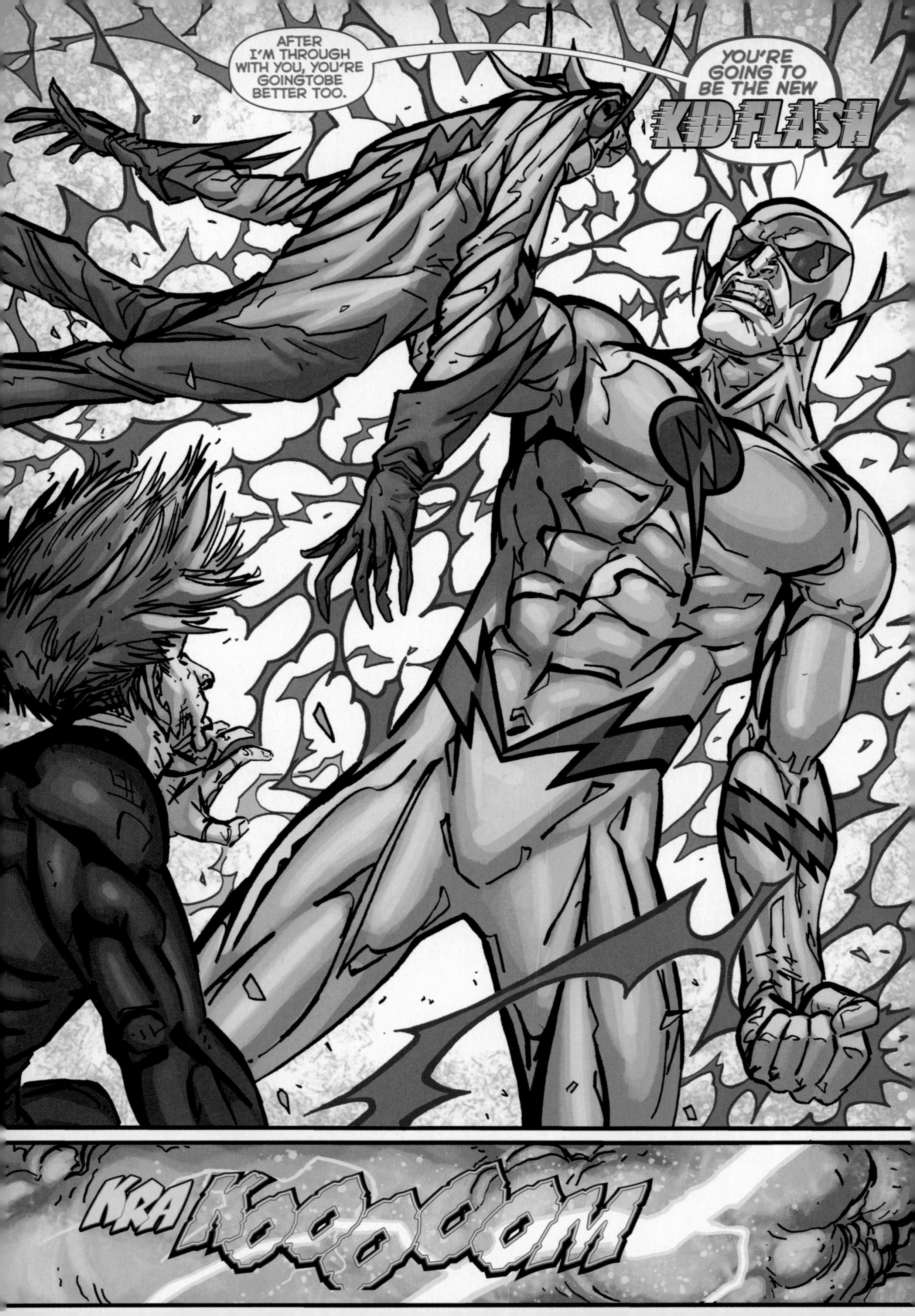
YOU'RE GOING TO BE THE NEW KID FLASH
AFTER I'M THROUGH WITH YOU, YOU'RE GOINGTOBE BETTER TOO.
KRA KOOOOOOM

Cover to FINAL CRISIS: ROGUES' REVENGE #2

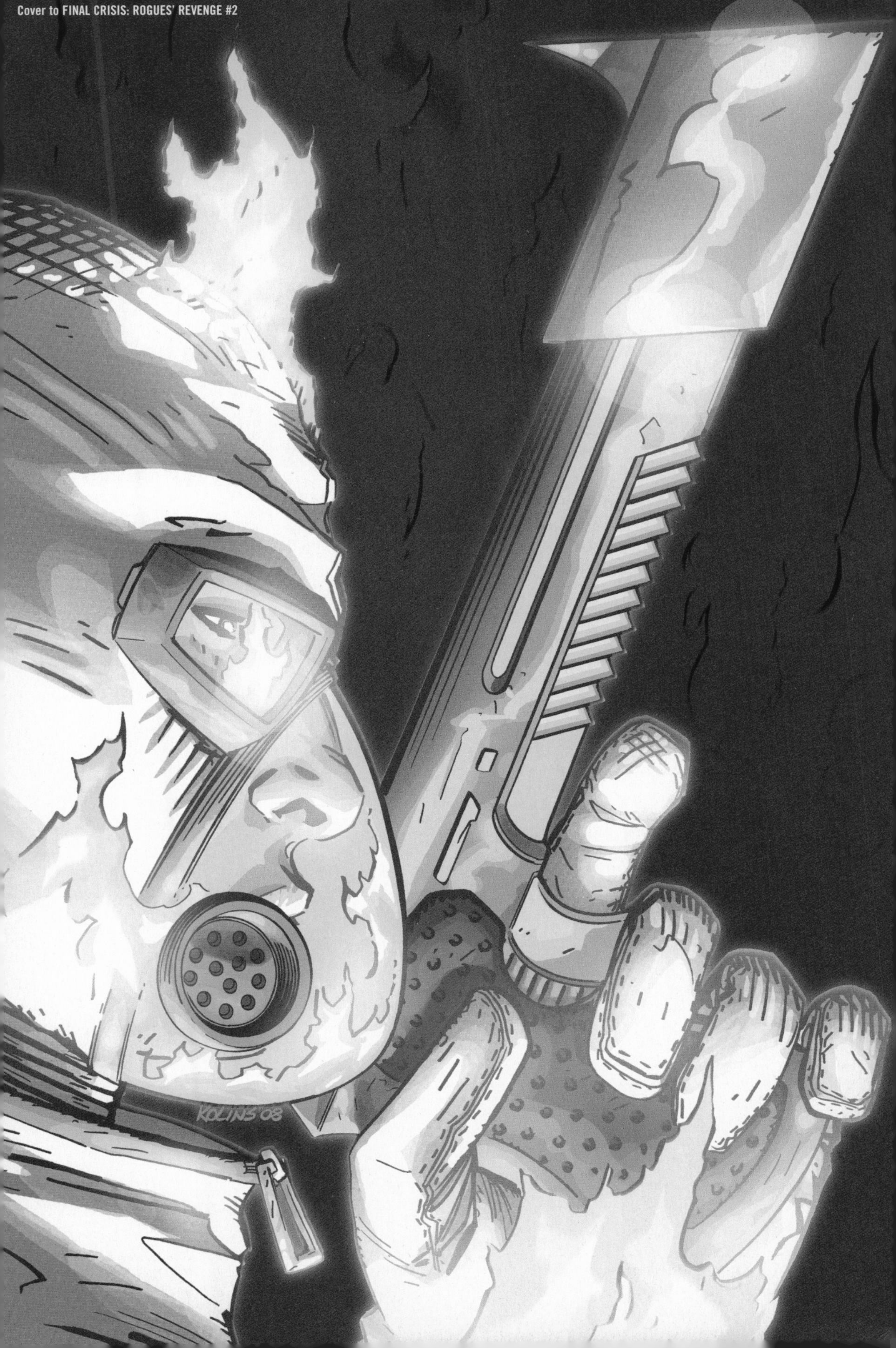
KOLINS '08

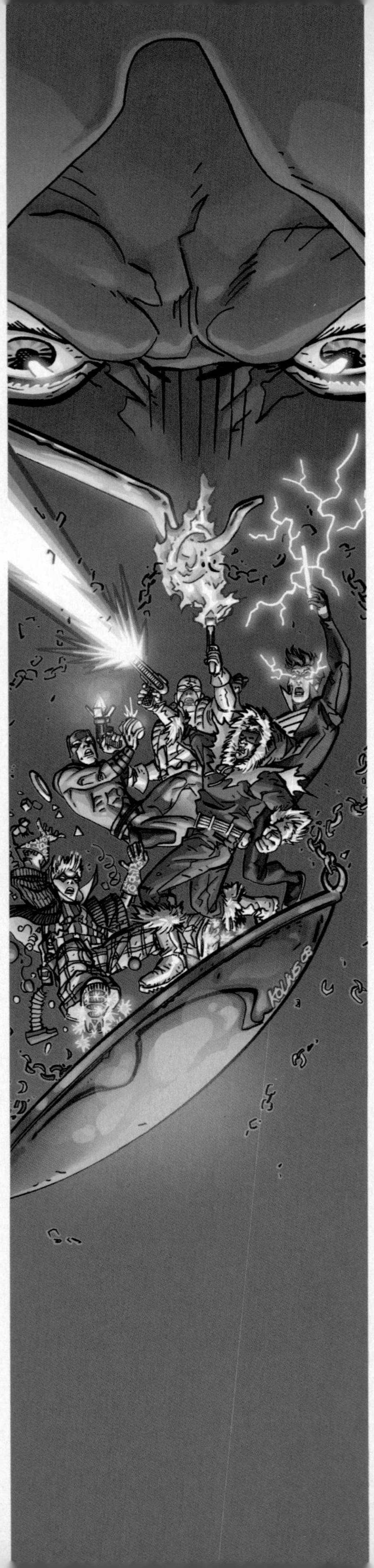

Sliver cover to FINAL CRISIS: ROGUES' REVENGE #2

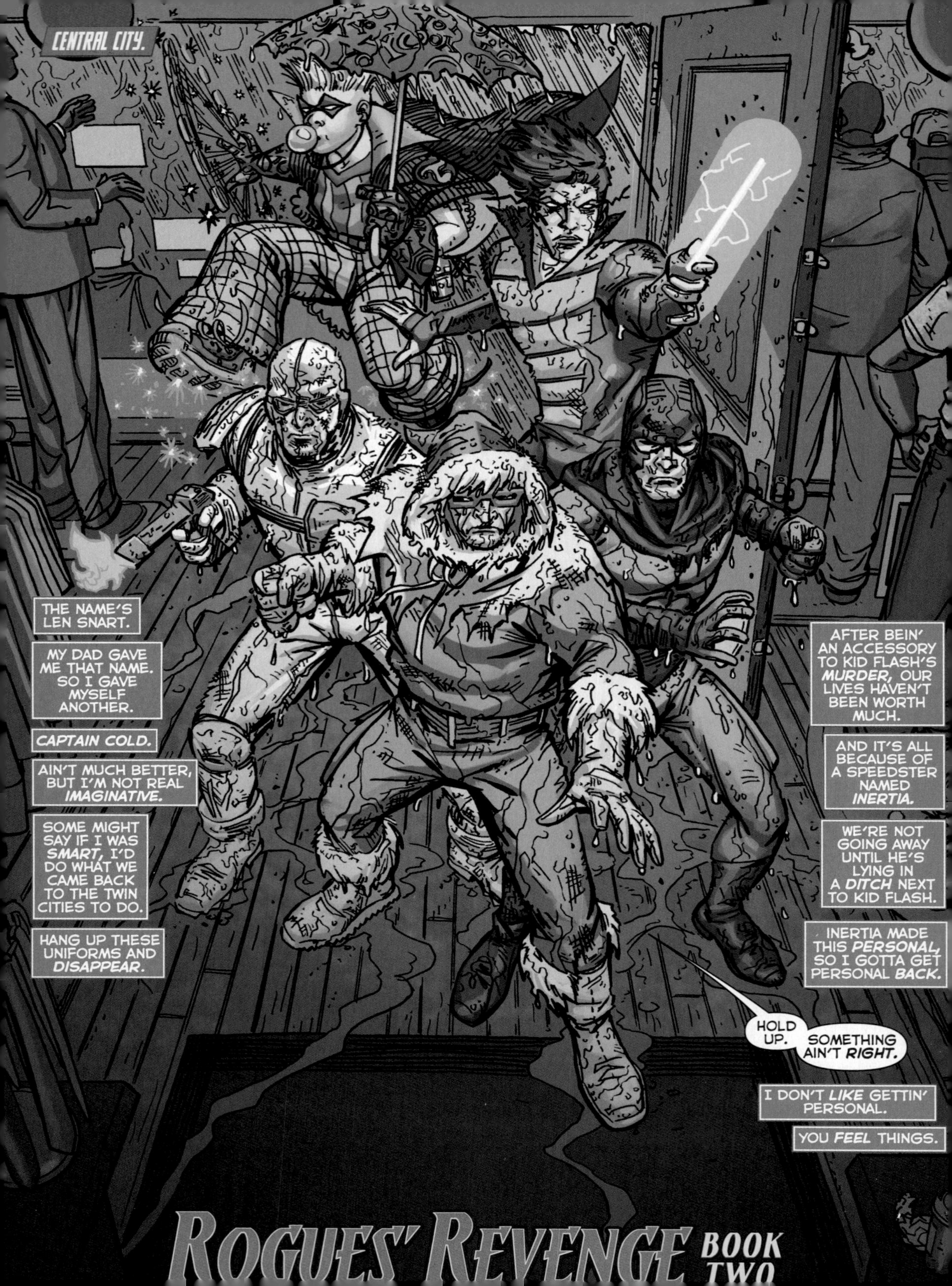

CENTRAL CITY.
THE NAME'S LEN SNART.
MY DAD GAVE ME THAT NAME. SO I GAVE MYSELF ANOTHER.
CAPTAIN COLD.
AIN'T MUCH BETTER, BUT I'M NOT REAL IMAGINATIVE.
SOME MIGHT SAY IF I WAS SMART, I'D DO WHAT WE CAME BACK TO THE TWIN CITIES TO DO.
HANG UP THESE UNIFORMS AND DISAPPEAR.
AFTER BEIN' AN ACCESSORY TO KID FLASH'S MURDER, OUR LIVES HAVEN'T BEEN WORTH MUCH.
AND IT'S ALL BECAUSE OF A SPEEDSTER NAMED INERTIA.
WE'RE NOT GOING AWAY UNTIL HE'S LYING IN A DITCH NEXT TO KID FLASH.
INERTIA MADE THIS PERSONAL, SO I GOTTA GET PERSONAL BACK.
HOLD UP. SOMETHING AIN'T RIGHT.
I DON'T LIKE GETTIN' PERSONAL.
YOU FEEL THINGS.
ROGUES' REVENGE BOOK TWO

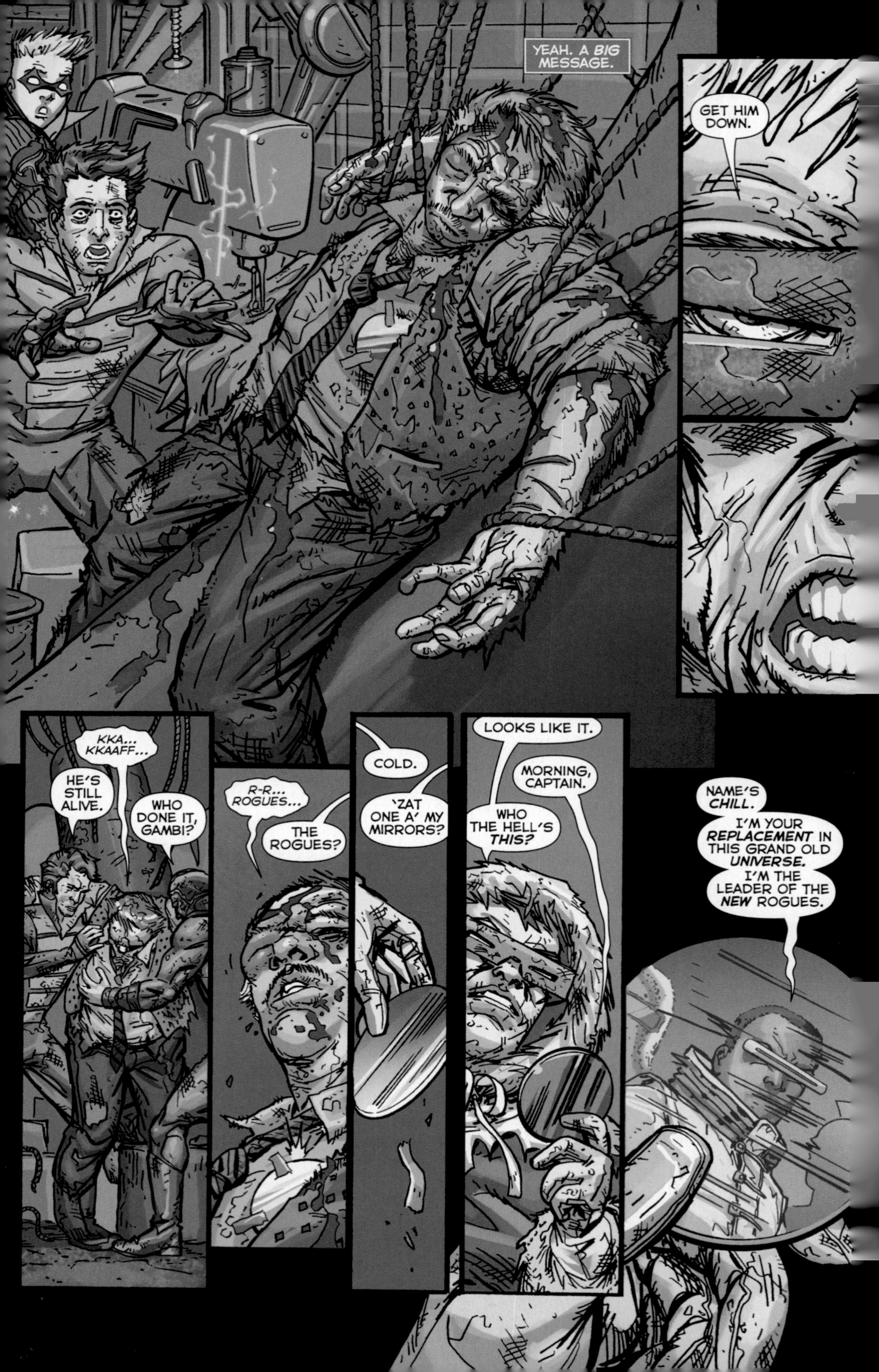
YEAH. A BIG MESSAGE.
GET HIM DOWN.
KKA... KKAAFF...
HE'S STILL ALIVE.
WHO DONE IT, GAMBI?
R-R... ROGUES...
THE ROGUES?
COLD.
'ZAT ONE A' MY MIRRORS?
LOOKS LIKE IT.
WHO THE HELL'S THIS?
MORNING, CAPTAIN.
NAME'S CHILL.
I'M YOUR REPLACEMENT IN THIS GRAND OLD UNIVERSE.
I'M THE LEADER OF THE NEW ROGUES.

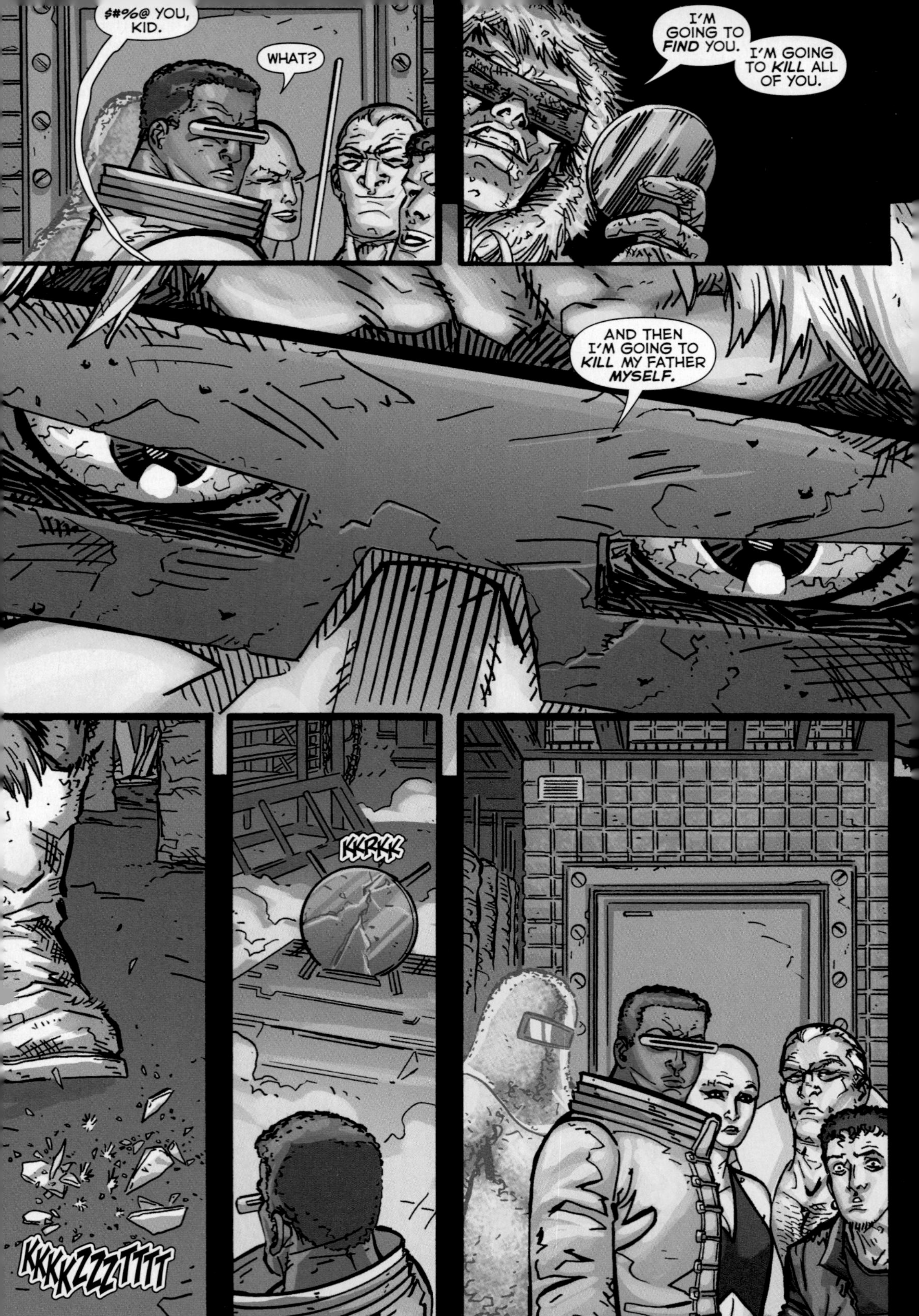
$#%@ YOU, KID.
WHAT?
I'M GOING TO FIND YOU.
I'M GOING TO KILL ALL OF YOU.
AND THEN I'M GOING TO KILL MY FATHER MYSELF.
KKRKK
KKKKZZZTTTT

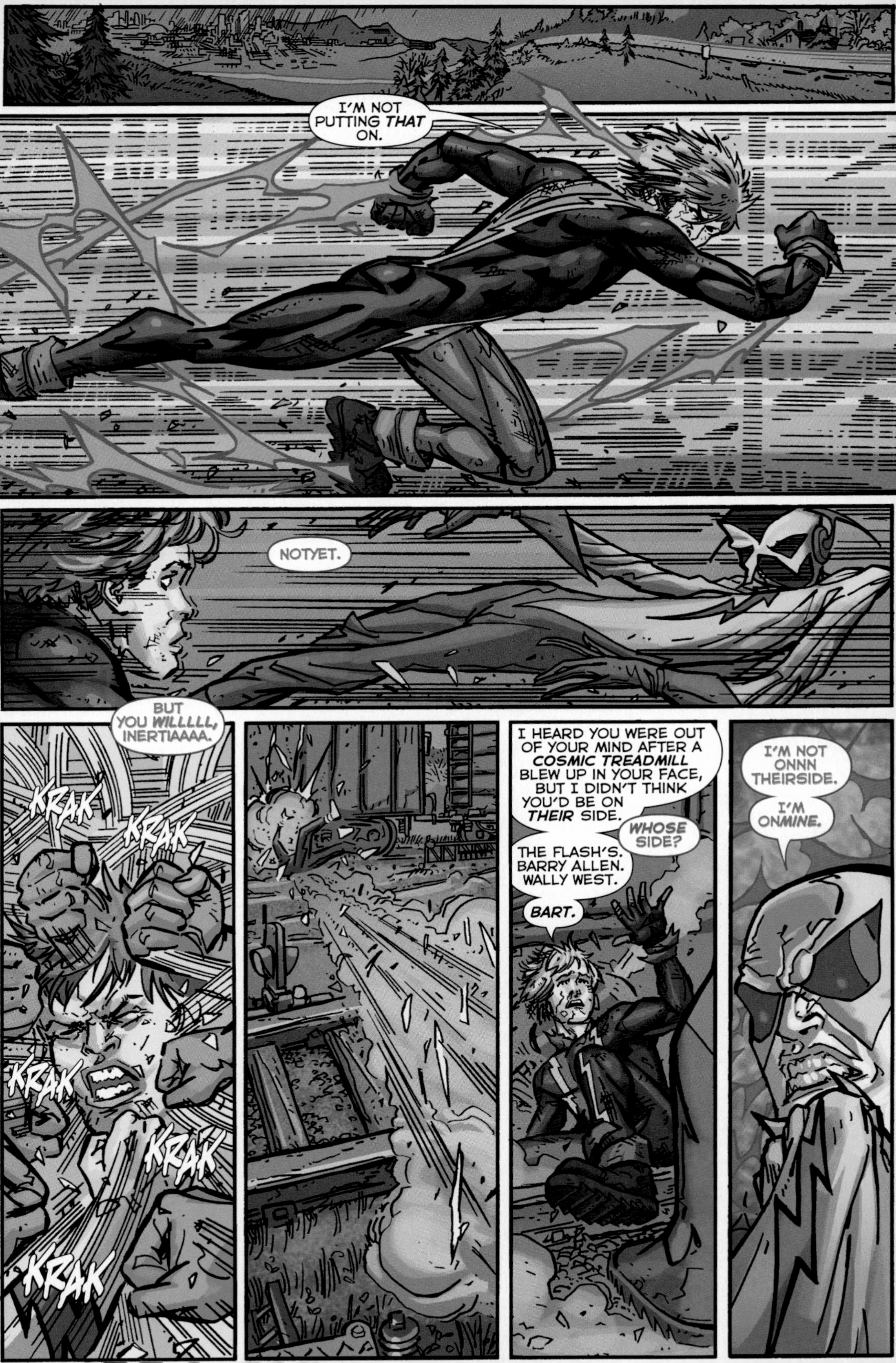
I'M NOT PUTTING THAT ON.
NOTYET.
BUT YOU WILLLLL, INERTIAAAA.
KRAK
KRAK
KRAK
KRAK
KRAK
I HEARD YOU WERE OUT OF YOUR MIND AFTER A COSMIC TREADMILL BLEW UP IN YOUR FACE, BUT I DIDN'T THINK YOU'D BE ON THEIR SIDE.
WHOSE SIDE?
THE FLASH'S. BARRY ALLEN. WALLY WEST.
BART.
I'M NOT ONNN THEIRSIDE.
I'M ONMINE.

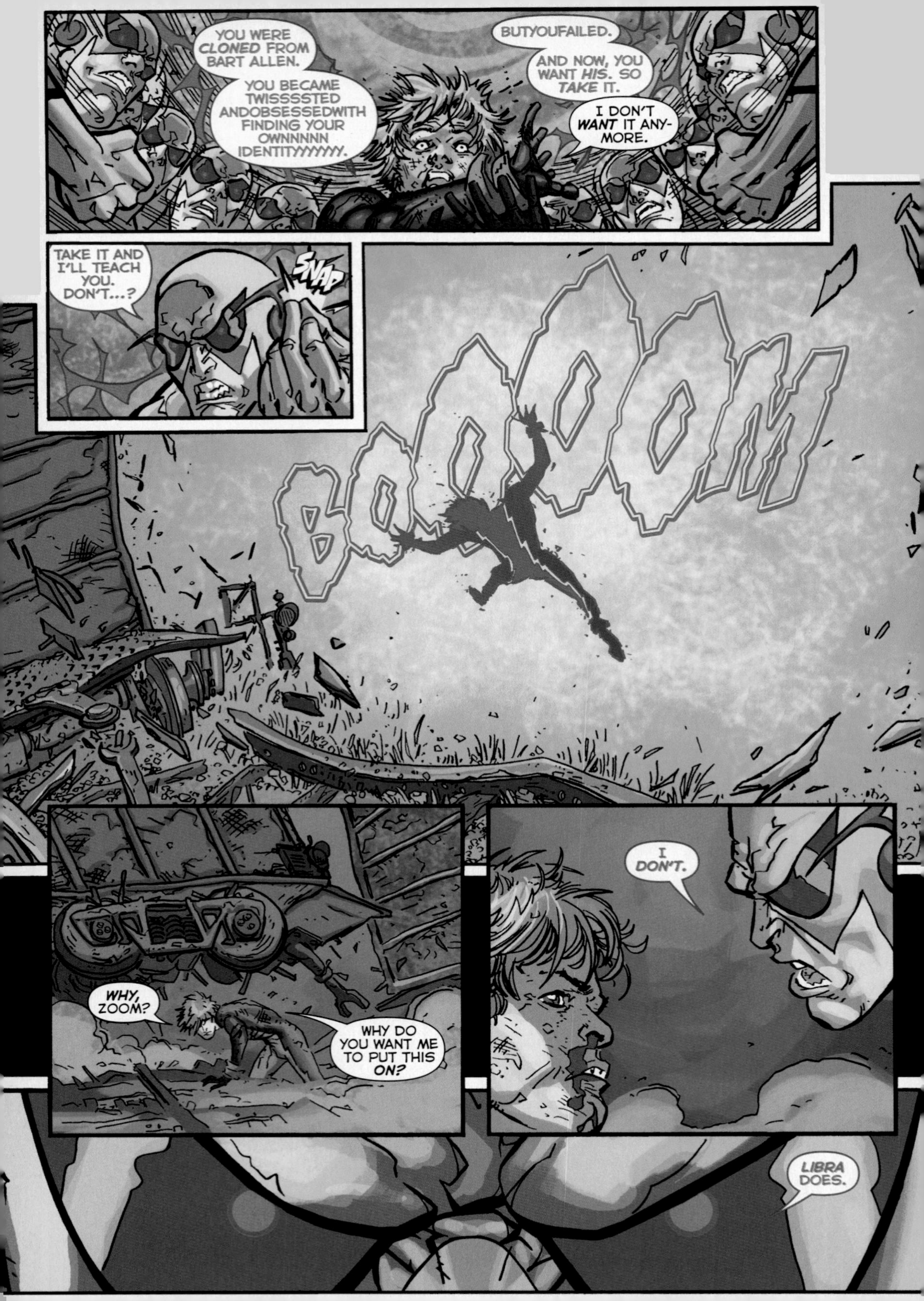
YOU WERE CLONED FROM BART ALLEN.
YOU BECAME TWISSSSTED ANDOBSESSEDWITH FINDING YOUR OWNNNNN IDENTITYYYYYYY.
BUTYOUFAILED.
AND NOW, YOU WANT HIS. SO TAKE IT.
I DON'T WANT IT ANY-MORE.
TAKE IT AND I'LL TEACH YOU. DON'T...?
SNAP
BOOOOOM
WHY, ZOOM?
WHY DO YOU WANT ME TO PUT THIS ON?
I DON'T.
LIBRA DOES.

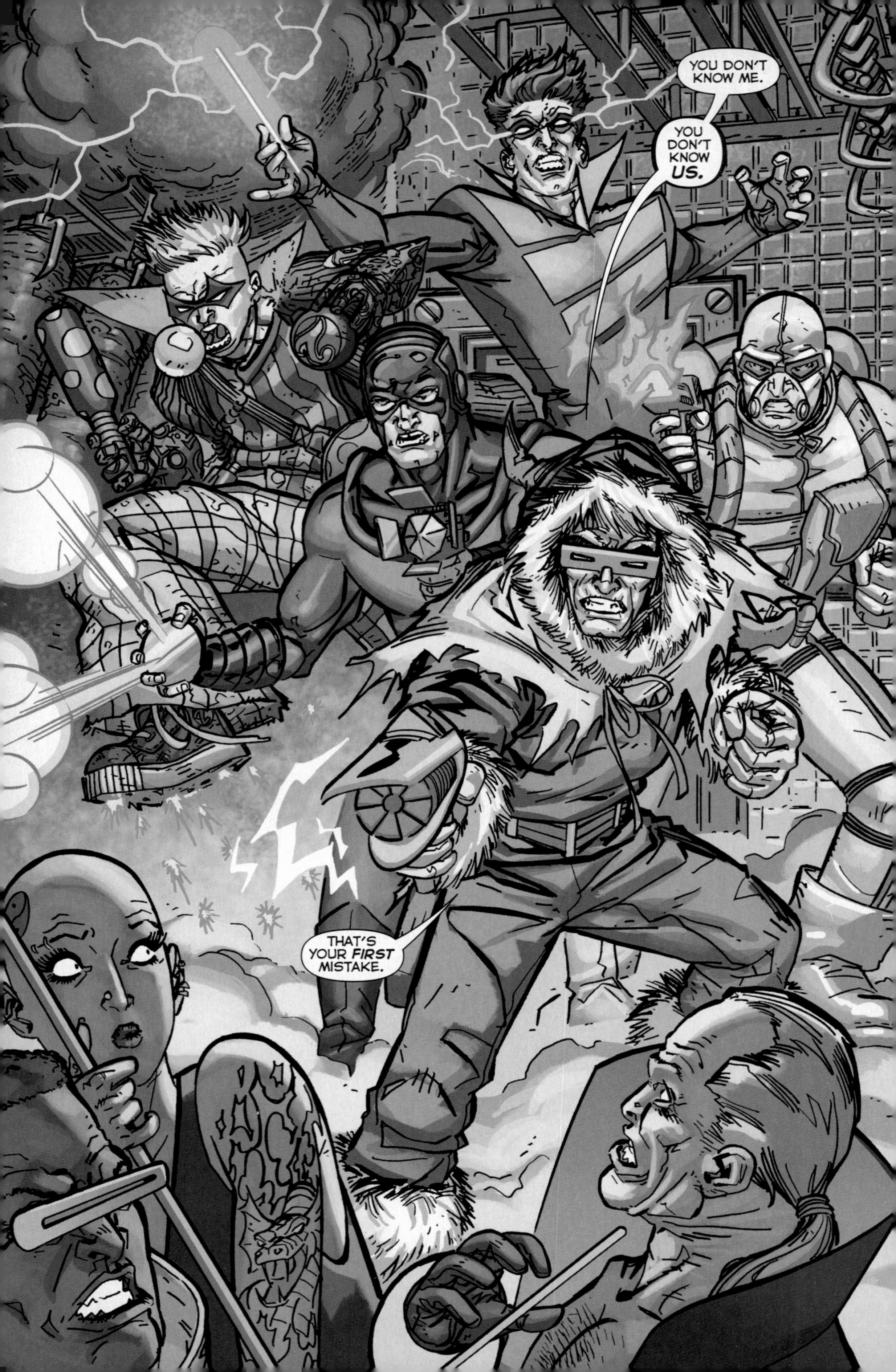
YOU DON'T KNOW ME.
YOU DON'T KNOW US.
THAT'S YOUR FIRST MISTAKE.

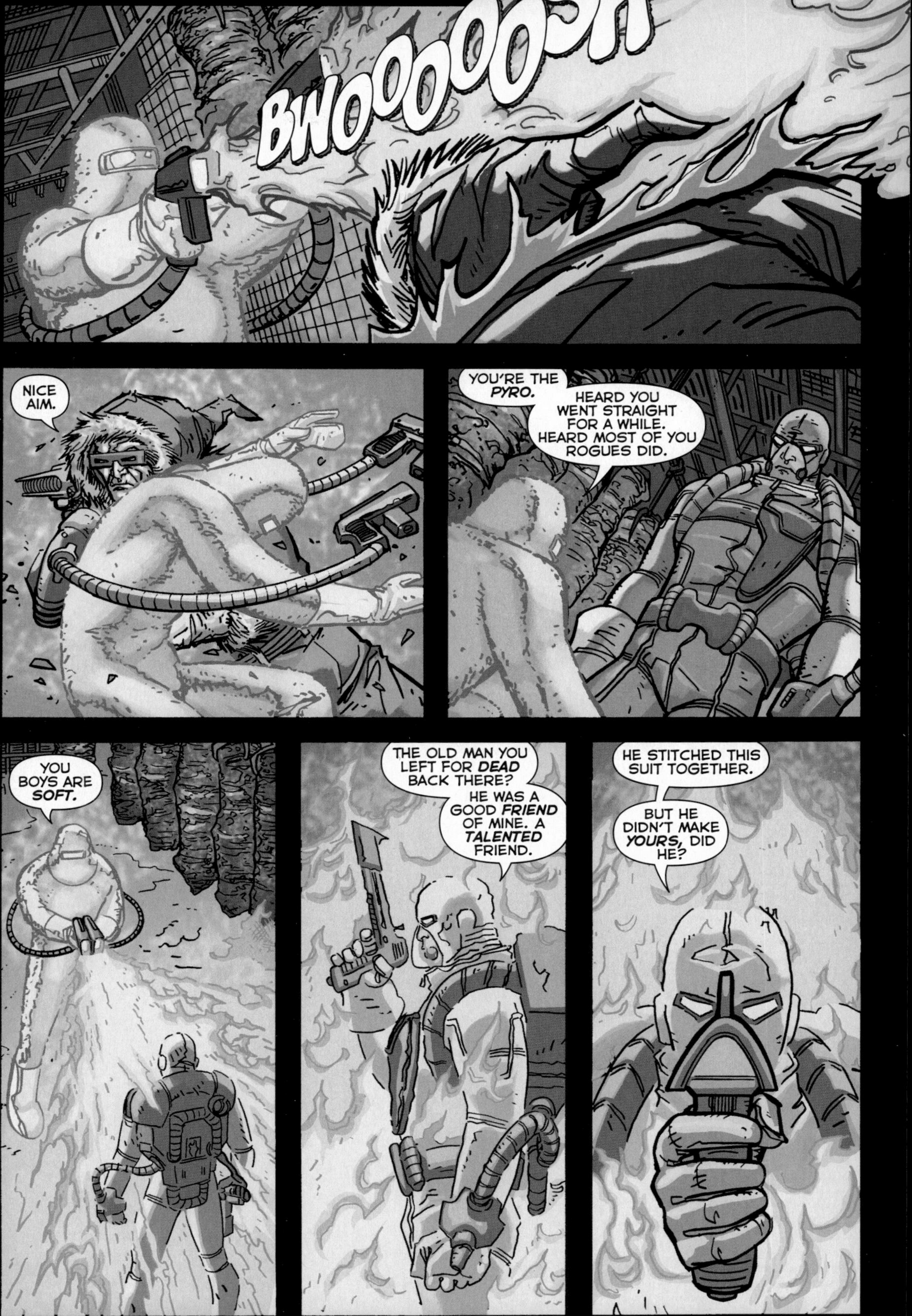
BWOOOOOOSH
NICE AIM.
YOU'RE THE PYRO.
HEARD YOU WENT STRAIGHT FOR A WHILE. HEARD MOST OF YOU ROGUES DID.
YOU BOYS ARE SOFT.
THE OLD MAN YOU LEFT FOR DEAD BACK THERE?
HE WAS A GOOD FRIEND OF MINE. A TALENTED FRIEND.
HE STITCHED THIS SUIT TOGETHER.
BUT HE DIDN'T MAKE YOURS, DID HE?

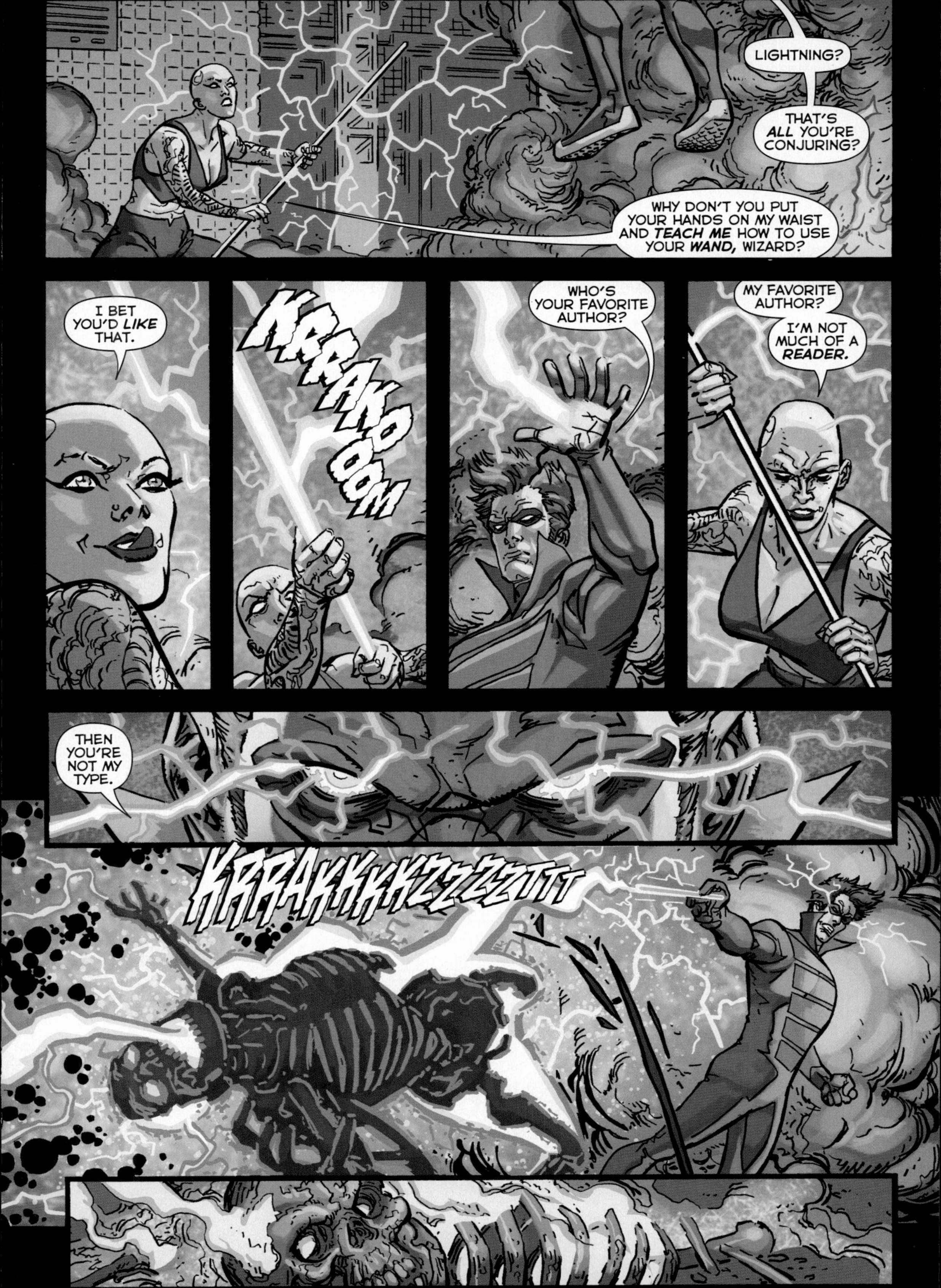
LIGHTNING?
THAT'S ALL YOU'RE CONJURING?
WHY DON'T YOU PUT YOUR HANDS ON MY WAIST AND TEACH ME HOW TO USE YOUR WAND, WIZARD?
I BET YOU'D LIKE THAT.
KRRAKOOOM
WHO'S YOUR FAVORITE AUTHOR?
MY FAVORITE AUTHOR?
I'M NOT MUCH OF A READER.
THEN YOU'RE NOT MY TYPE.
KRRAKKKKKZZZZZTTT

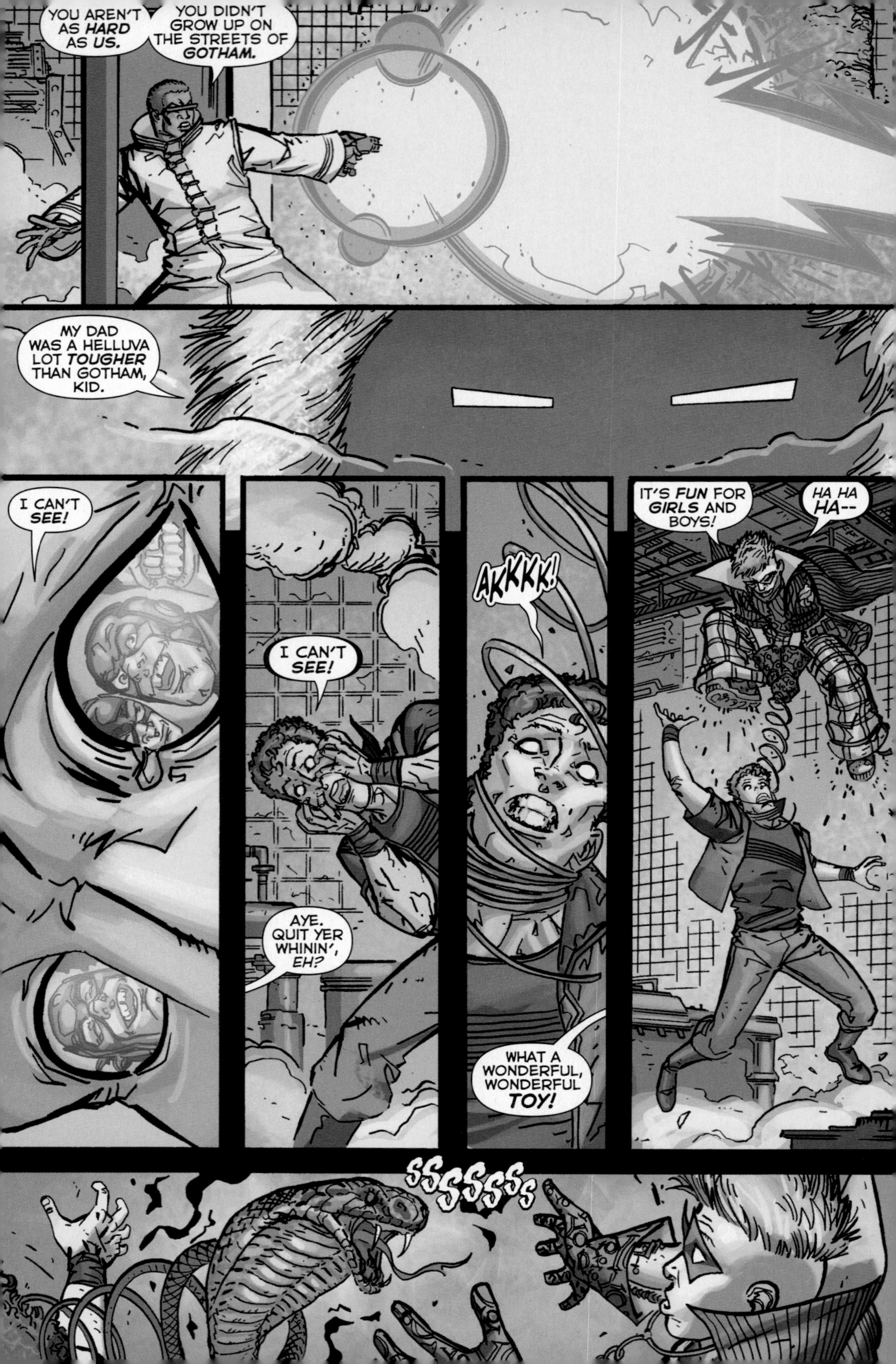
YOU AREN'T AS HARD AS US.
YOU DIDN'T GROW UP ON THE STREETS OF GOTHAM.
MY DAD WAS A HELLUVA LOT TOUGHER THAN GOTHAM, KID.
I CAN'T SEE!
I CAN'T SEE!
AYE. QUIT YER WHININ', EH?
AKKKK!
WHAT A WONDERFUL, WONDERFUL TOY!
IT'S FUN FOR GIRLS AND BOYS!
HA HA HA--
SSSSSSS

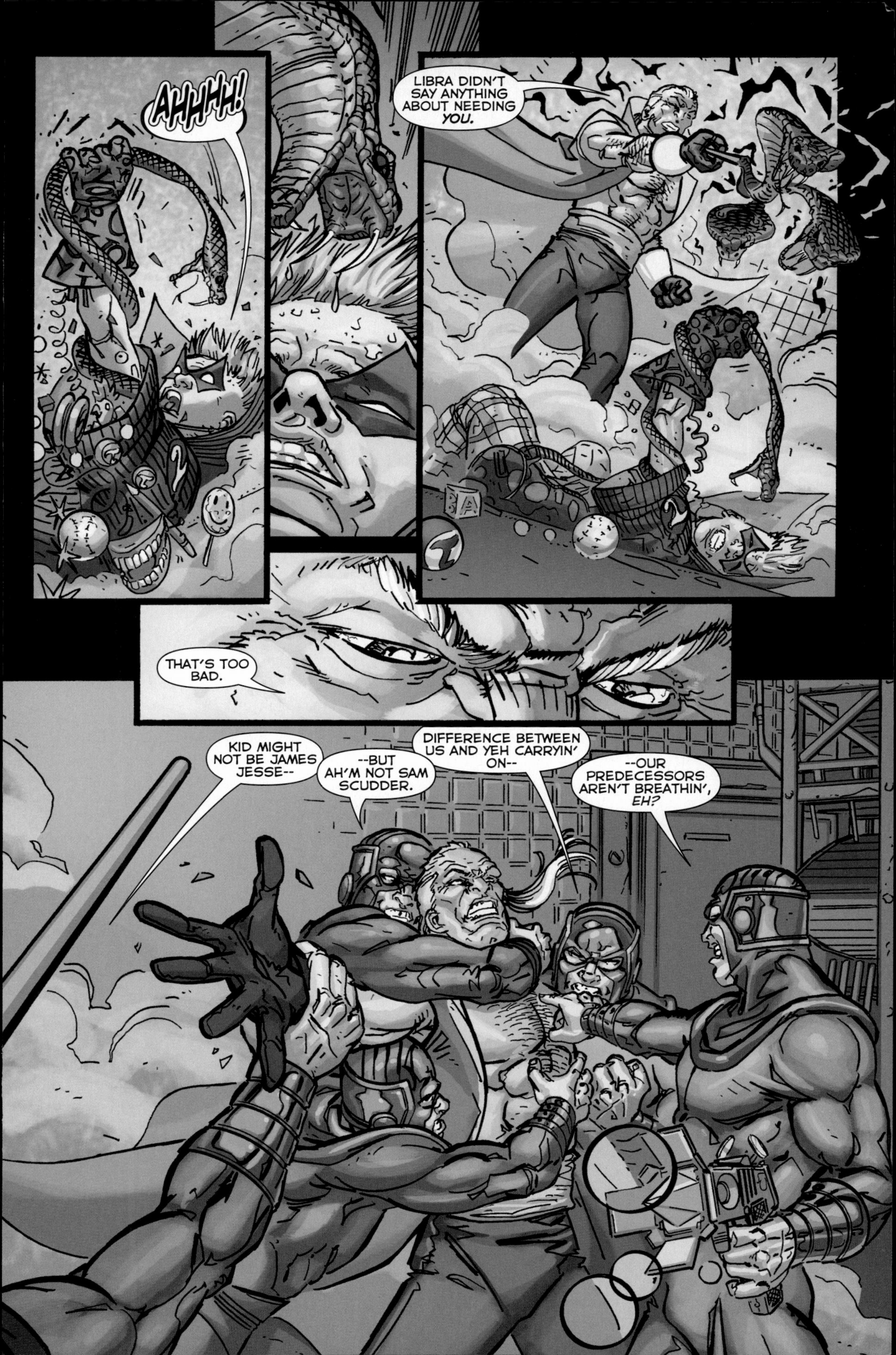
AHHHH!
LIBRA DIDN'T SAY ANYTHING ABOUT NEEDING YOU.
THAT'S TOO BAD.
KID MIGHT NOT BE JAMES JESSE--
--BUT AH'M NOT SAM SCUDDER.
DIFFERENCE BETWEEN US AND YEH CARRYIN' ON--
--OUR PREDECESSORS AREN'T BREATHIN', EH?

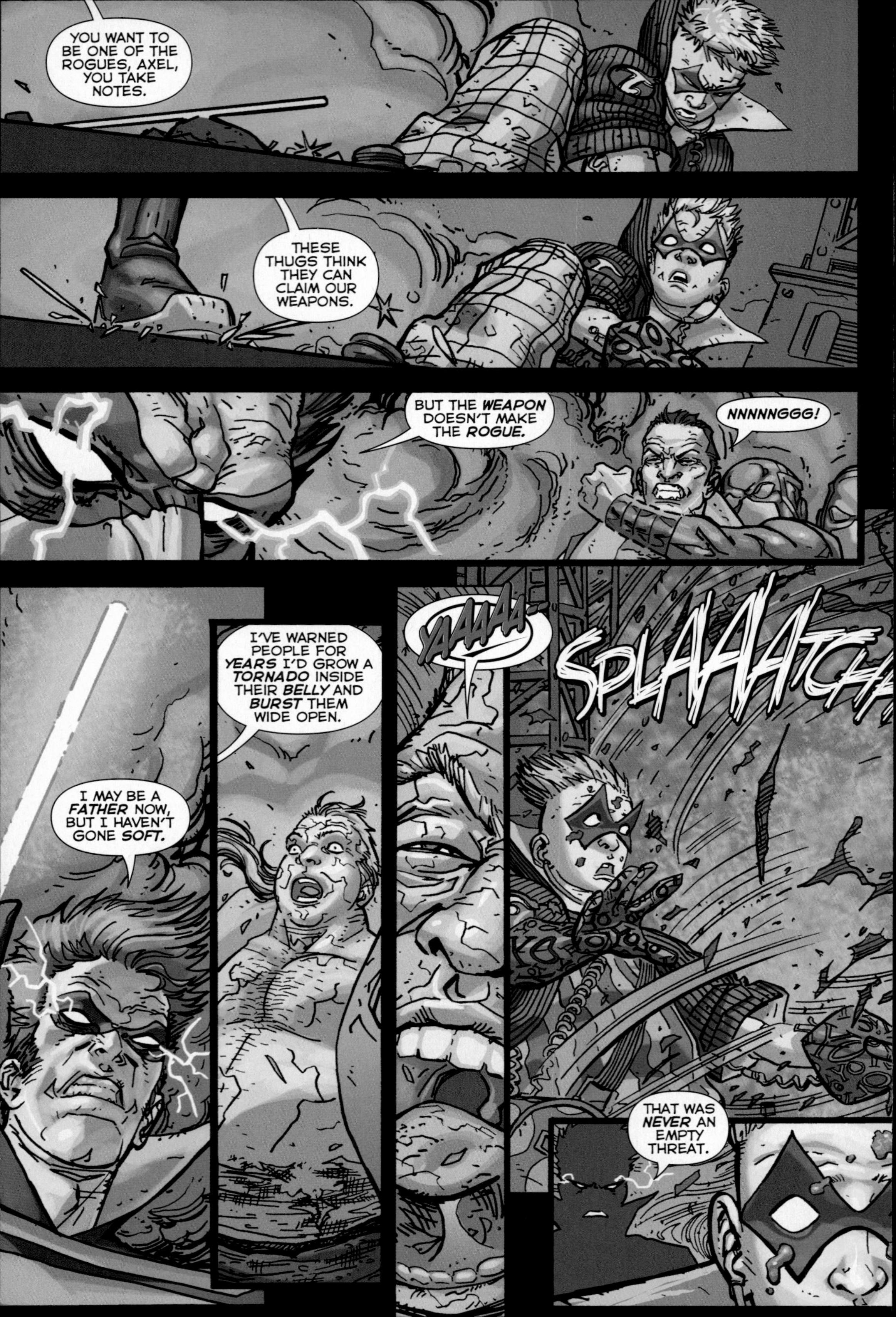

YOU WANT TO BE ONE OF THE ROGUES, AXEL, YOU TAKE NOTES.
THESE THUGS THINK THEY CAN CLAIM OUR WEAPONS.
BUT THE WEAPON DOESN'T MAKE THE ROGUE.
NNNNNGGG!
I MAY BE A FATHER NOW, BUT I HAVEN'T GONE SOFT.
I'VE WARNED PEOPLE FOR YEARS I'D GROW A TORNADO INSIDE THEIR BELLY AND BURST THEM WIDE OPEN.
YAAAAA
SPLAAATCH
THAT WAS NEVER AN EMPTY THREAT.

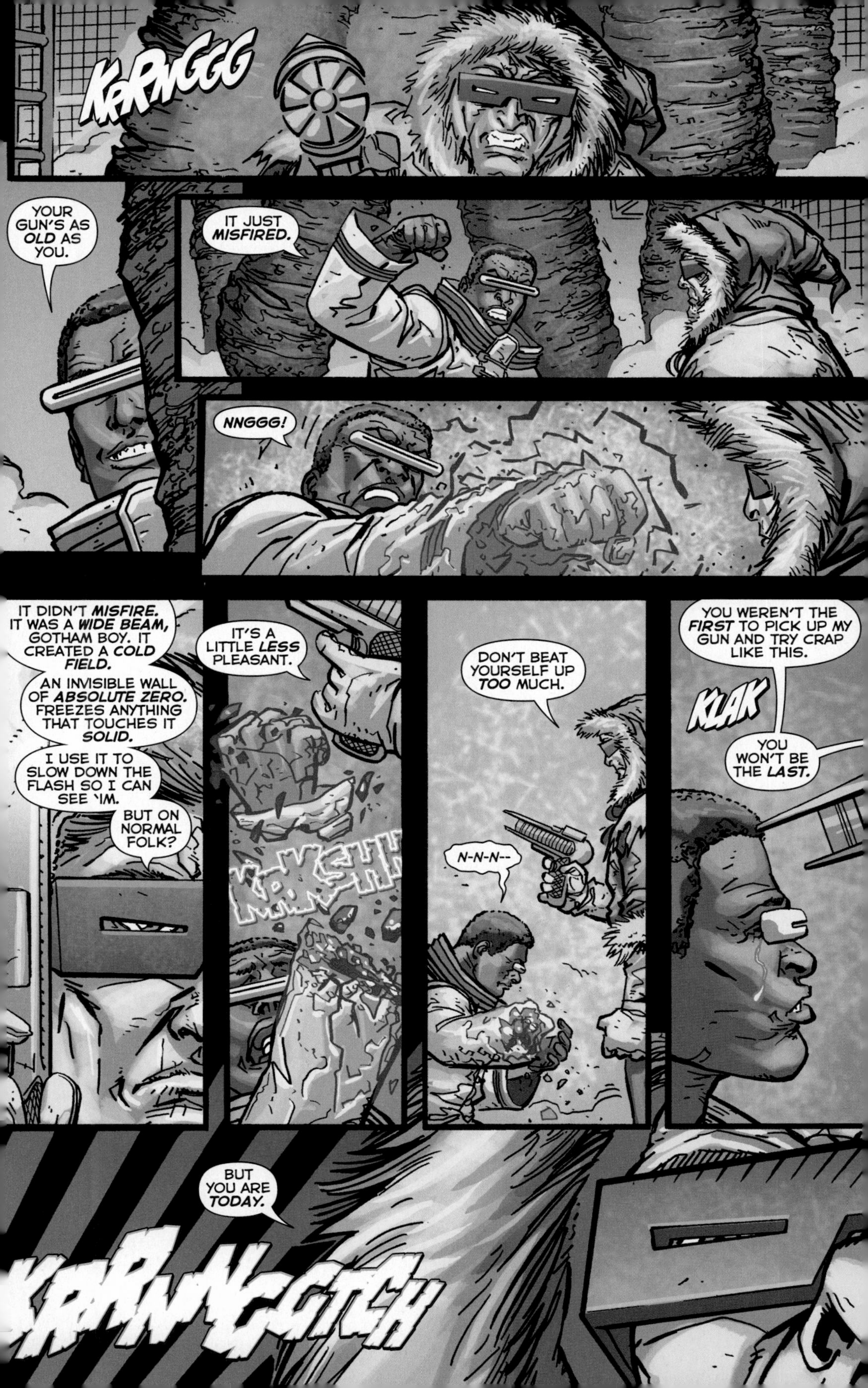
KRRNGGG
YOUR GUN'S AS OLD AS YOU.
IT JUST MISFIRED.
NNGGG!
IT DIDN'T MISFIRE. IT WAS A WIDE BEAM, GOTHAM BOY. IT CREATED A COLD FIELD.
AN INVISIBLE WALL OF ABSOLUTE ZERO. FREEZES ANYTHING THAT TOUCHES IT SOLID.
I USE IT TO SLOW DOWN THE FLASH SO I CAN SEE 'IM.
BUT ON NORMAL FOLK?
IT'S A LITTLE LESS PLEASANT.
KRKSHH
DON'T BEAT YOURSELF UP TOO MUCH.
N-N-N--
YOU WEREN'T THE FIRST TO PICK UP MY GUN AND TRY CRAP LIKE THIS.
KLAK
YOU WON'T BE THE LAST.
BUT YOU ARE TODAY.
KRRNGGTCH

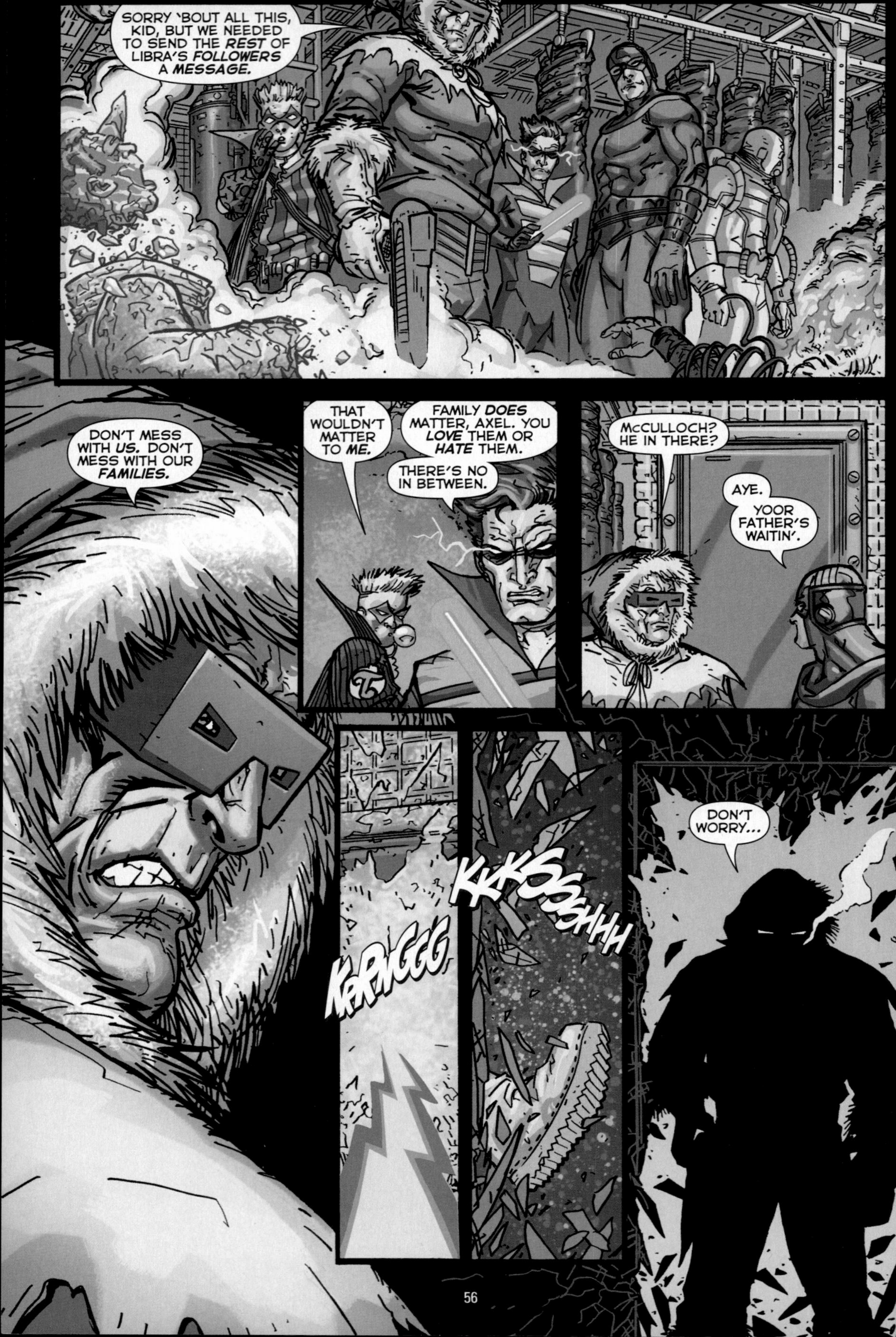
SORRY 'BOUT ALL THIS, KID, BUT WE NEEDED TO SEND THE REST OF LIBRA'S FOLLOWERS A MESSAGE.
DON'T MESS WITH US. DON'T MESS WITH OUR FAMILIES.
THAT WOULDN'T MATTER TO ME.
FAMILY DOES MATTER, AXEL. YOU LOVE THEM OR HATE THEM.
THERE'S NO IN BETWEEN.
McCULLOCH? HE IN THERE?
AYE.
YOOR FATHER'S WAITIN'.
KRRNGGG
KKKSSSSHHHH
DON'T WORRY...

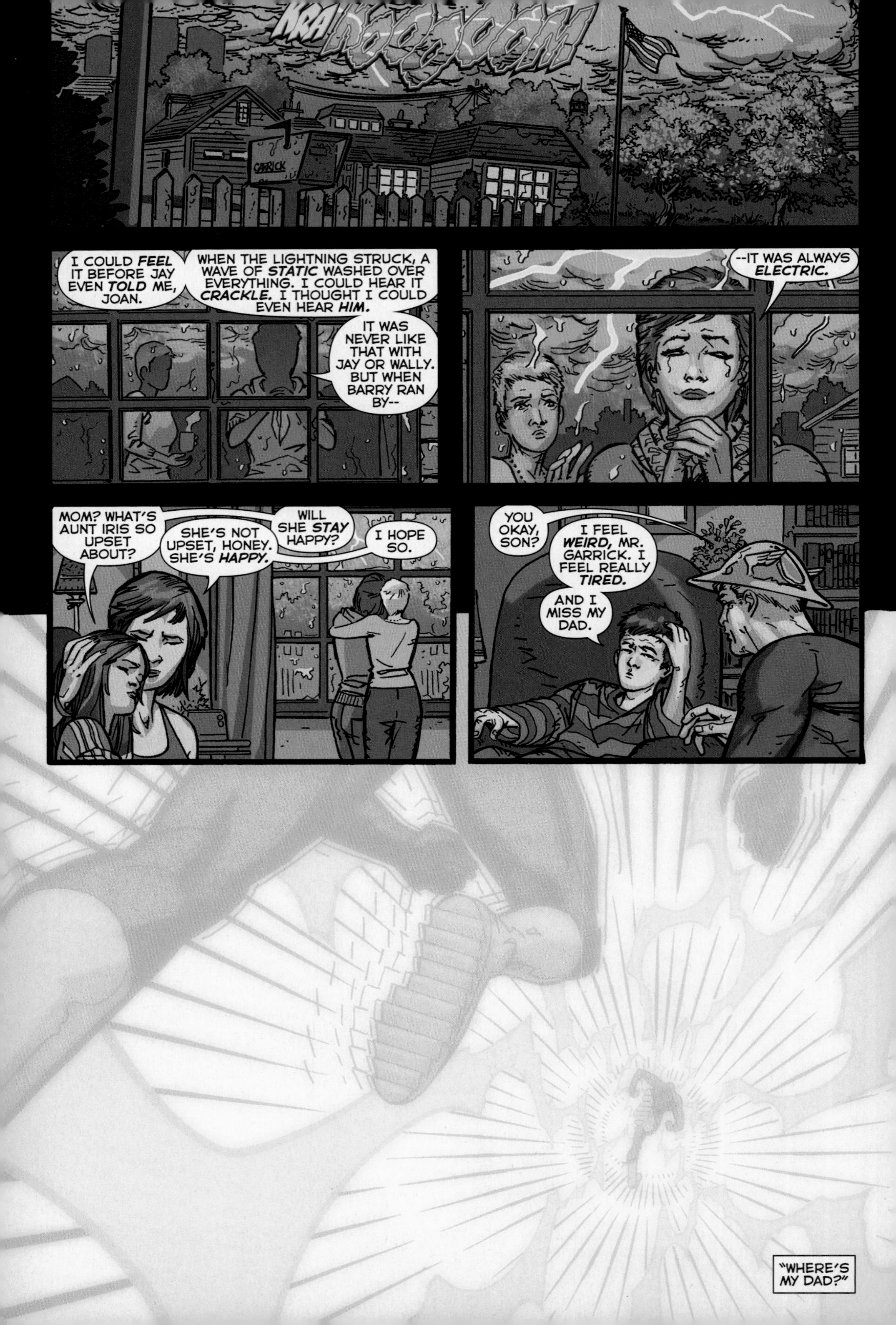
KRA KOOOOOM
GARRICK
I COULD FEEL IT BEFORE JAY EVEN TOLD ME, JOAN.
WHEN THE LIGHTNING STRUCK, A WAVE OF STATIC WASHED OVER EVERYTHING. I COULD HEAR IT CRACKLE. I THOUGHT I COULD EVEN HEAR HIM.
IT WAS NEVER LIKE THAT WITH JAY OR WALLY. BUT WHEN BARRY RAN BY--
--IT WAS ALWAYS ELECTRIC.
MOM? WHAT'S AUNT IRIS SO UPSET ABOUT?
SHE'S NOT UPSET, HONEY. SHE'S HAPPY.
WILL SHE STAY HAPPY?
I HOPE SO.
YOU OKAY, SON?
I FEEL WEIRD, MR. GARRICK. I FEEL REALLY TIRED.
AND I MISS MY DAD.
"WHERE'S MY DAD?"

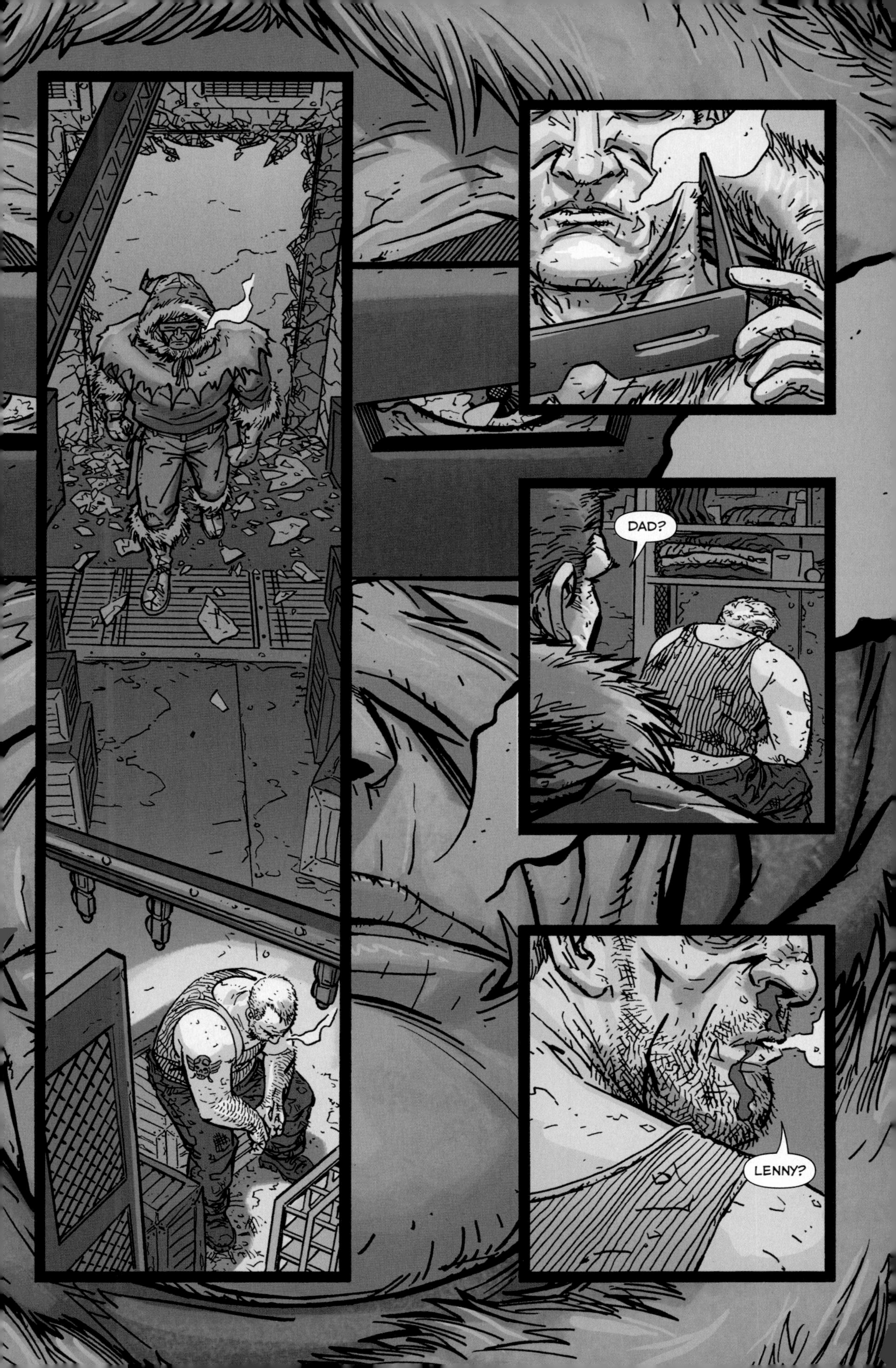
DAD?
LENNY?

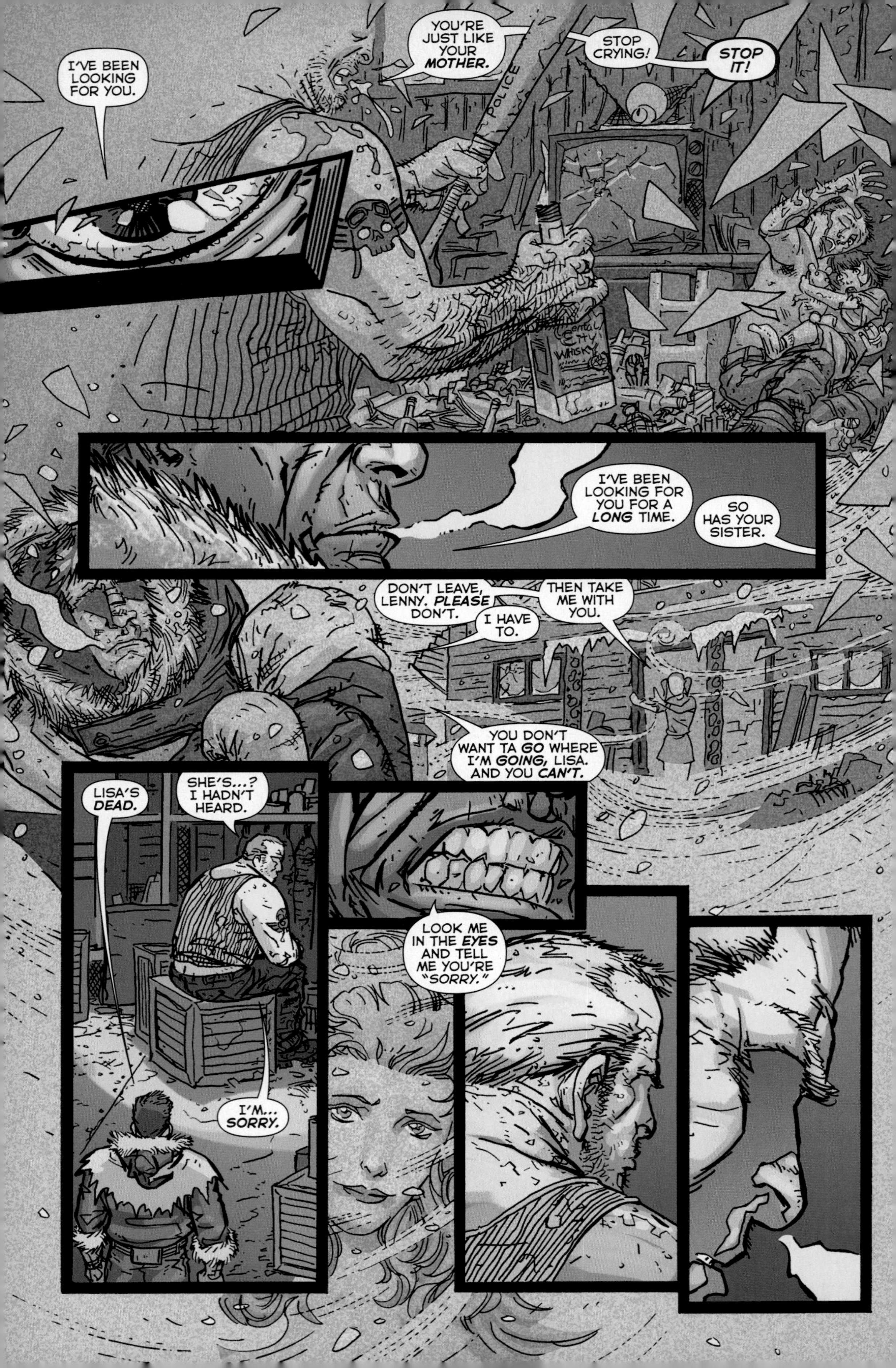
I'VE BEEN LOOKING FOR YOU.
YOU'RE JUST LIKE YOUR MOTHER.
STOP CRYING!
STOP IT!
POLICE
Central City WHISKY
I'VE BEEN LOOKING FOR YOU FOR A LONG TIME.
SO HAS YOUR SISTER.
DON'T LEAVE, LENNY. PLEASE DON'T.
I HAVE TO.
THEN TAKE ME WITH YOU.
YOU DON'T WANT TA GO WHERE I'M GOING, LISA. AND YOU CAN'T.
LISA'S DEAD.
SHE'S...? I HADN'T HEARD.
I'M... SORRY.
LOOK ME IN THE EYES AND TELL ME YOU'RE "SORRY."

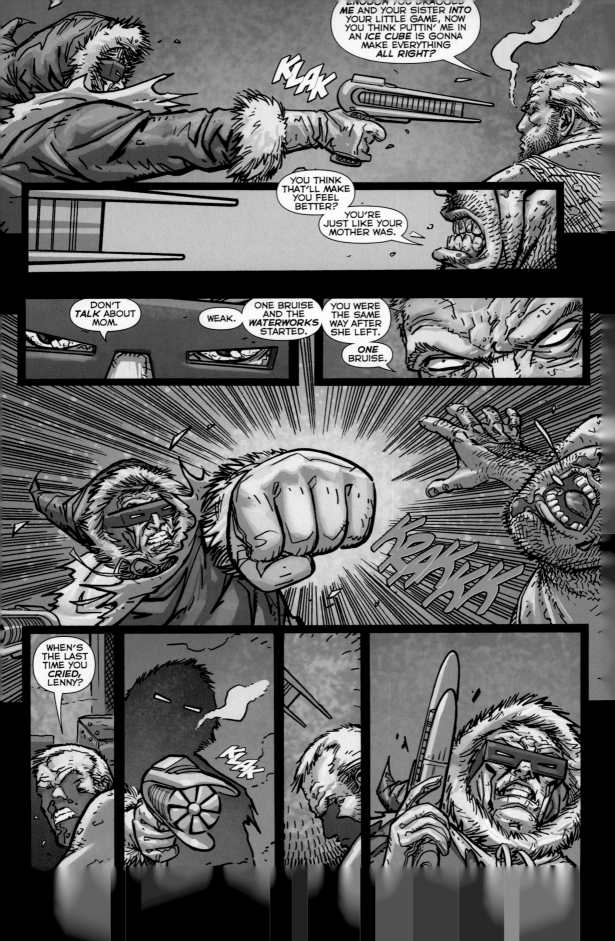

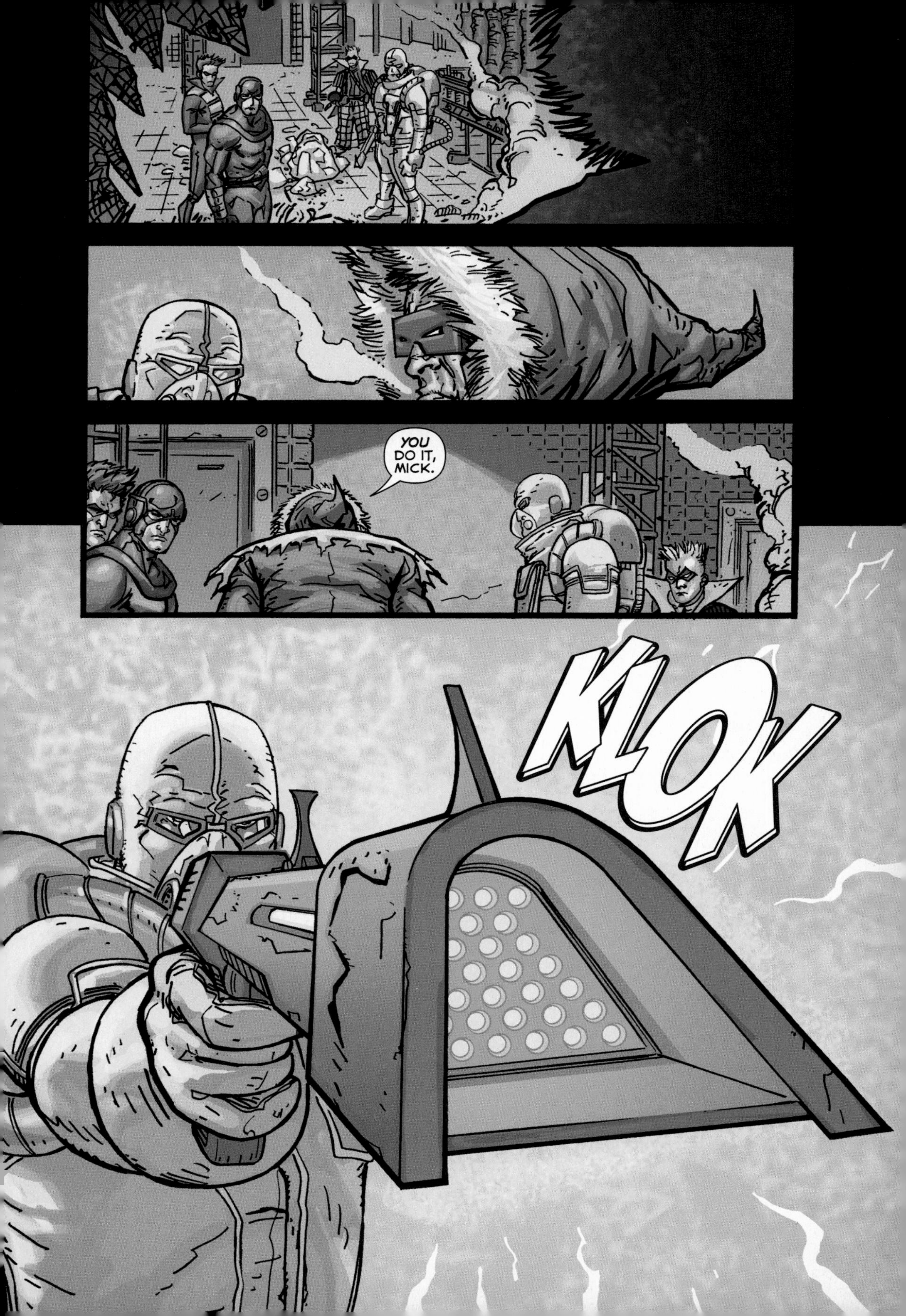
YOU DO IT, MICK.
KLOK

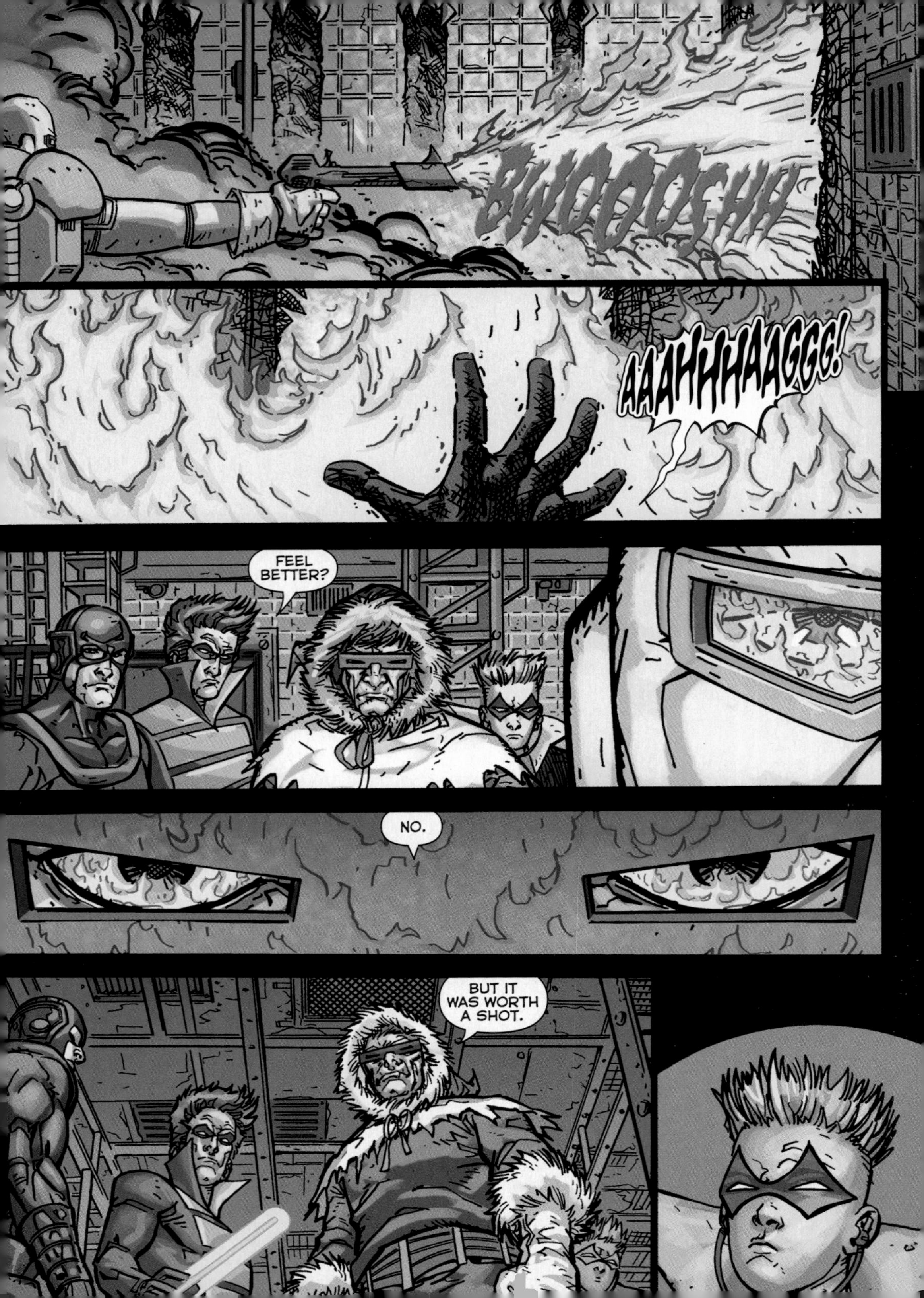
BWOOOSHH
AAAHHHAAGGG!
FEEL BETTER?
NO.
BUT IT WAS WORTH A SHOT.

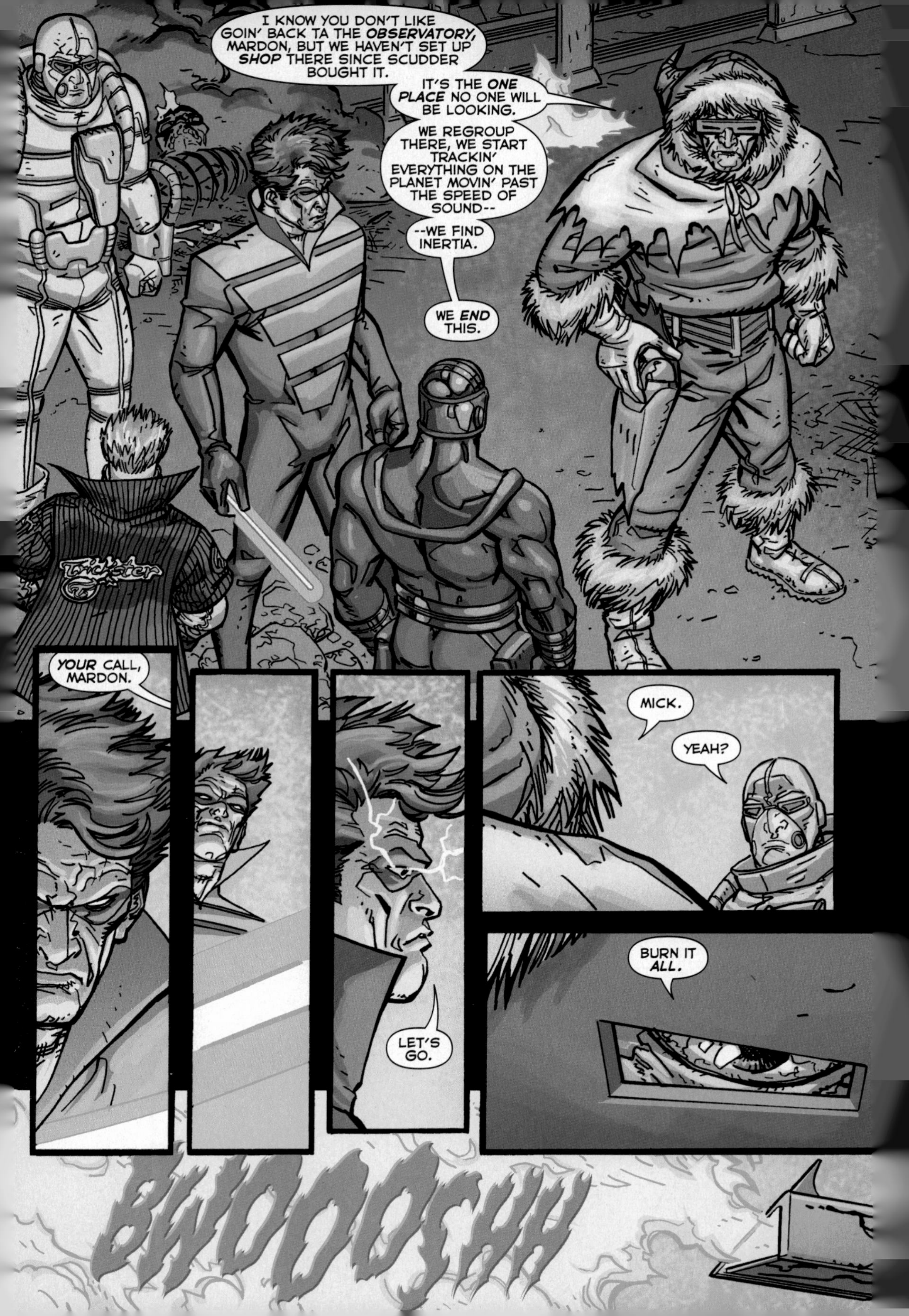
I KNOW YOU DON'T LIKE GOIN' BACK TA THE *OBSERVATORY*, MARDON, BUT WE HAVEN'T SET UP *SHOP* THERE SINCE SCUDDER BOUGHT IT.
IT'S THE *ONE PLACE* NO ONE WILL BE LOOKING.
WE REGROUP THERE, WE START TRACKIN' EVERYTHING ON THE PLANET MOVIN' PAST THE SPEED OF SOUND--
--WE FIND INERTIA.
WE *END* THIS.
Trickster
YOUR CALL, MARDON.
LET'S GO.
MICK.
YEAH?
BURN IT *ALL*.
BWOOOSHH

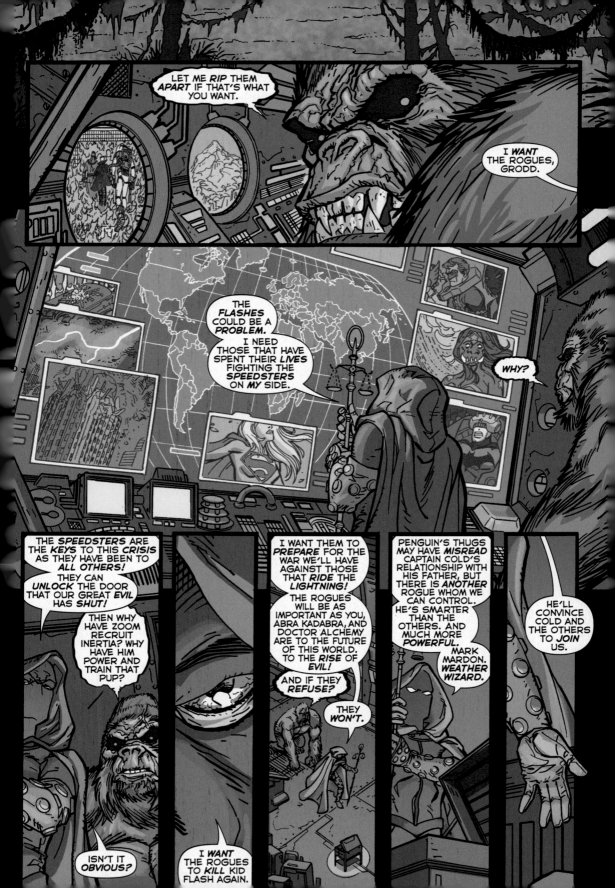

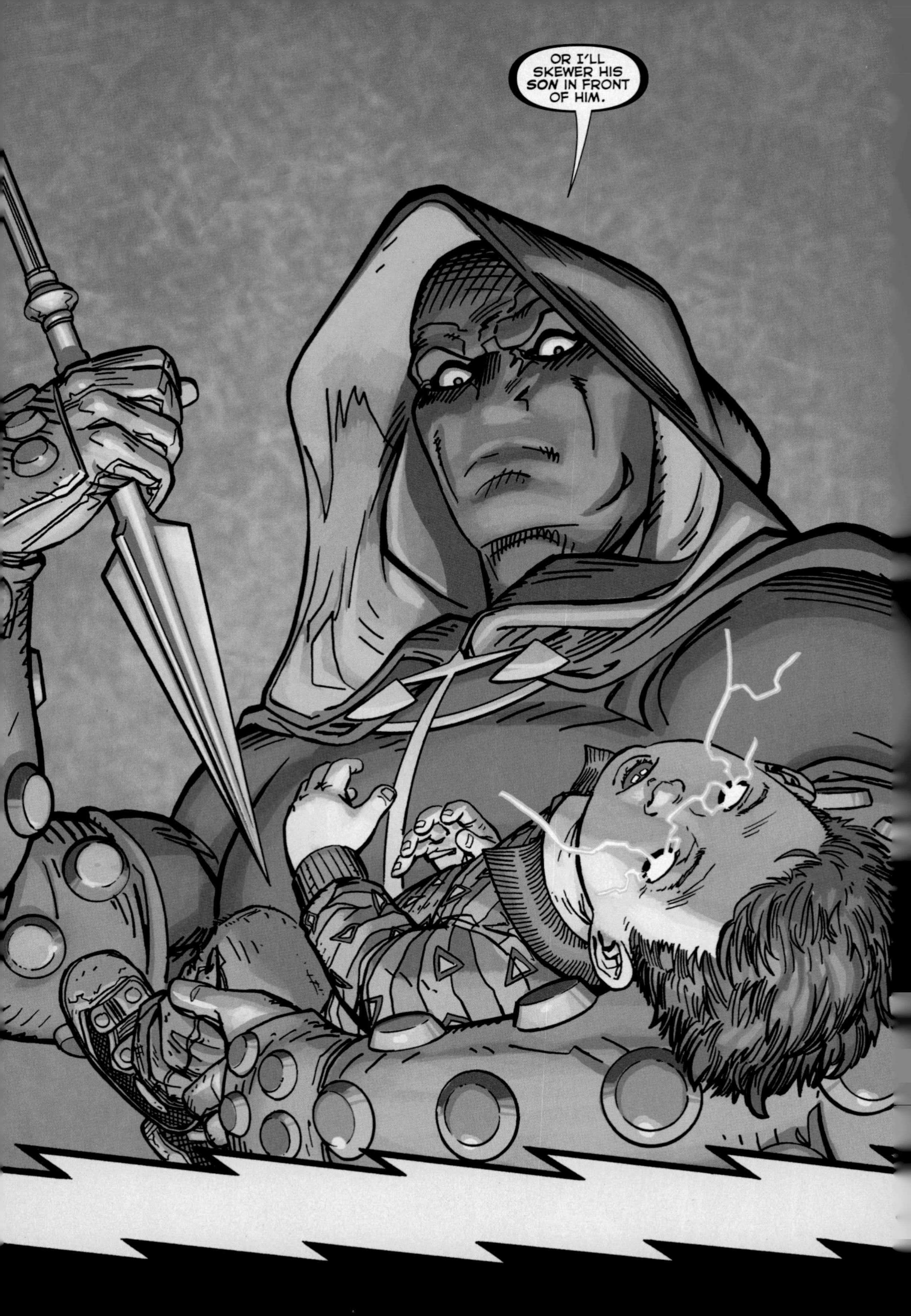
OR I'LL SKEWER HIS SON IN FRONT OF HIM.

Cover to FINAL CRISIS: ROGUES' REVENGE #3

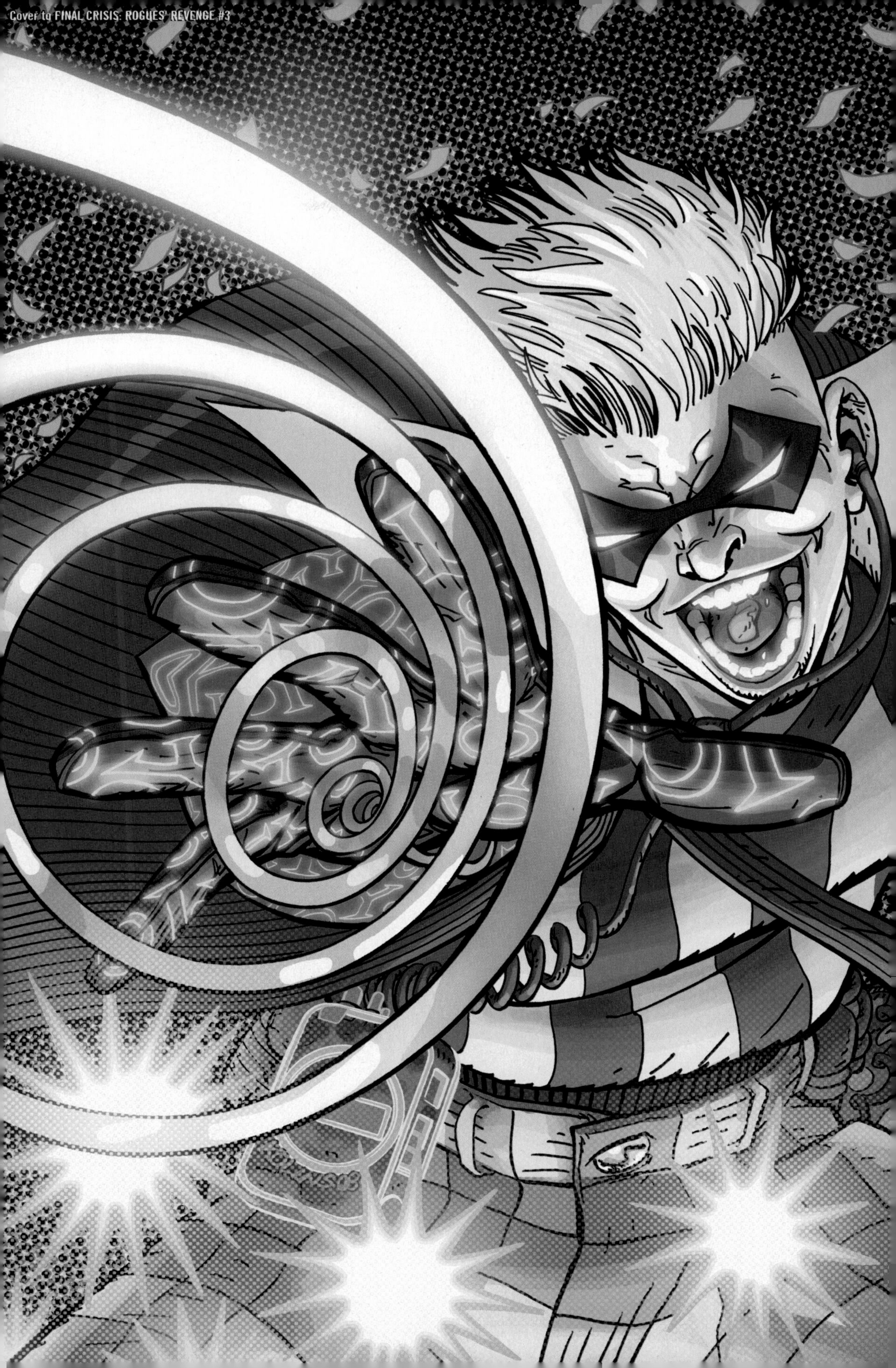

Sliver cover to FINAL CRISIS: ROGUES' REVENGE #3

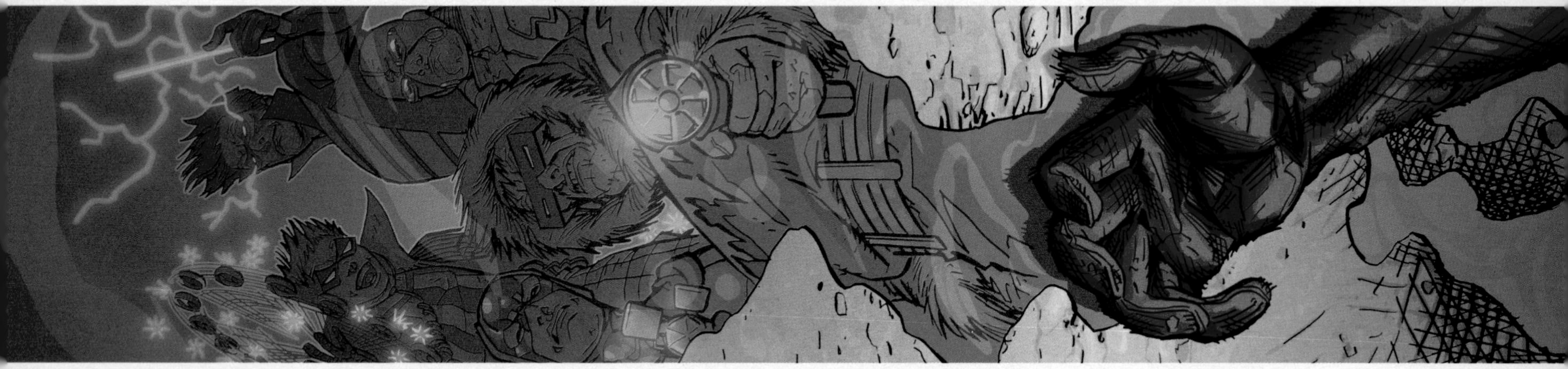

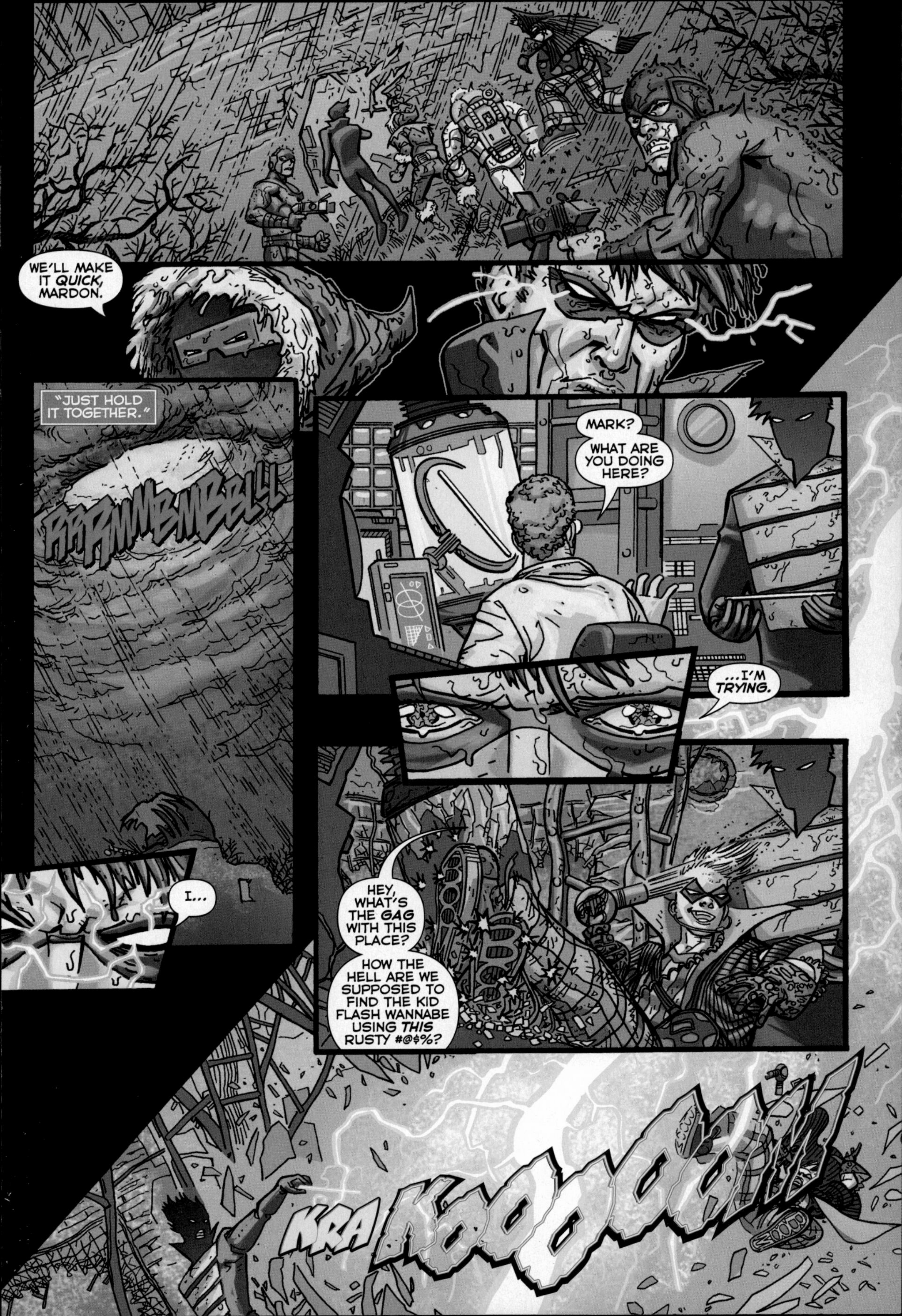

WE'LL MAKE IT QUICK, MARDON.
"JUST HOLD IT TOGETHER."
RRRMMMBMBBLLL
MARK? WHAT ARE YOU DOING HERE?
...I'M TRYING.
I...
HEY, WHAT'S THE GAG WITH THIS PLACE?
HOW THE HELL ARE WE SUPPOSED TO FIND THE KID FLASH WANNABE USING THIS RUSTY #@$%?
KRAKOOOOOM

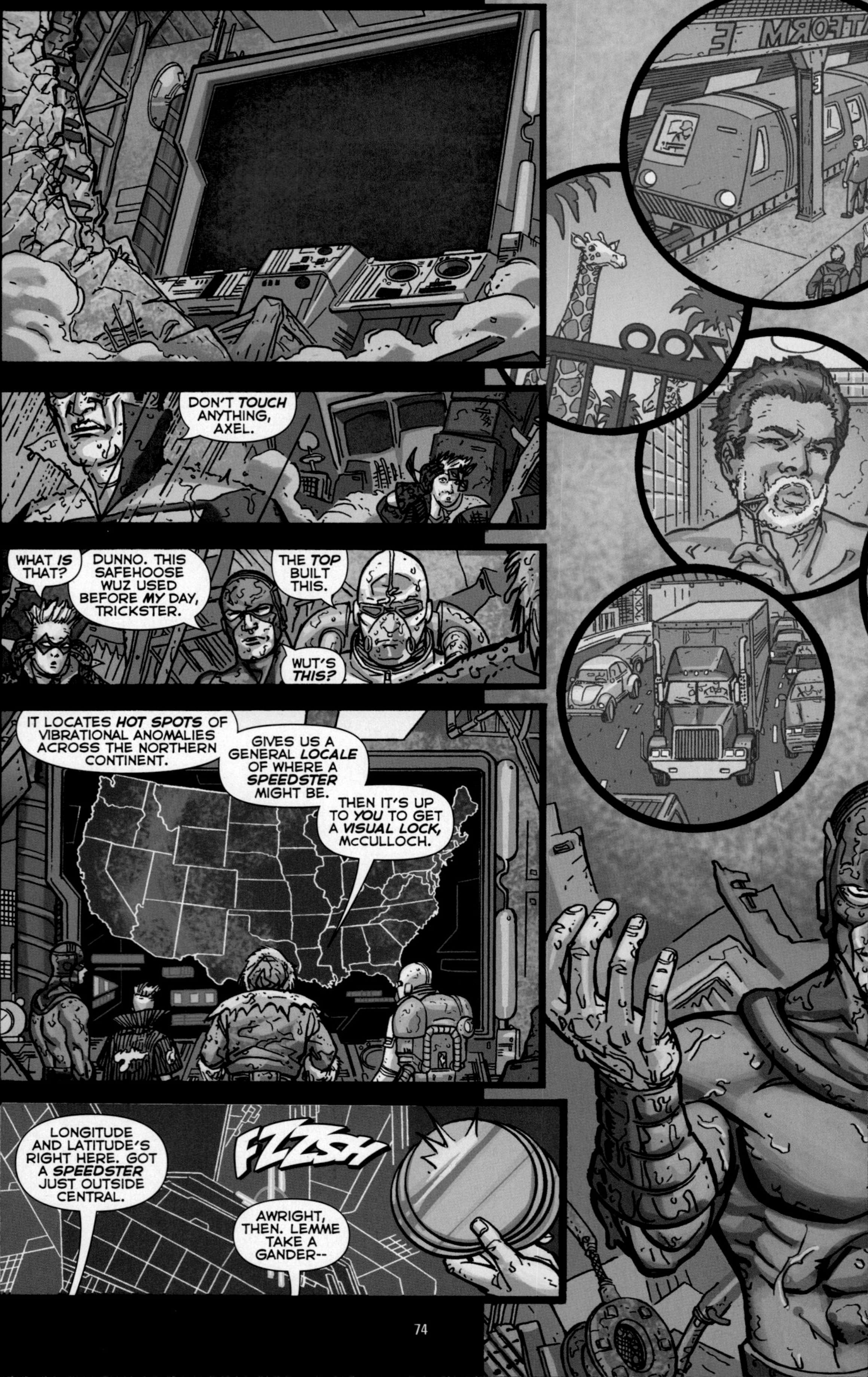
ATFORM E
ZOO
DON'T TOUCH ANYTHING, AXEL.
WHAT IS THAT?
DUNNO. THIS SAFEHOOSE WUZ USED BEFORE MY DAY, TRICKSTER.
THE TOP BUILT THIS.
WUT'S THIS?
IT LOCATES HOT SPOTS OF VIBRATIONAL ANOMALIES ACROSS THE NORTHERN CONTINENT.
GIVES US A GENERAL LOCALE OF WHERE A SPEEDSTER MIGHT BE.
THEN IT'S UP TO YOU TO GET A VISUAL LOCK, McCULLOCH.
LONGITUDE AND LATITUDE'S RIGHT HERE. GOT A SPEEDSTER JUST OUTSIDE CENTRAL.
FZZSH
AWRIGHT, THEN. LEMME TAKE A GANDER--

--THROUGH THE *LOOKING GLASS.*

WHAT'S DONE IS DONE, MARDON.

MY BROTHER WASN'T LIKE YOUR FATHER, COLD.

IT WAS *TRAGIC* WHAT HAPPENED HERE.

THAT'S WHAT IT *WAS.* THAT'S ALL YOU GOTTA THINK.

AYE. I THINK I GOT THE LITTLE *BUGGER.*

HEY, HOLD *UP!* THAT'S *KID FLASH!* HE'S--

NAW. THAT'S OUR WEE KILLER RIGHT THERE. JUS' WEARIN' KID FLASH'S SOOT.

KLAK

LET'S GO *ASK* HIM.

'CUZ KID FLASH WOULDN'T BE RUNNIN' WITH THE LIKES OF *HIM.*

ZOOM? WE'RE NOT GOING TO GO UP AGAINST *HIM,* ARE WE? NOT *THAT* GUY.

WHAT'S INERTIA DOING WITH ZOOM?

HOW CAN YOU BE *SURE,* McCULLOCH?

HEY. YOU WANT ME TO BURN THIS PLACE, MARK?

NO.

COVER OUR TRACKS?

NO, MICK.

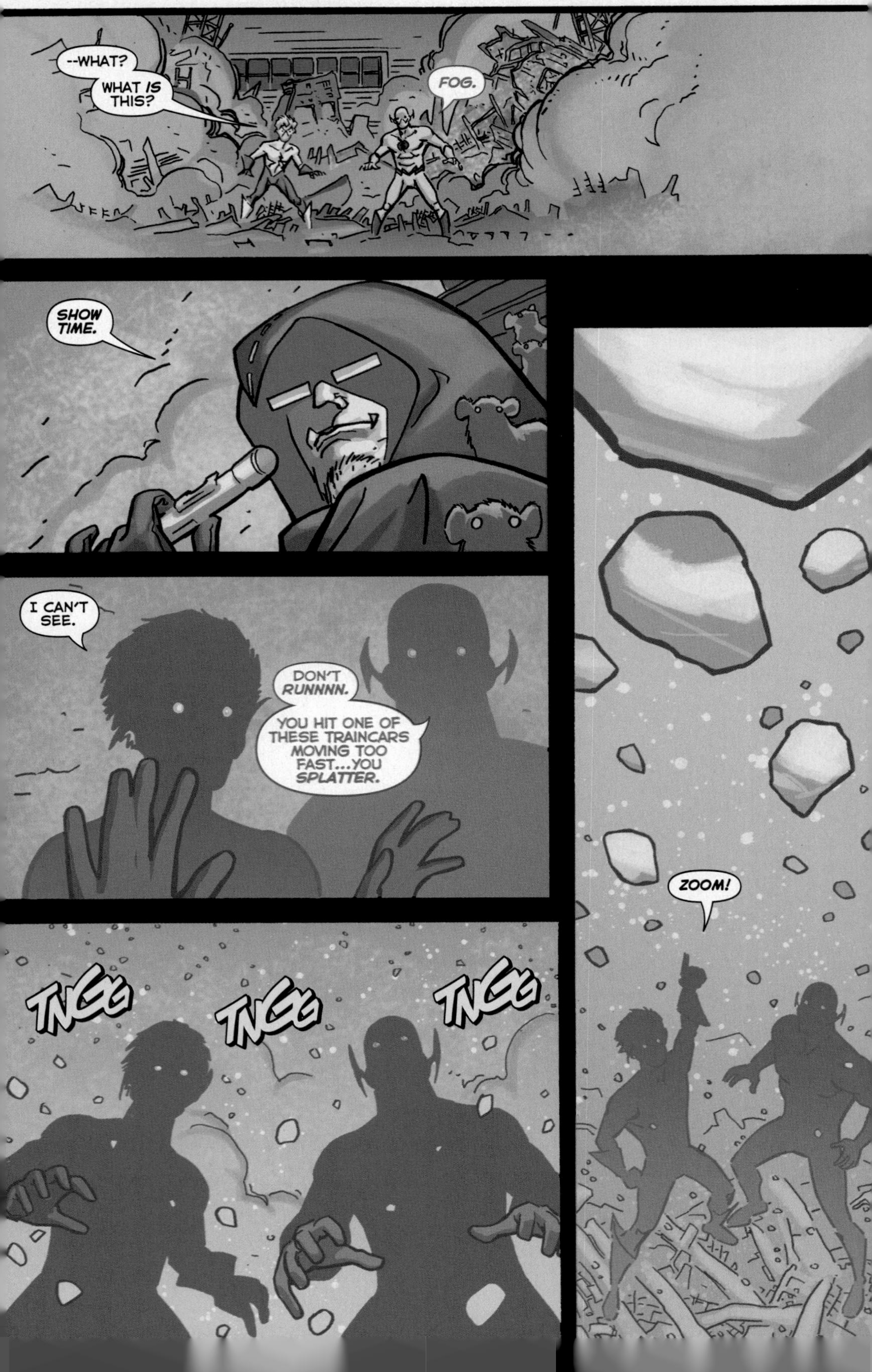
--WHAT?
WHAT IS THIS?
FOG.
SHOW TIME.
I CAN'T SEE.
DON'T RUNNNN.
YOU HIT ONE OF THESE TRAINCARS MOVING TOO FAST...YOU SPLATTER.
TNGG
TNGG
TNGG
ZOOM!

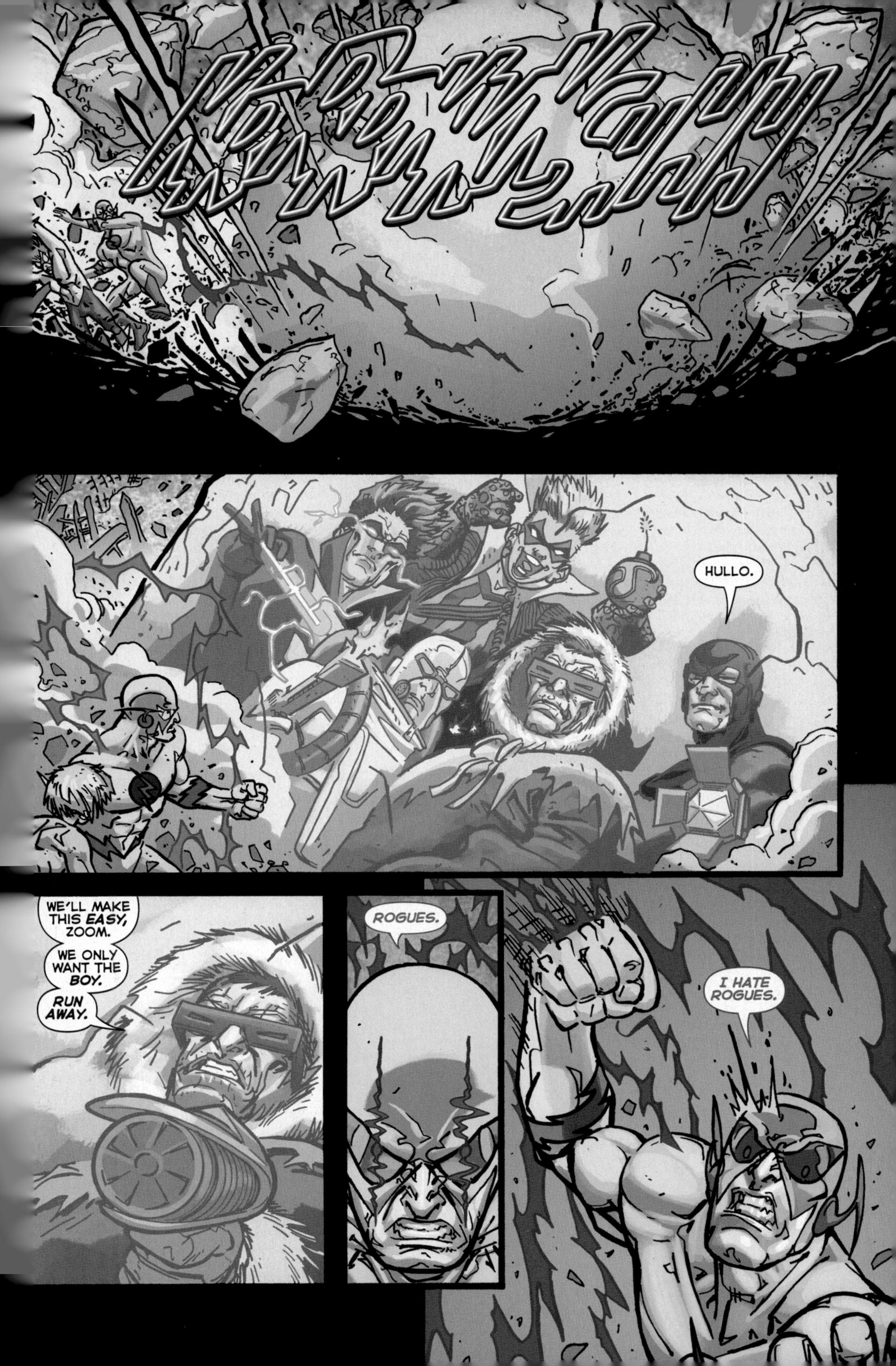
HULLO.
WE'LL MAKE THIS EASY, ZOOM.
WE ONLY WANT THE BOY.
RUN AWAY.
ROGUES.
I HATE ROGUES.

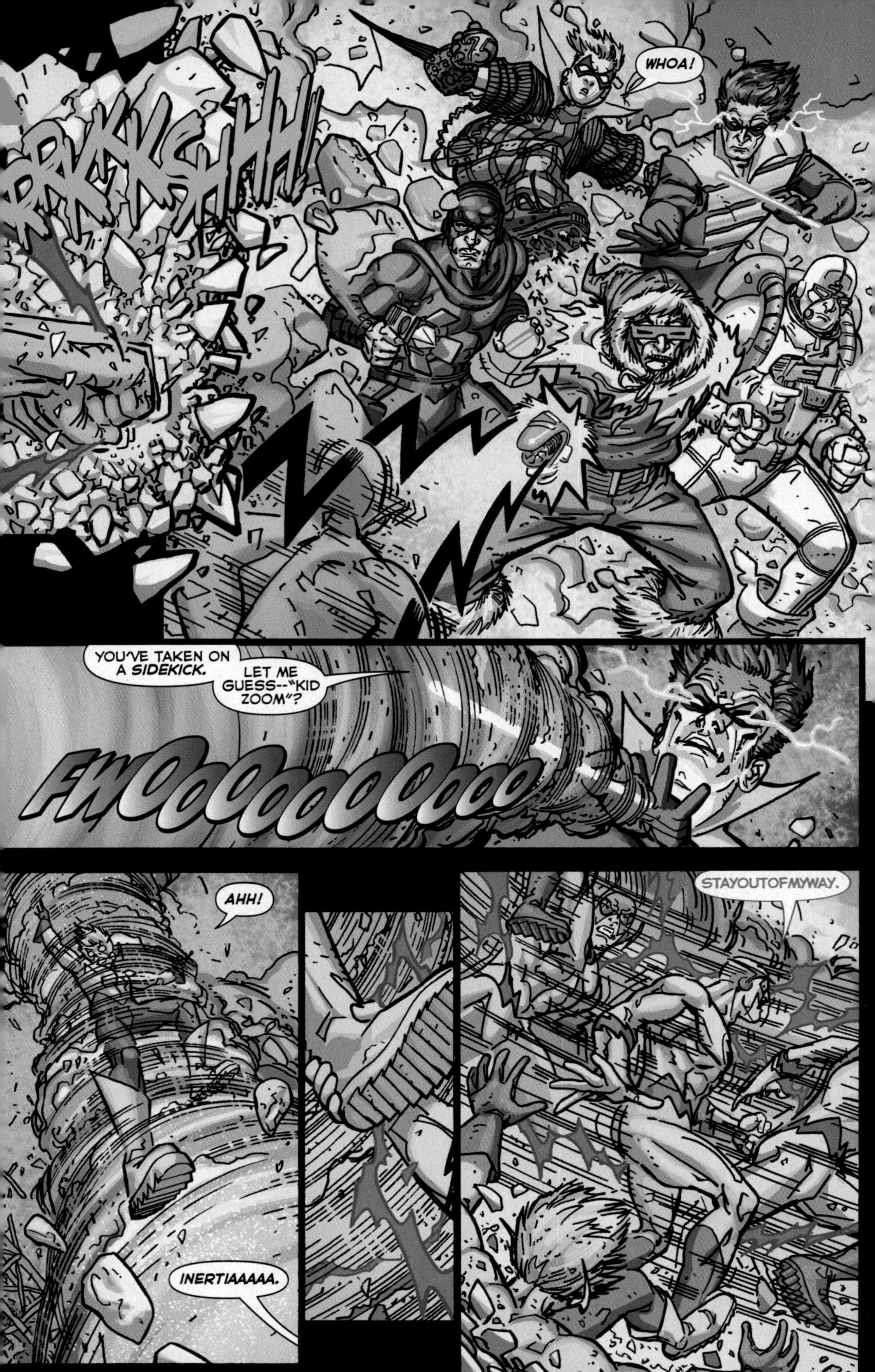
BRKKSHHH!
WHOA!
YOU'VE TAKEN ON A *SIDEKICK.*
LET ME GUESS--"KID ZOOM"?
FWOOOOOOOOOOO
AHH!
INERTIAAAAA.
STAYOUTOFMYWAY.

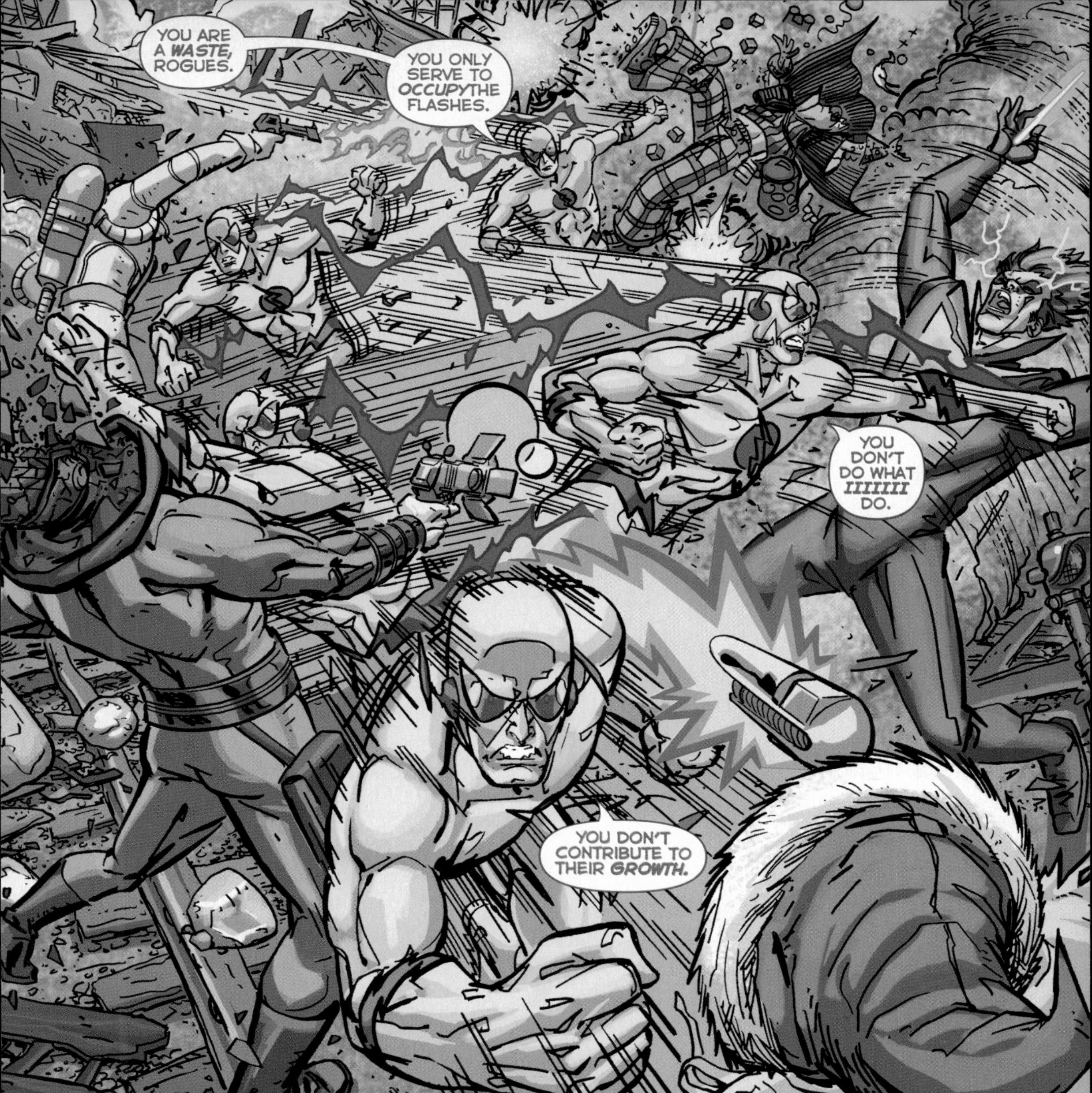
YOU ARE A WASTE, ROGUES.
YOU ONLY SERVE TO OCCUPY THE FLASHES.
YOU DON'T DO WHAT IIIIIII DO.
YOU DON'T CONTRIBUTE TO THEIR GROWTH.

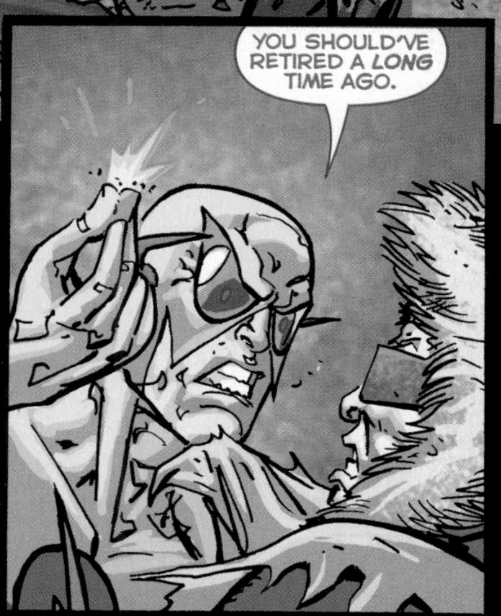
YOU SHOULD'VE RETIRED A LONG TIME AGO.

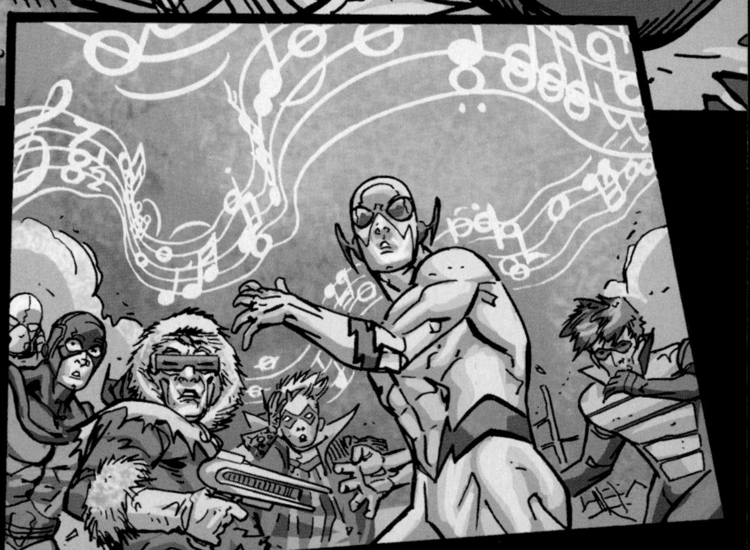

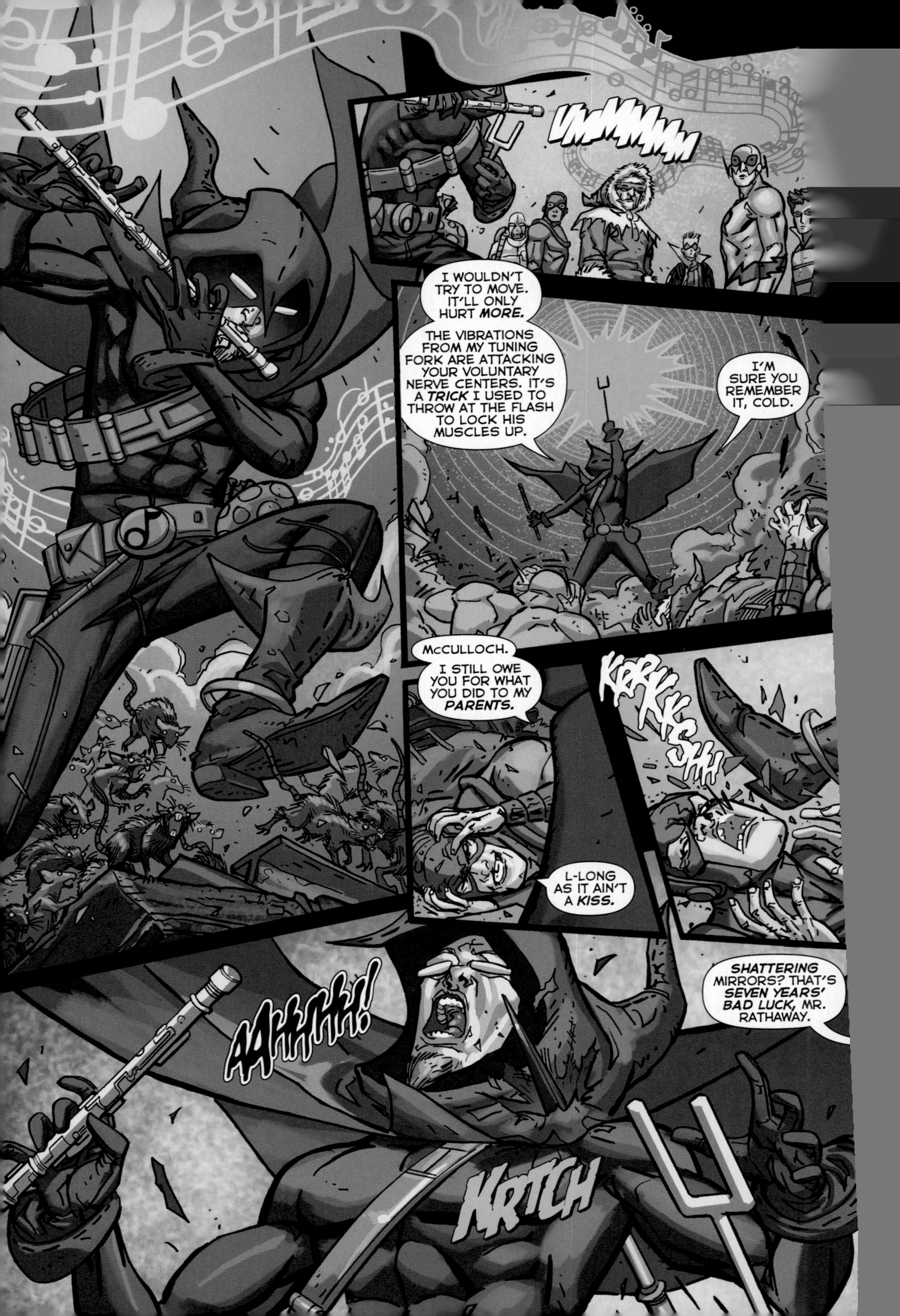

VMMMMMM
I WOULDN'T TRY TO MOVE. IT'LL ONLY HURT MORE.
THE VIBRATIONS FROM MY TUNING FORK ARE ATTACKING YOUR VOLUNTARY NERVE CENTERS. IT'S A TRICK I USED TO THROW AT THE FLASH TO LOCK HIS MUSCLES UP.
I'M SURE YOU REMEMBER IT, COLD.
McCULLOCH.
I STILL OWE YOU FOR WHAT YOU DID TO MY PARENTS.
L-LONG AS IT AIN'T A KISS.
KRRKKSHH
AAHHHH!
SHATTERING MIRRORS? THAT'S SEVEN YEARS' BAD LUCK, MR. RATHAWAY.
KRTCH

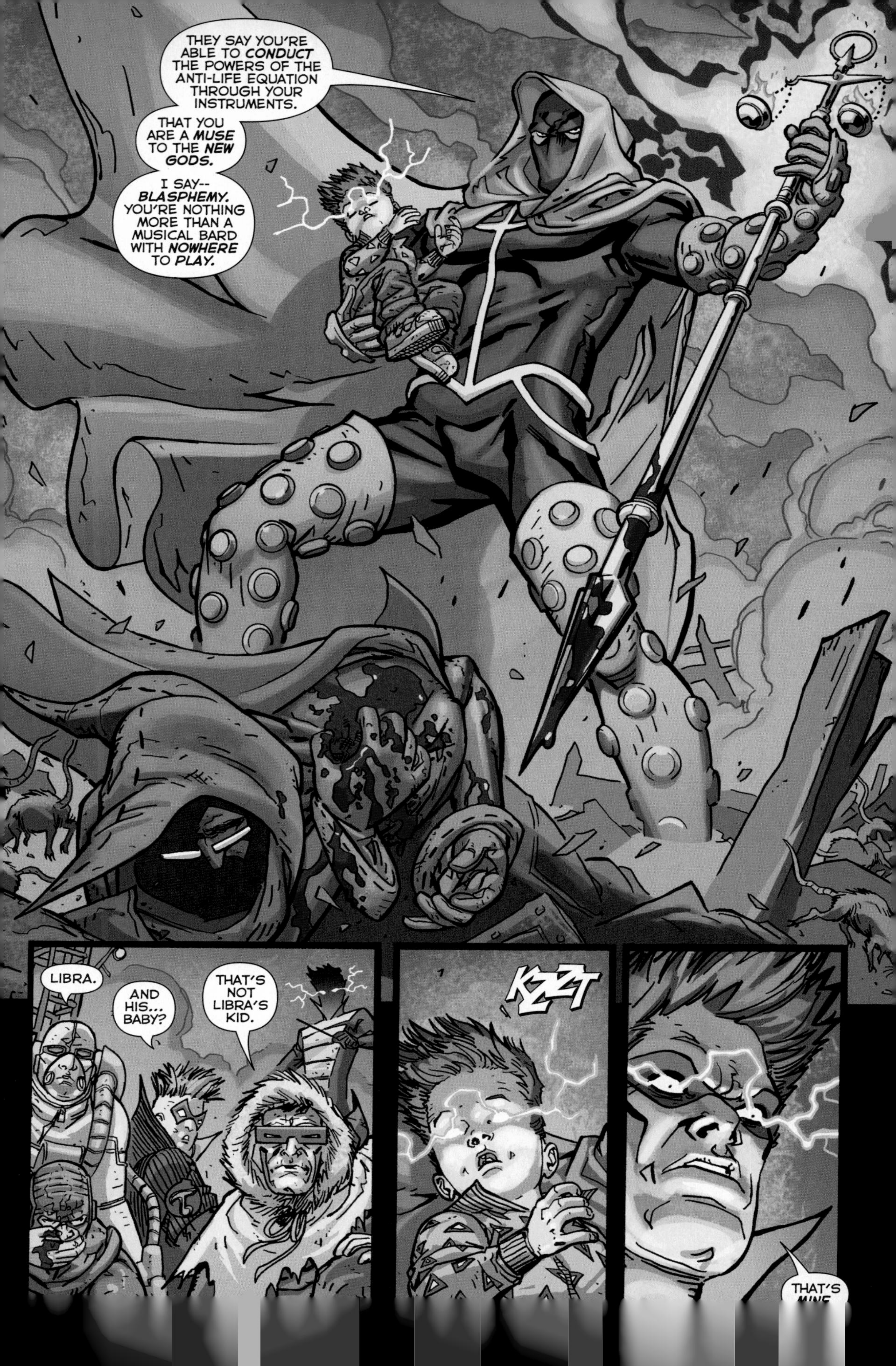
THEY SAY YOU'RE ABLE TO CONDUCT THE POWERS OF THE ANTI-LIFE EQUATION THROUGH YOUR INSTRUMENTS.
THAT YOU ARE A MUSE TO THE NEW GODS.
I SAY-- BLASPHEMY. YOU'RE NOTHING MORE THAN A MUSICAL BARD WITH NOWHERE TO PLAY.
LIBRA.
AND HIS... BABY?
THAT'S NOT LIBRA'S KID.
KZZT
THAT'S

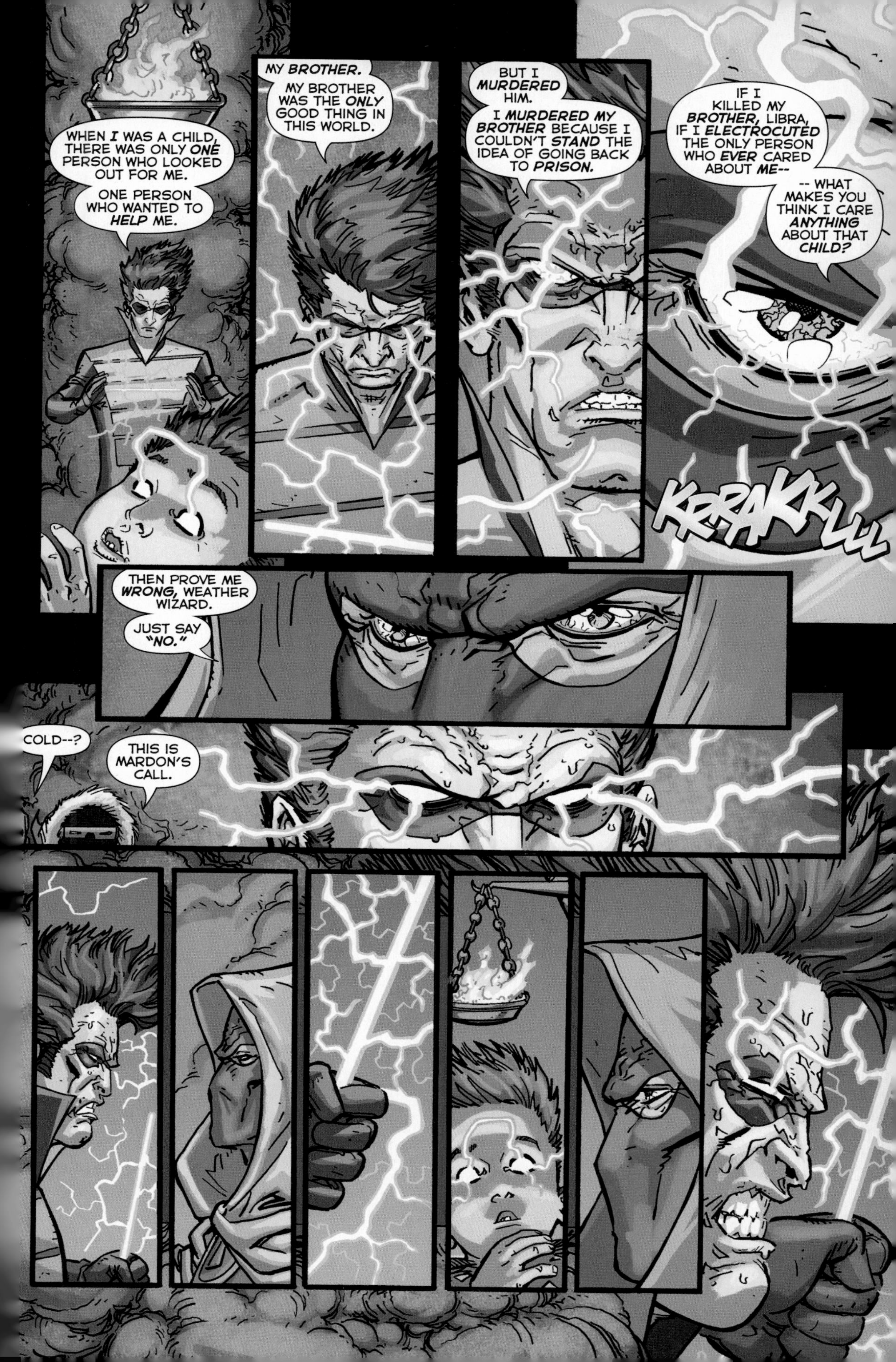
WHEN I WAS A CHILD, THERE WAS ONLY ONE PERSON WHO LOOKED OUT FOR ME.
ONE PERSON WHO WANTED TO HELP ME.
MY BROTHER.
MY BROTHER WAS THE ONLY GOOD THING IN THIS WORLD.
BUT I MURDERED HIM.
I MURDERED MY BROTHER BECAUSE I COULDN'T STAND THE IDEA OF GOING BACK TO PRISON.
IF I KILLED MY BROTHER, LIBRA, IF I ELECTROCUTED THE ONLY PERSON WHO EVER CARED ABOUT ME--
-- WHAT MAKES YOU THINK I CARE ANYTHING ABOUT THAT CHILD?
KRRAKKLLL
THEN PROVE ME WRONG, WEATHER WIZARD.
JUST SAY "NO."
COLD--?
THIS IS MARDON'S CALL.

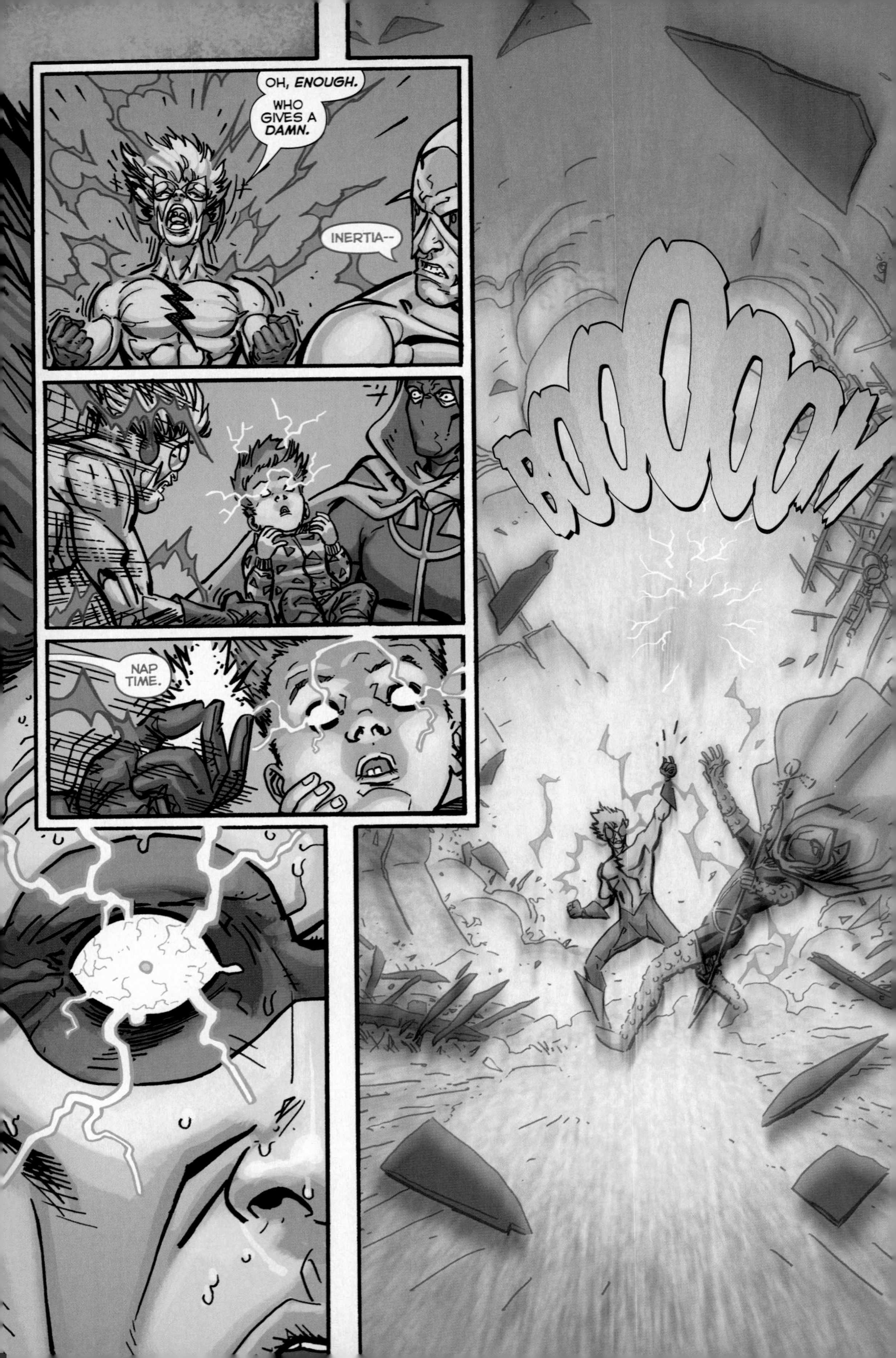

OH, *ENOUGH.*
WHO GIVES A *DAMN.*
INERTIA--
NAP TIME.
BOOOOOM

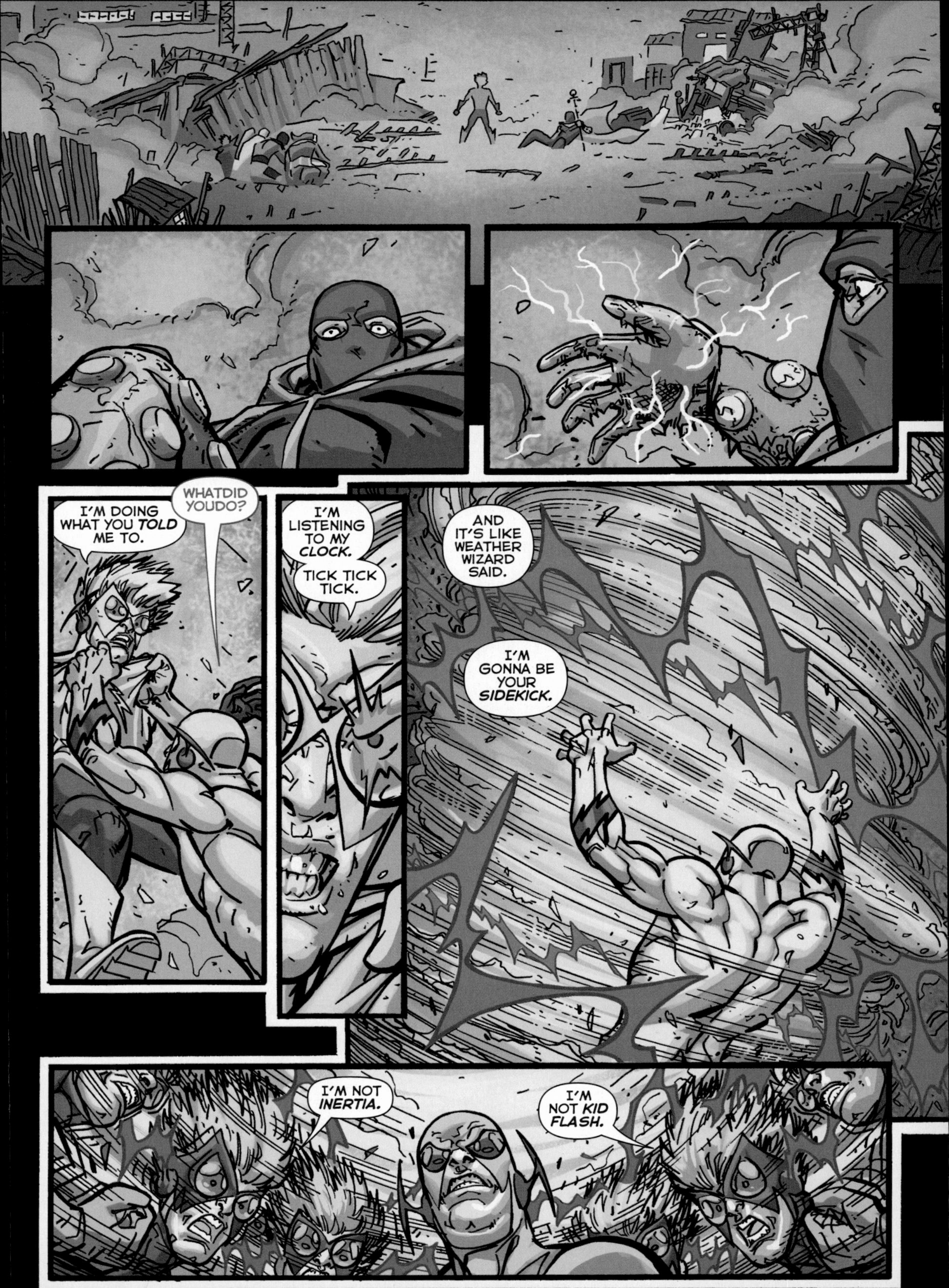
I'M DOING WHAT YOU TOLD ME TO.
WHATDID YOUDO?
I'M LISTENING TO MY CLOCK.
TICK TICK TICK.
AND IT'S LIKE WEATHER WIZARD SAID.
I'M GONNA BE YOUR SIDEKICK.
I'M NOT INERTIA.
I'M NOT KID FLASH.

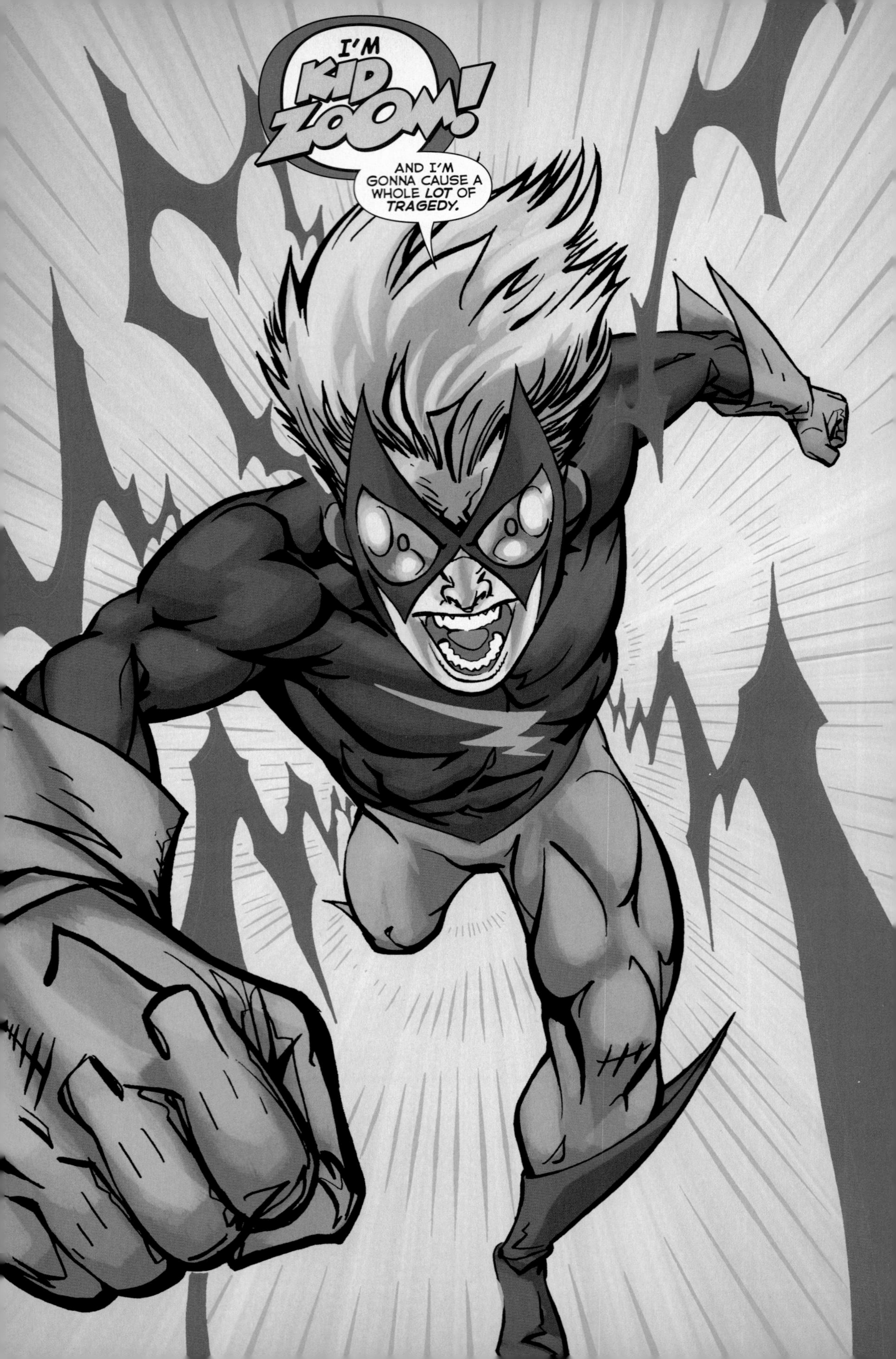
I'M KID ZOOM!
AND I'M GONNA CAUSE A WHOLE LOT OF TRAGEDY.

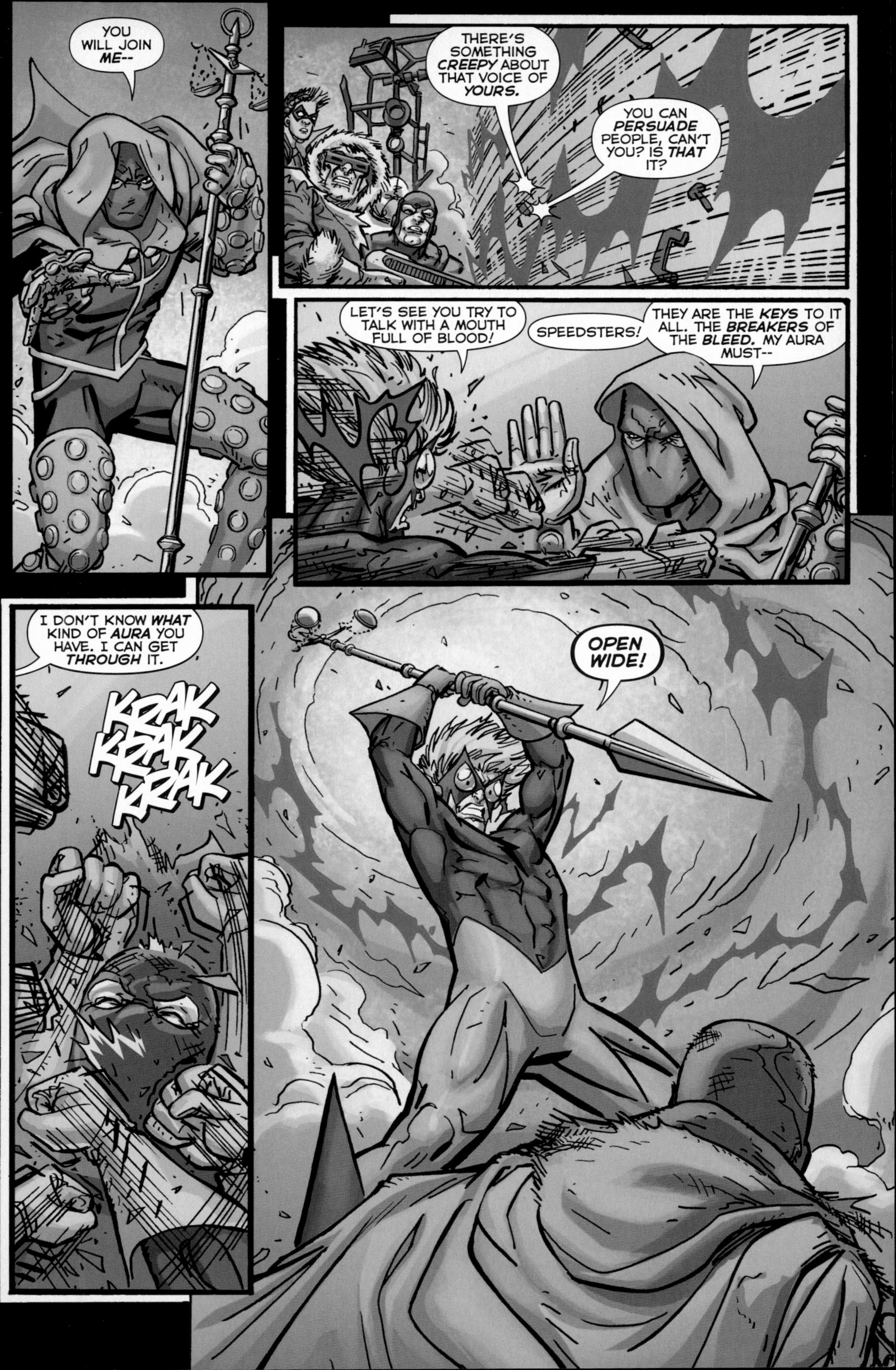
YOU WILL JOIN ME--
THERE'S SOMETHING CREEPY ABOUT THAT VOICE OF YOURS.
YOU CAN PERSUADE PEOPLE, CAN'T YOU? IS THAT IT?
LET'S SEE YOU TRY TO TALK WITH A MOUTH FULL OF BLOOD!
SPEEDSTERS!
THEY ARE THE KEYS TO IT ALL. THE BREAKERS OF THE BLEED. MY AURA MUST--
I DON'T KNOW WHAT KIND OF AURA YOU HAVE. I CAN GET THROUGH IT.
KRAK KRAK KRAK
OPEN WIDE!

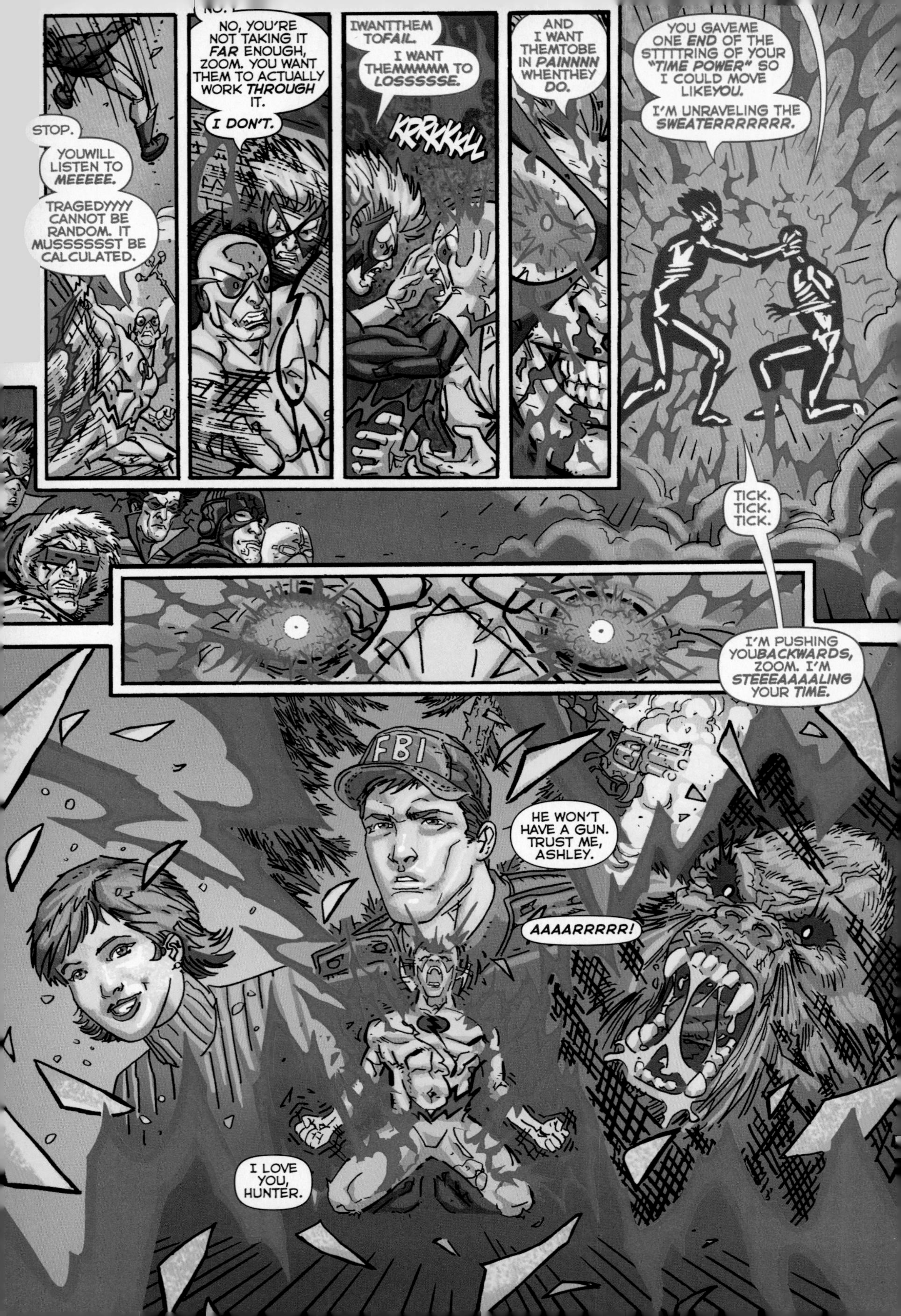
STOP.
YOUWILL LISTEN TO MEEEEE.
TRAGEDYYYY CANNOT BE RANDOM. IT MUSSSSSST BE CALCULATED.
NO, YOU'RE NOT TAKING IT FAR ENOUGH, ZOOM. YOU WANT THEM TO ACTUALLY WORK THROUGH IT.
I DON'T.
IWANTTHEM TOFAIL.
I WANT THEMMMMM TO LOSSSSSE.
KRRKKKLL
AND I WANT THEMTOBE IN PAINNNN WHENTHEY DO.
YOU GAVEME ONE END OF THE STTTTRING OF YOUR "TIME POWER" SO I COULD MOVE LIKEYOU.
I'M UNRAVELING THE SWEATERRRRRRR.
TICK. TICK. TICK.
I'M PUSHING YOUBACKWARDS, ZOOM. I'M STEEEAAAALING YOUR TIME.
HE WON'T HAVE A GUN. TRUST ME, ASHLEY.
AAAARRRRR!
I LOVE YOU, HUNTER.

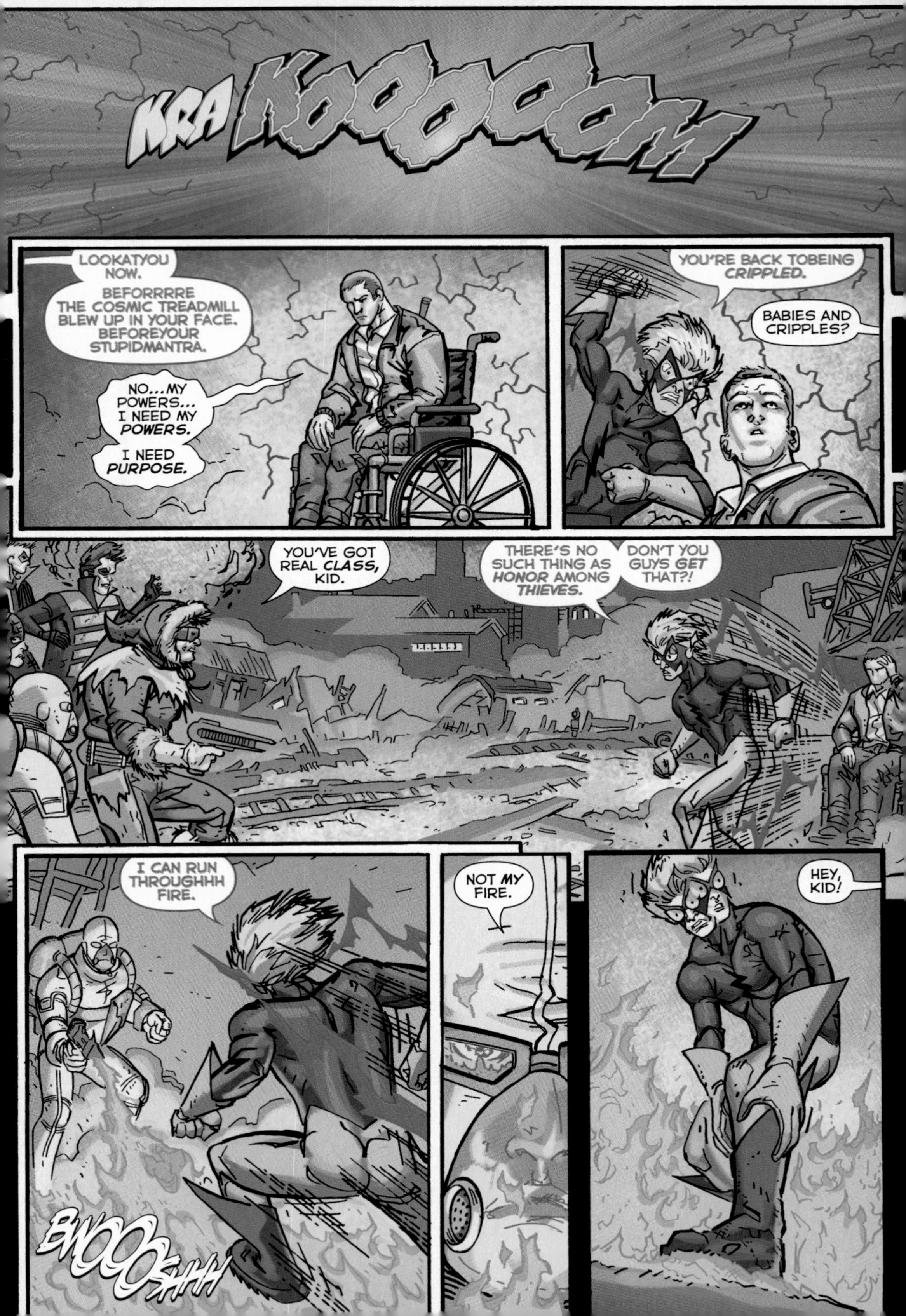
KRA KOOOOOM
LOOKATYOU NOW.
BEFORRRRE THE COSMIC TREADMILL BLEW UP IN YOUR FACE. BEFOREYOUR STUPIDMANTRA.
NO...MY POWERS... I NEED MY POWERS.
I NEED PURPOSE.
YOU'RE BACK TOBEING CRIPPLED.
BABIES AND CRIPPLES?
YOU'VE GOT REAL CLASS, KID.
THERE'S NO SUCH THING AS HONOR AMONG THIEVES.
DON'T YOU GUYS GET THAT?!
I CAN RUN THROUGHHH FIRE.
BWOOOSHHH
NOT MY FIRE.
HEY, KID!

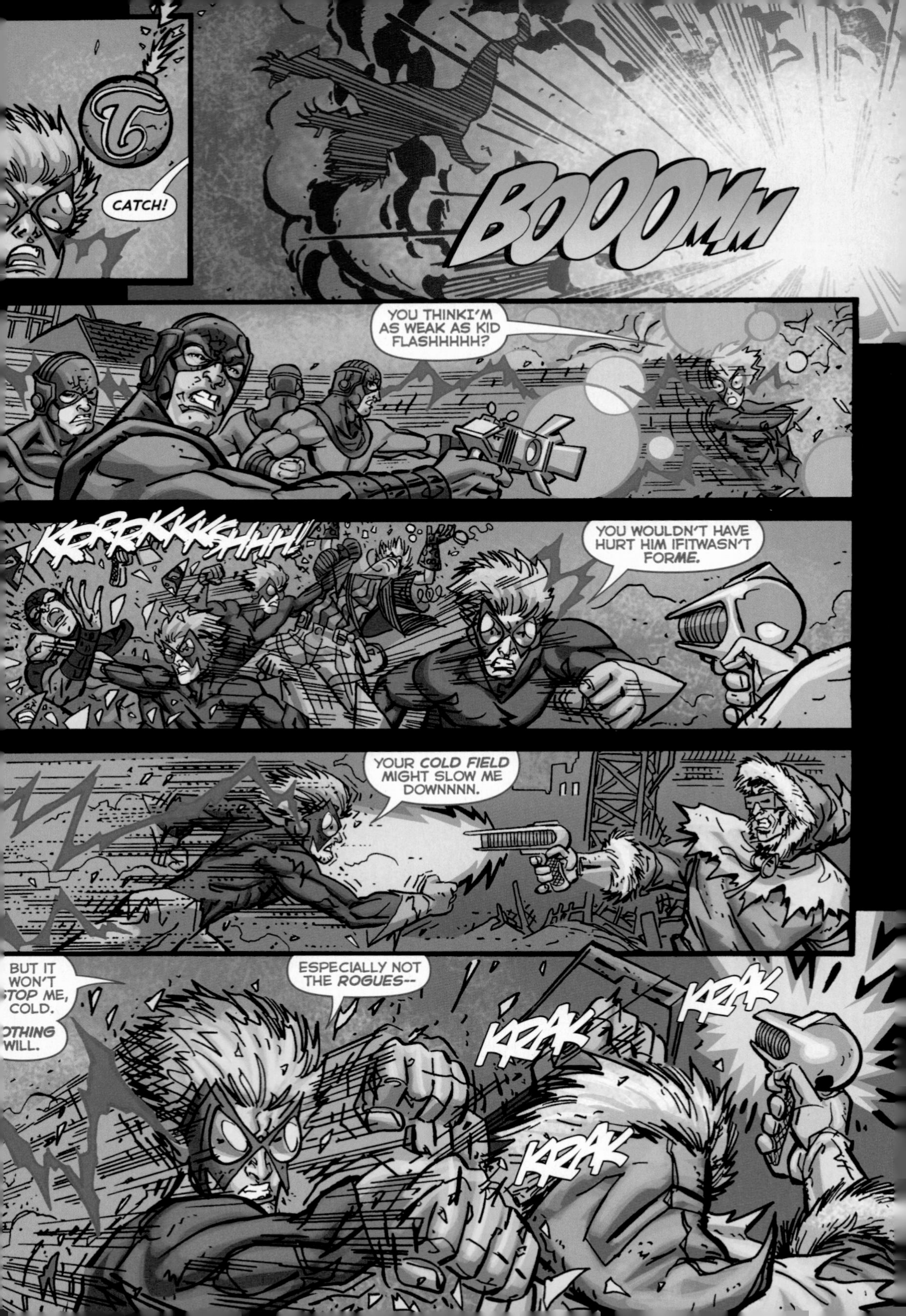
CATCH!
BOOOOMM
YOU THINK I'M AS WEAK AS KID FLASHHHHHH?
KRRRKKKSHHH!
YOU WOULDN'T HAVE HURT HIM IF IT WASN'T FOR ME.
YOUR COLD FIELD MIGHT SLOW ME DOWNNNN.
BUT IT WON'T STOP ME, COLD.
OTHING WILL.
ESPECIALLY NOT THE ROGUES--
KRAK
KRAK
KRAK

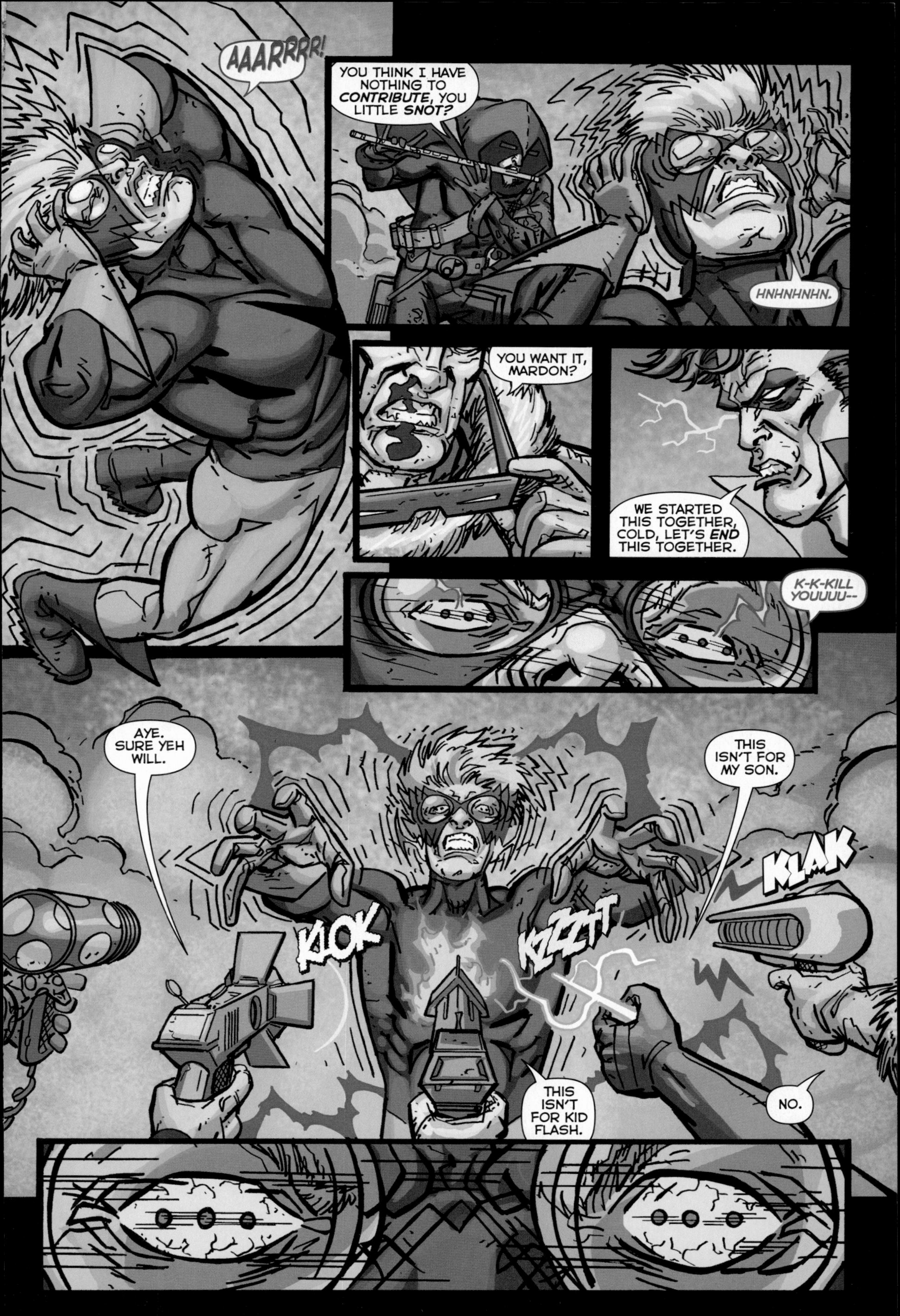
AAARRRR!
YOU THINK I HAVE NOTHING TO CONTRIBUTE, YOU LITTLE SNOT?
HNHNHNHN.
YOU WANT IT, MARDON?
WE STARTED THIS TOGETHER, COLD, LET'S END THIS TOGETHER.
K-K-KILL YOUUUU--
AYE. SURE YEH WILL.
THIS ISN'T FOR MY SON.
KLAK
KLOK
KZZZTT
THIS ISN'T FOR KID FLASH.
NO.

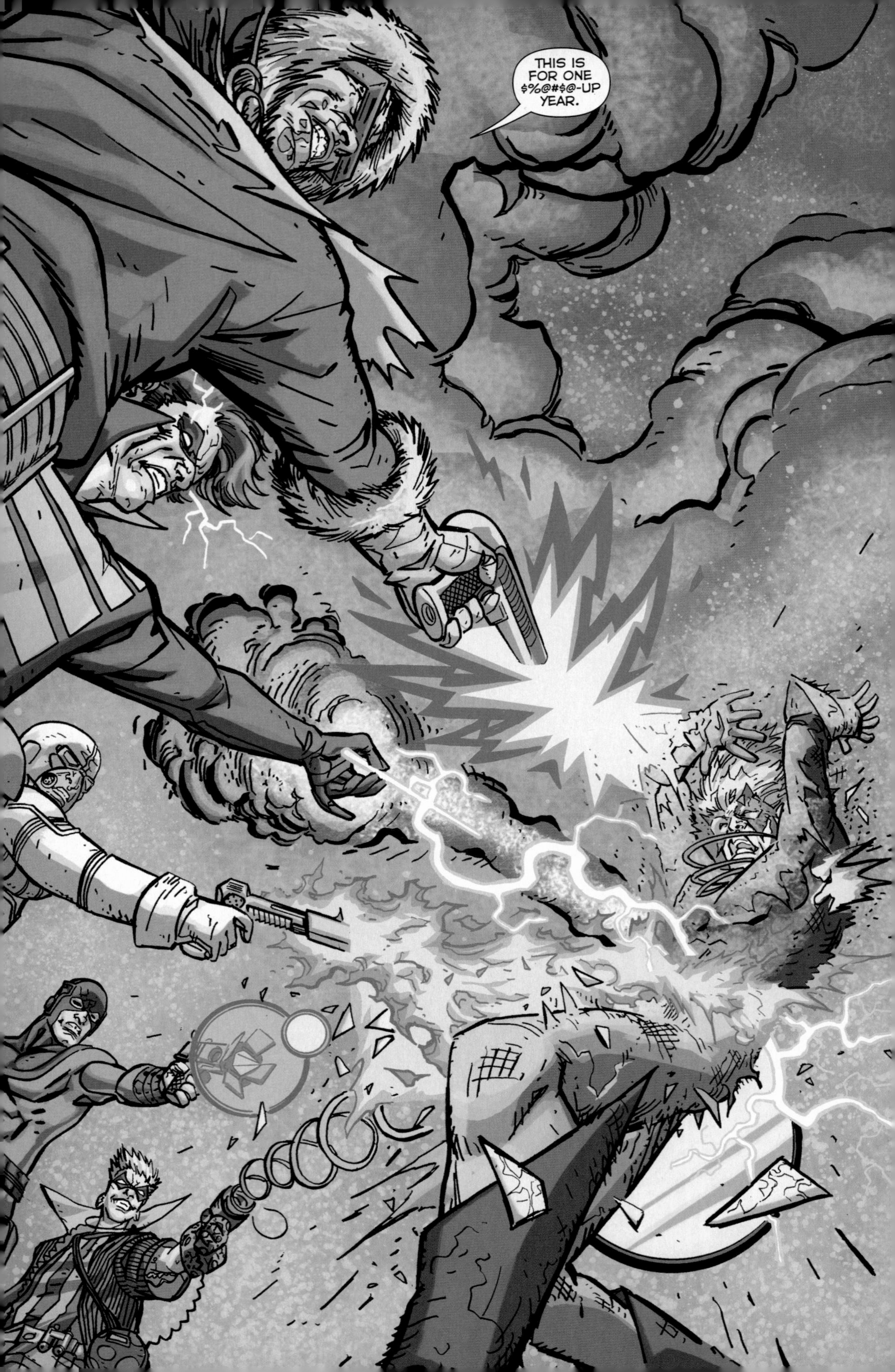
THIS IS FOR ONE $%@#$@-UP YEAR.

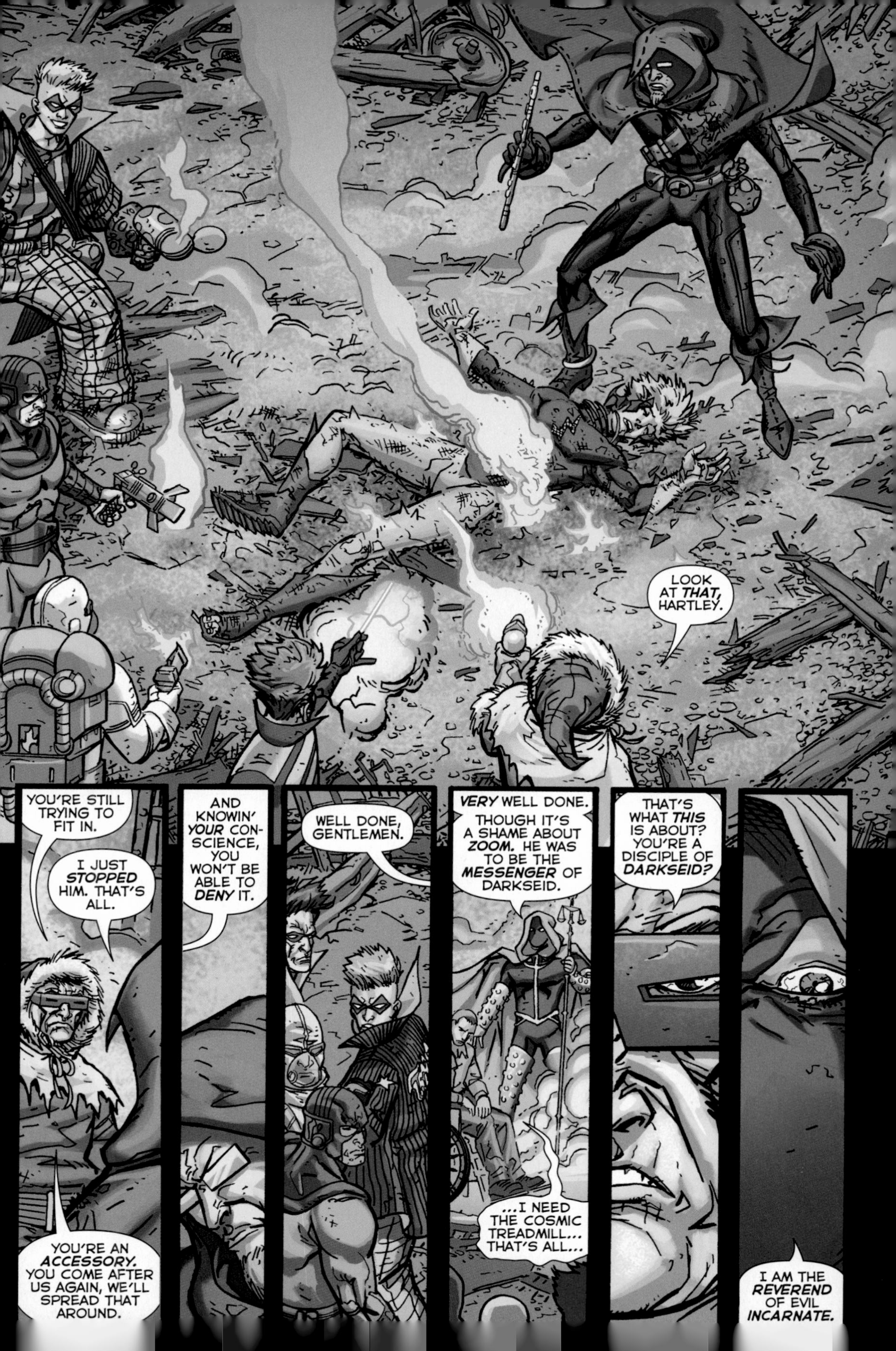
LOOK AT THAT, HARTLEY.
YOU'RE STILL TRYING TO FIT IN.
I JUST STOPPED HIM. THAT'S ALL.
YOU'RE AN ACCESSORY. YOU COME AFTER US AGAIN, WE'LL SPREAD THAT AROUND.
AND KNOWIN' YOUR CONSCIENCE, YOU WON'T BE ABLE TO DENY IT.
WELL DONE, GENTLEMEN.
VERY WELL DONE.
THOUGH IT'S A SHAME ABOUT ZOOM. HE WAS TO BE THE MESSENGER OF DARKSEID.
...I NEED THE COSMIC TREADMILL... THAT'S ALL...
THAT'S WHAT THIS IS ABOUT? YOU'RE A DISCIPLE OF DARKSEID?
I AM THE REVEREND OF EVIL INCARNATE.

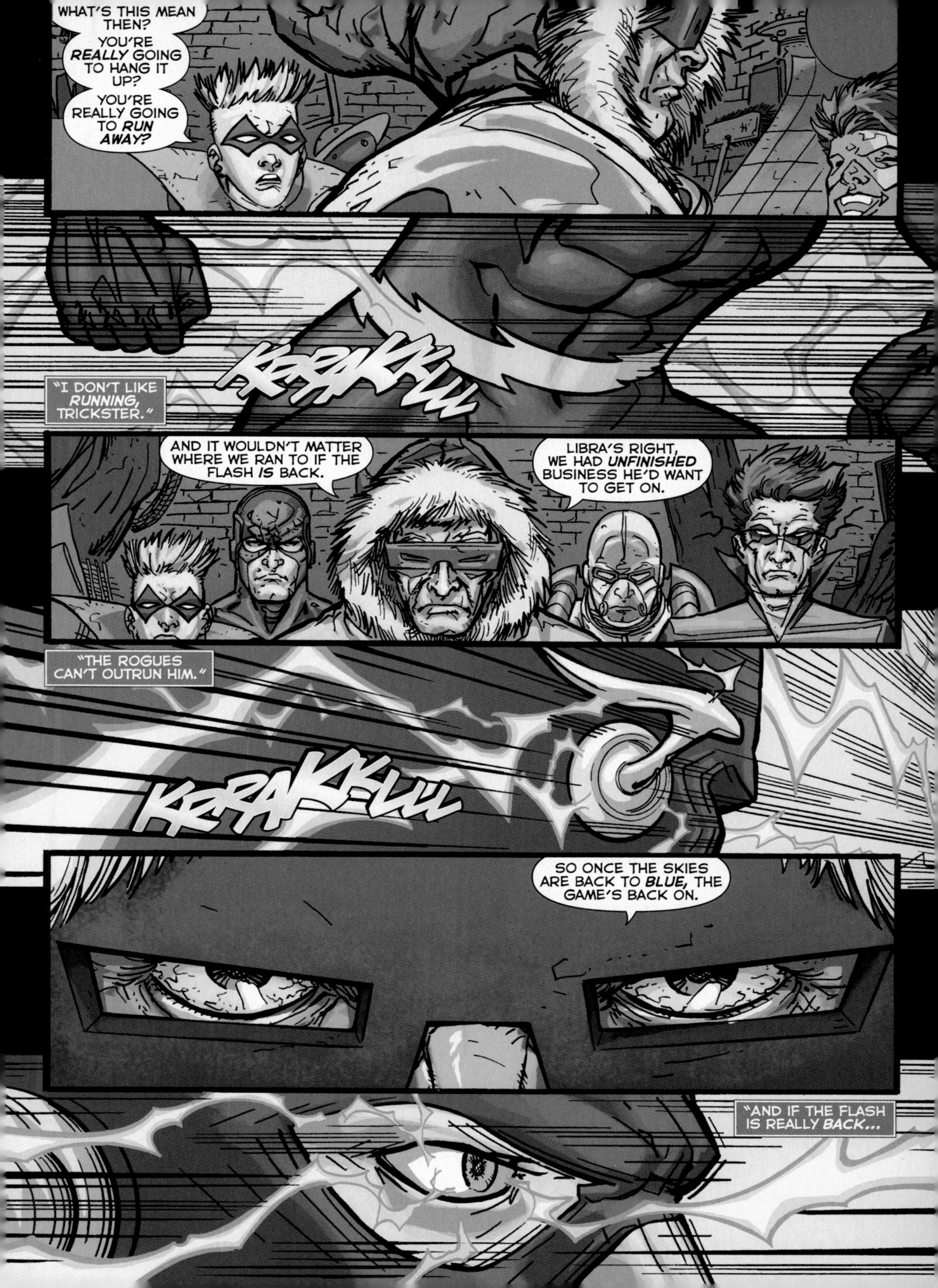

WHAT'S THIS MEAN THEN? YOU'RE *REALLY* GOING TO HANG IT UP? YOU'RE REALLY GOING TO *RUN AWAY?*
KRRAKKKLLL
"I DON'T LIKE *RUNNING,* TRICKSTER."
AND IT WOULDN'T MATTER WHERE WE RAN TO IF THE FLASH *IS* BACK.
LIBRA'S RIGHT, WE HAD *UNFINISHED* BUSINESS HE'D WANT TO GET ON.
"THE ROGUES CAN'T OUTRUN HIM."
KRRAKK-LLL
SO ONCE THE SKIES ARE BACK TO *BLUE,* THE GAME'S BACK ON.
"AND IF THE FLASH IS REALLY *BACK...*

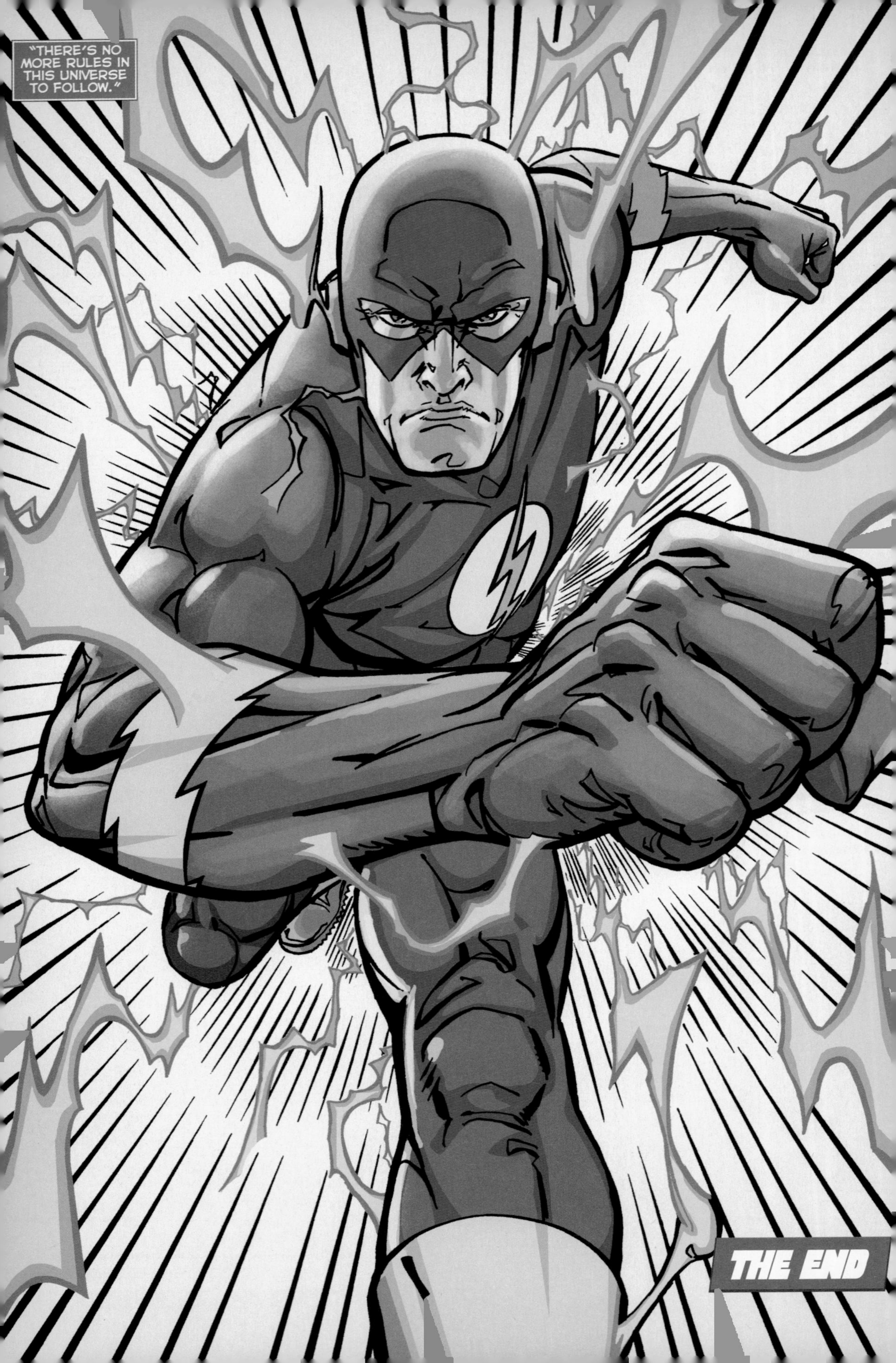
"THERE'S NO MORE RULES IN THIS UNIVERSE TO FOLLOW."
THE END

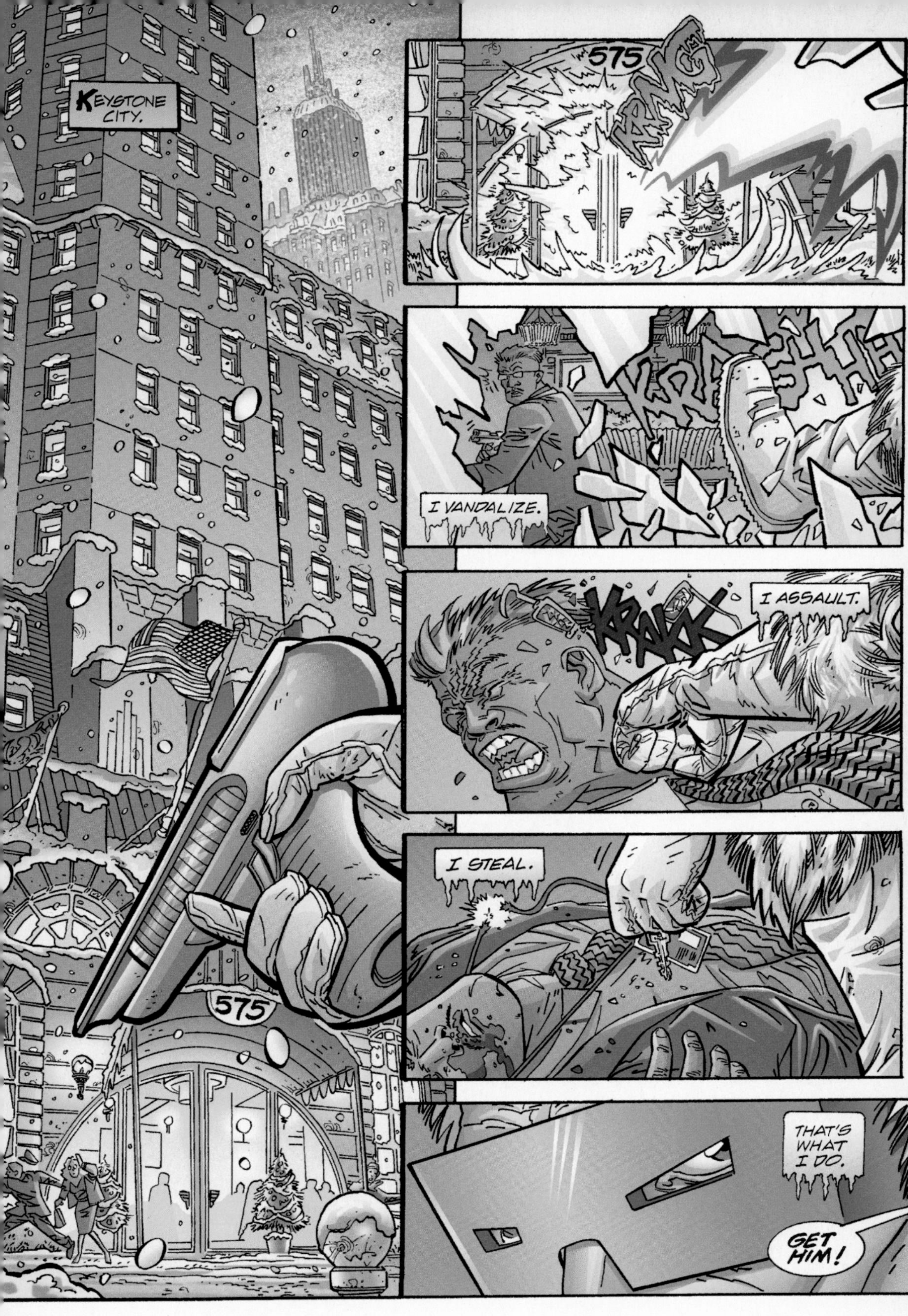
KEYSTONE CITY.
575
KRANG
575
I VANDALIZE.
KRASHH
KRAKK
I ASSAULT.
I STEAL.
THAT'S WHAT I DO.
GET HIM!

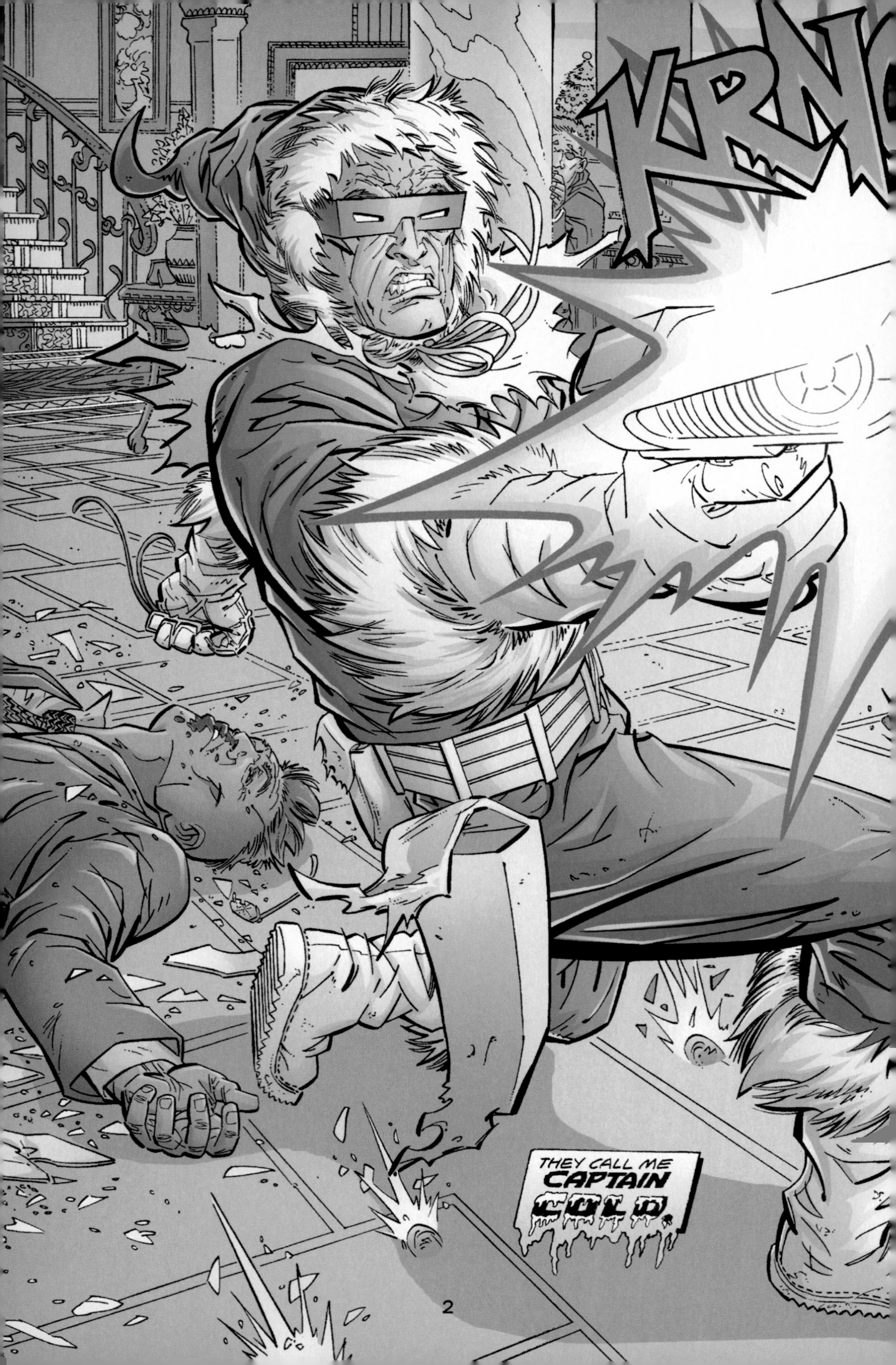
KRNC
THEY CALL ME
CAPTAIN
COLD.

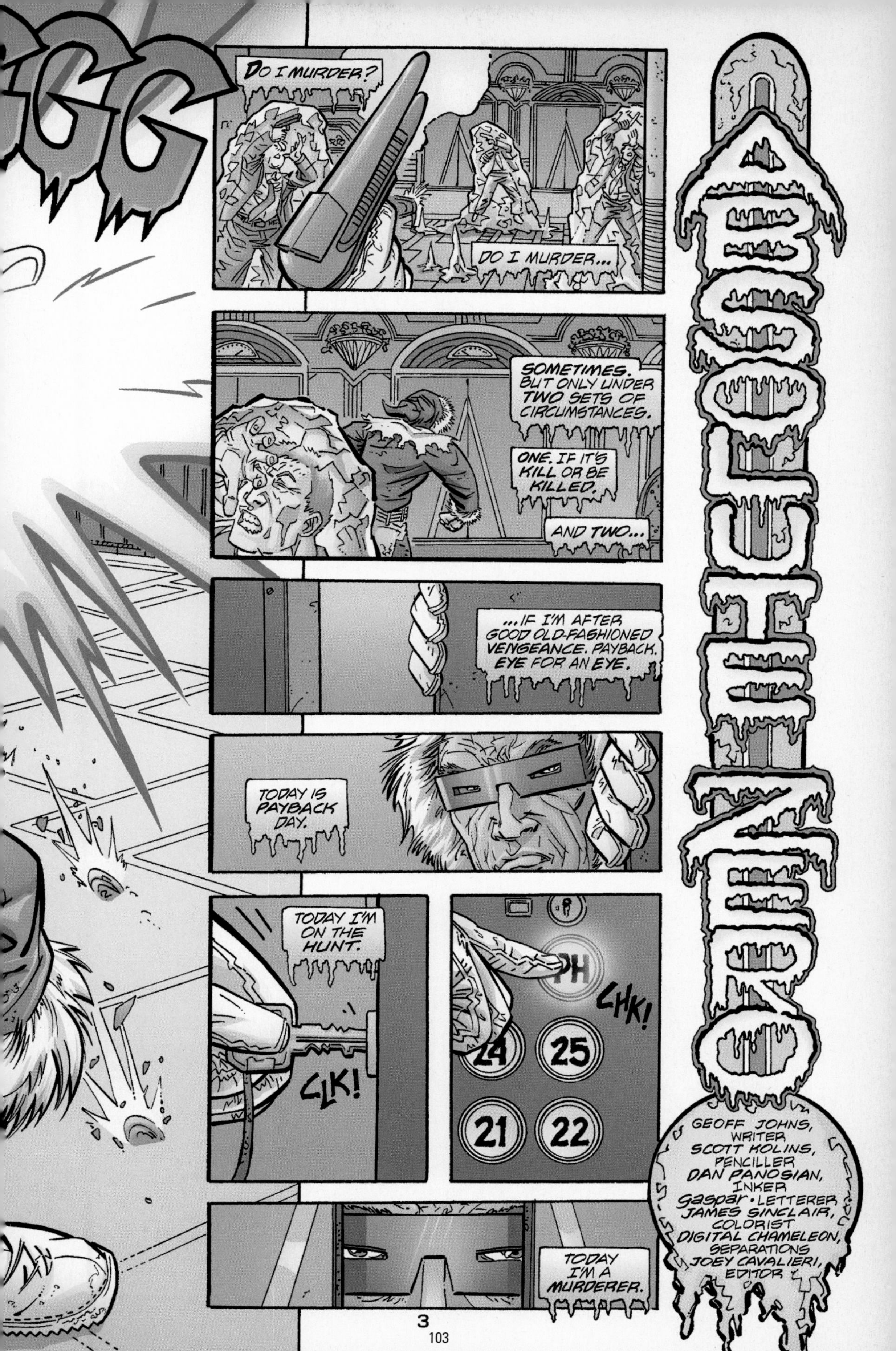
DO I MURDER?
DO I MURDER...
SOMETIMES. BUT ONLY UNDER TWO SETS OF CIRCUMSTANCES.
ONE. IF IT'S KILL OR BE KILLED.
AND TWO...
...IF I'M AFTER GOOD OLD-FASHIONED VENGEANCE. PAYBACK. EYE FOR AN EYE.
TODAY IS PAYBACK DAY.
TODAY I'M ON THE HUNT.
CLK!
PH
CHK!
24
25
21
22
TODAY I'M A MURDERER.
GEOFF JOHNS, WRITER
SCOTT KOLINS, PENCILLER
DAN PANOSIAN, INKER
Gaspar • LETTERER
JAMES SINCLAIR, COLORIST
DIGITAL CHAMELEON, SEPARATIONS
JOEY CAVALIERI, EDITOR

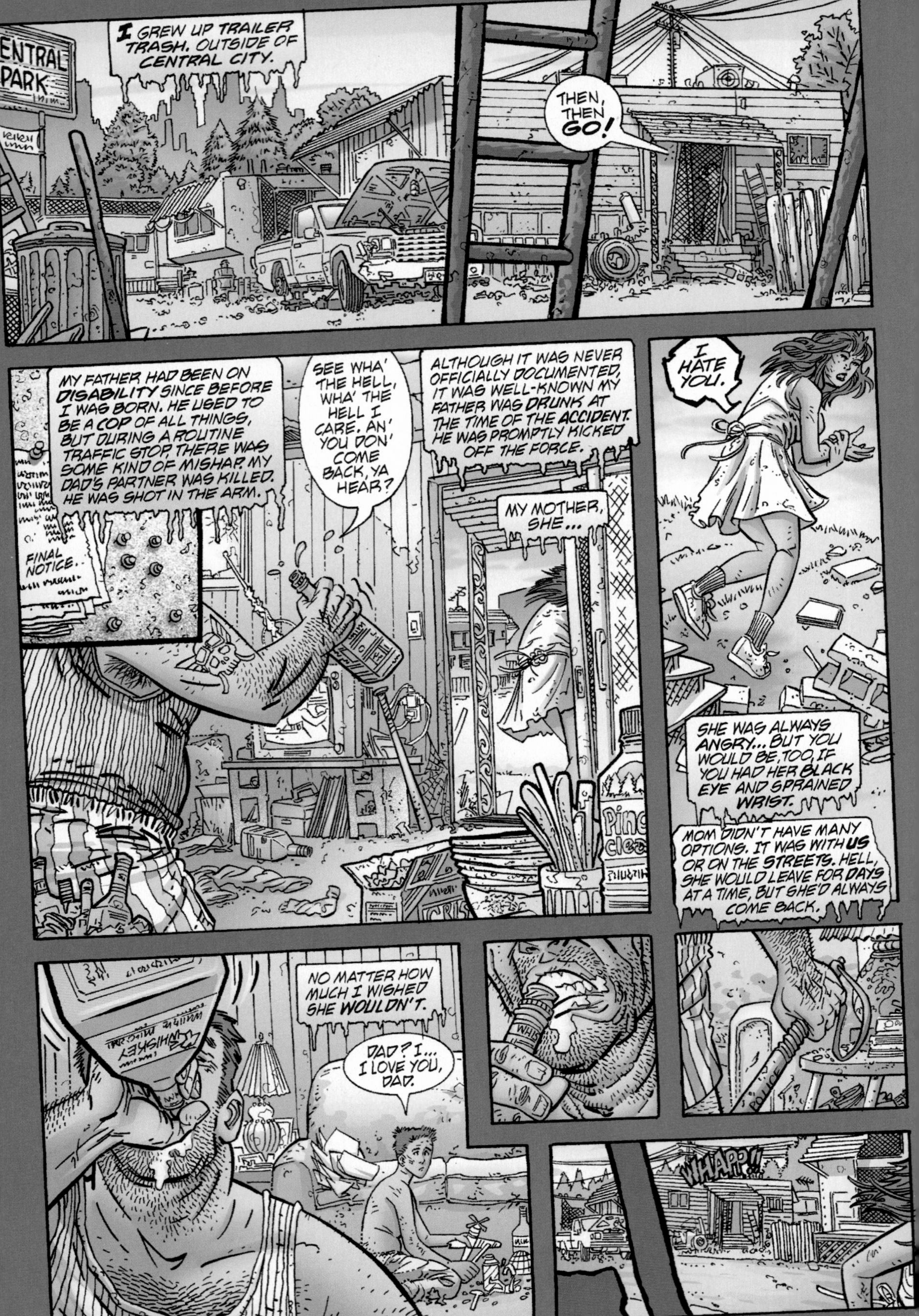
CENTRAL PARK
I GREW UP TRAILER TRASH. OUTSIDE OF CENTRAL CITY.
THEN, THEN GO!
MY FATHER HAD BEEN ON DISABILITY SINCE BEFORE I WAS BORN. HE USED TO BE A COP OF ALL THINGS, BUT DURING A ROUTINE TRAFFIC STOP, THERE WAS SOME KIND OF MISHAP. MY DAD'S PARTNER WAS KILLED. HE WAS SHOT IN THE ARM.
FINAL NOTICE.
SEE WHA' THE HELL, WHA' THE HELL I CARE. AN' YOU DON' COME BACK, YA HEAR?
ALTHOUGH IT WAS NEVER OFFICIALLY DOCUMENTED, IT WAS WELL-KNOWN MY FATHER WAS DRUNK AT THE TIME OF THE ACCIDENT. HE WAS PROMPTLY KICKED OFF THE FORCE.
MY MOTHER, SHE...
I HATE YOU.
SHE WAS ALWAYS ANGRY... BUT YOU WOULD BE, TOO, IF YOU HAD HER BLACK EYE AND SPRAINED WRIST.
MOM DIDN'T HAVE MANY OPTIONS. IT WAS WITH US OR ON THE STREETS. HELL, SHE WOULD LEAVE FOR DAYS AT A TIME, BUT SHE'D ALWAYS COME BACK.
WHISKEY
NO MATTER HOW MUCH I WISHED SHE WOULDN'T.
DAD? I... I LOVE YOU, DAD.
POLICE
WHAPP!!

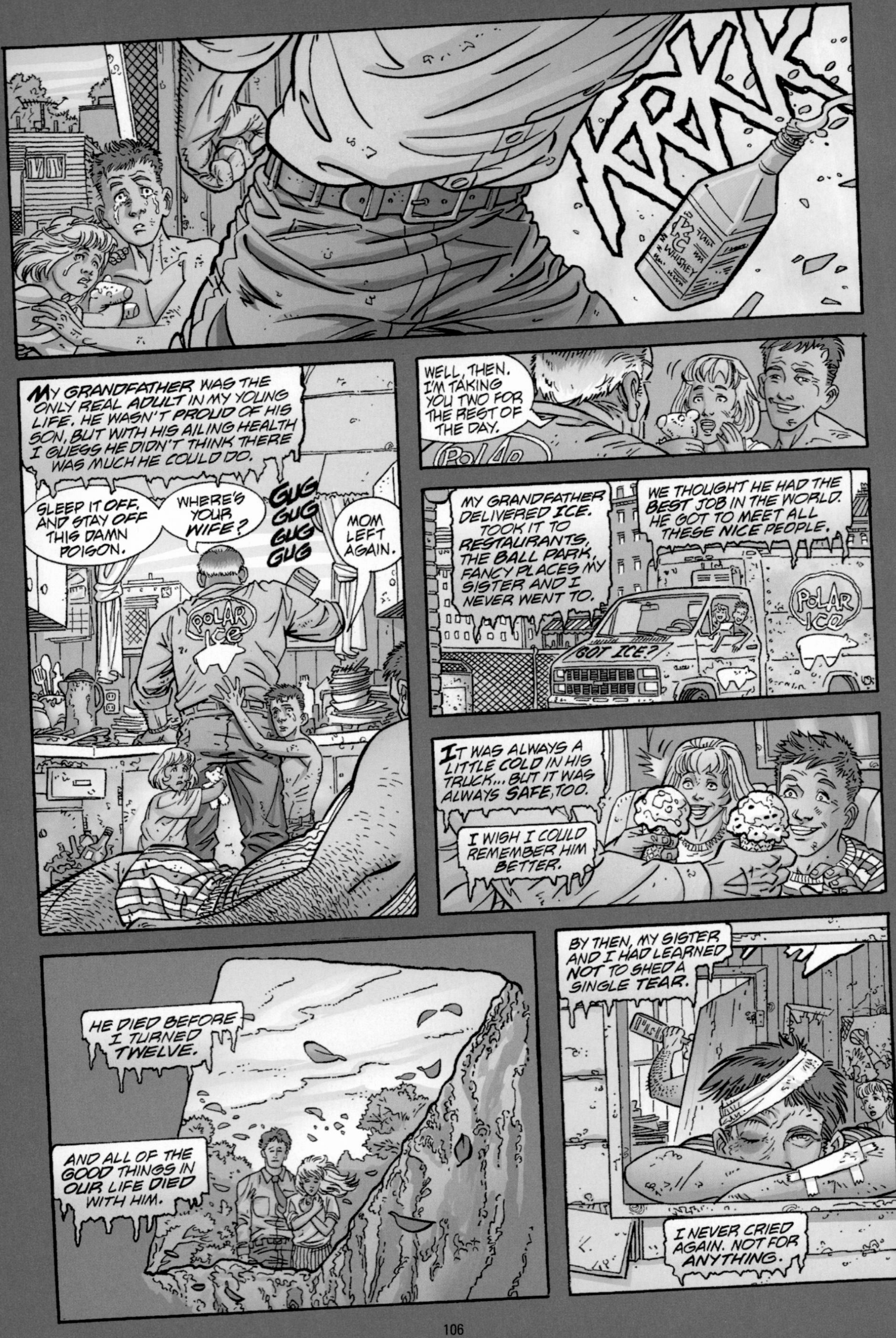
MY GRANDFATHER WAS THE ONLY REAL ADULT IN MY YOUNG LIFE. HE WASN'T PROUD OF HIS SON, BUT WITH HIS AILING HEALTH I GUESS HE DIDN'T THINK THERE WAS MUCH HE COULD DO.
SLEEP IT OFF, AND STAY OFF THIS DAMN POISON.
WHERE'S YOUR WIFE?
GUG GUG GUG GUG
MOM LEFT AGAIN.
POLAR ICE
WELL, THEN. I'M TAKING YOU TWO FOR THE REST OF THE DAY.
MY GRANDFATHER DELIVERED ICE. TOOK IT TO RESTAURANTS, THE BALL PARK, FANCY PLACES MY SISTER AND I NEVER WENT TO.
WE THOUGHT HE HAD THE BEST JOB IN THE WORLD. HE GOT TO MEET ALL THESE NICE PEOPLE.
GOT ICE?
POLAR ICE
IT WAS ALWAYS A LITTLE COLD IN HIS TRUCK... BUT IT WAS ALWAYS SAFE, TOO.
I WISH I COULD REMEMBER HIM BETTER.
HE DIED BEFORE I TURNED TWELVE.
AND ALL OF THE GOOD THINGS IN OUR LIFE DIED WITH HIM.
BY THEN, MY SISTER AND I HAD LEARNED NOT TO SHED A SINGLE TEAR.
I NEVER CRIED AGAIN. NOT FOR ANYTHING.

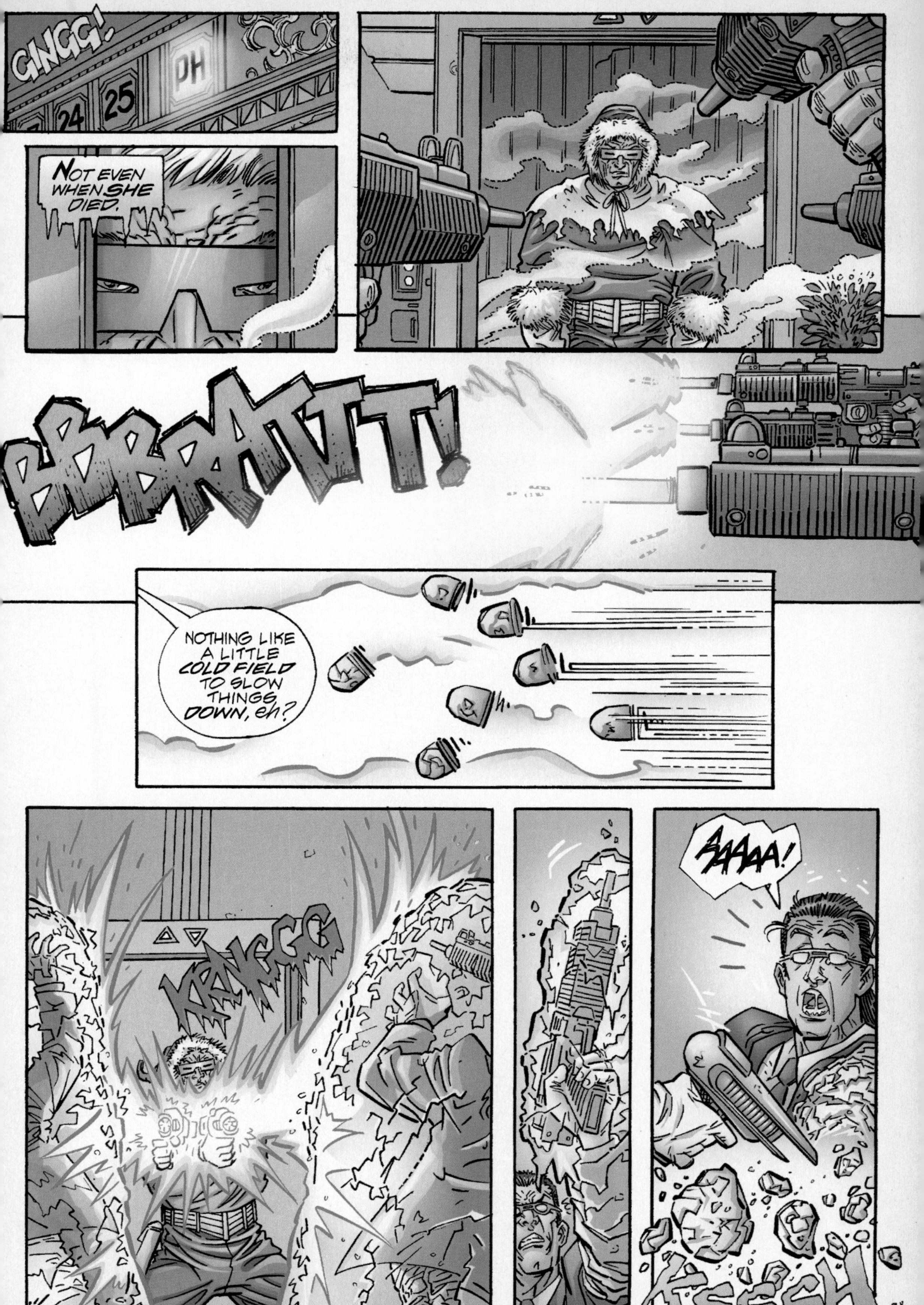
GINGG!
24
25
PH
NOT EVEN WHEN SHE DIED.
BBBRATTT!
NOTHING LIKE A LITTLE COLD FIELD TO SLOW THINGS DOWN, eh?
KRAKGG
AAAAA!
KSSSH

QUIT YOUR **WHINING**, LOOK AT ME AND **LISTEN.** I DON'T WANT YOU GOING INTO **SHOCK.** THE **PAIN** WON'T HIT FOR AT LEAST **TWENTY** MINUTES.

BY THEN, ONE OF YOUR **FELLOW** GUN-TOTING MORONS WILL PROBABLY HAVE YOU IN A NICE **WARM** ROOM AT ST. JOHN'S. IF YOU'RE **LUCKY,** THEY'LL BE ABLE TO PIECE TO-GETHER THAT ARM... AS LONG AS IT STAYS **FROZEN.**

IF YOU'RE NOT **LUCKY,** I'LL HELP SPREAD THE **FROSTBITE.** **UNDERSTAND?**

DAMMIT...

WHERE'S **CHILLBLAINE?**

CHILLBLAINE? I DON'T KNOW WHO YOU'RE--

WRONG ANSWER.

KRNNNGG

AARR **GH!**

LET'S TRY AGAIN. CHILLBLAINE. PLINK WITH A **COLD-GUN** JUST LIKE **THIS.**

I DON'T KNOW, MAN. SOMEWHERE AROUND. HE'S WITH THE **CANDYMAN.**

YEAH, THE **DRUG KING** OF KEYSTONE. I HEARD HE WAS WORKING FOR YOUR **BOSS** NOW. HIS **BODYGUARD,** RIGHT?

W-WHAT'S YOUR P-PROBLEM WITH HIM ANYWAY?

CHILLBLAINE WANTED EVERYONE TO THINK HE WAS **DEAD.** THE FLASH, DR. POLARIS, THE COPS... AND ESPECIALLY ME.

I FOUND OUT HE OFFED SOME OTHER POOR SAP, DRESSED HIM UP IN HIS COSTUME, TRACED DOWN SOME LEADS FOR MONTHS. TO HERE... THE STRONGHOLD OF THE CANDYMAN.

CHILLBLAINE KILLED MY SISTER.

KLAK!

CH-KAK! KAK!

AND NOW WE GONNA KILL **YOU!**

ALWAYS GETTING IN OVER MY HEAD. BEGINNING BACK IN THE DAY...

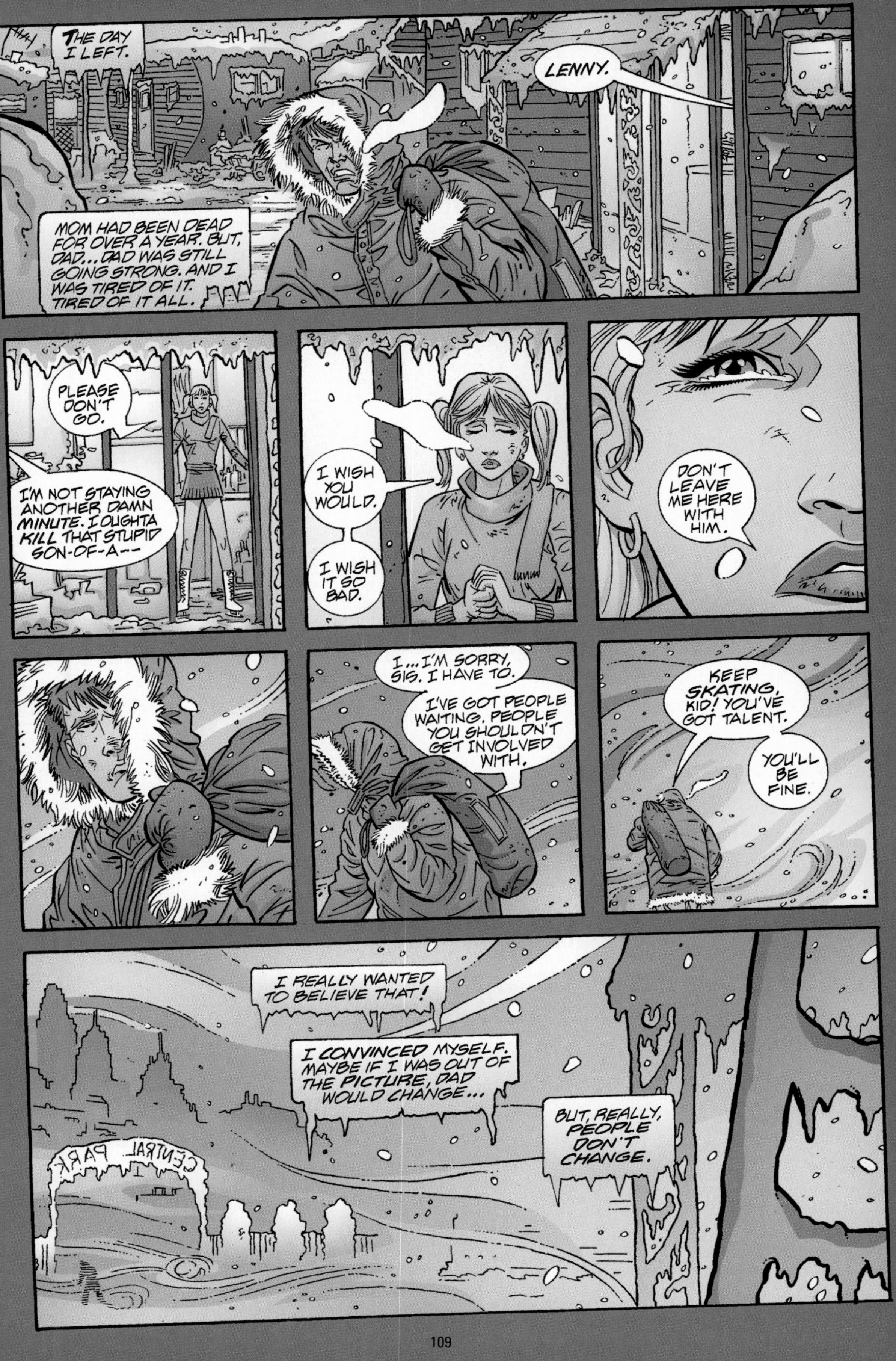
THE DAY I LEFT.
LENNY.
MOM HAD BEEN DEAD FOR OVER A YEAR. BUT, DAD... DAD WAS STILL GOING STRONG. AND I WAS TIRED OF IT. TIRED OF IT ALL.
PLEASE DON'T GO.
I'M NOT STAYING ANOTHER DAMN MINUTE. I OUGHTA KILL THAT STUPID SON-OF-A--
I WISH YOU WOULD.
I WISH IT SO BAD.
DON'T LEAVE ME HERE WITH HIM.
I... I'M SORRY, SIS. I HAVE TO.
I'VE GOT PEOPLE WAITING. PEOPLE YOU SHOULDN'T GET INVOLVED WITH.
KEEP SKATING, KID! YOU'VE GOT TALENT.
YOU'LL BE FINE.
I REALLY WANTED TO BELIEVE THAT!
I CONVINCED MYSELF. MAYBE IF I WAS OUT OF THE PICTURE, DAD WOULD CHANGE...
BUT, REALLY, PEOPLE DON'T CHANGE.

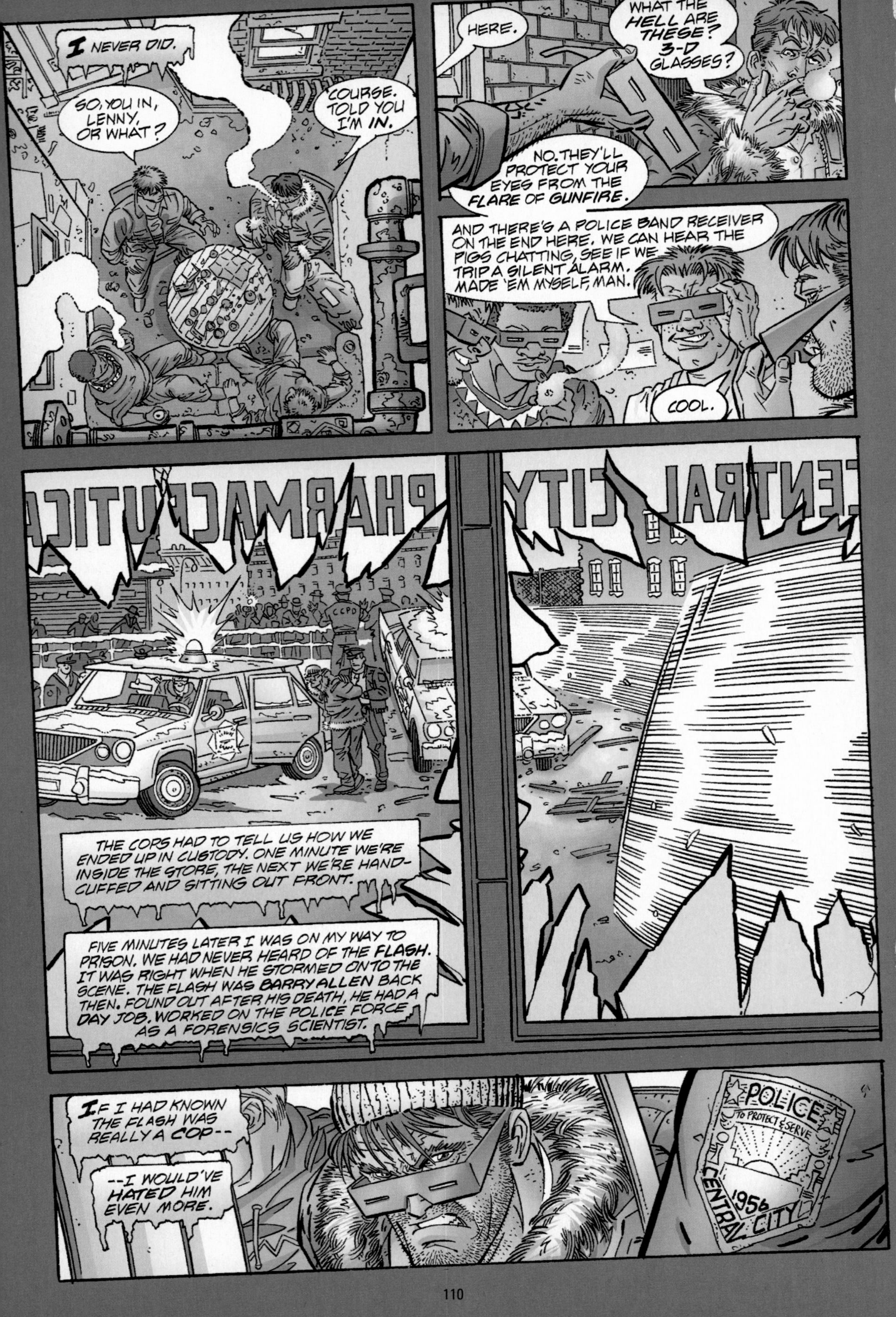
I NEVER DID.
SO, YOU IN, LENNY, OR WHAT?
COURSE. TOLD YOU I'M IN.
HERE.
WHAT THE HELL ARE THESE? 3-D GLASSES?
NO. THEY'LL PROTECT YOUR EYES FROM THE FLARE OF GUNFIRE.
AND THERE'S A POLICE BAND RECEIVER ON THE END HERE. WE CAN HEAR THE PIGS CHATTING, SEE IF WE TRIP A SILENT ALARM. MADE 'EM MYSELF, MAN.
COOL.
PHARMACEUTICA
CENTRAL CITY
CCPD
THE COPS HAD TO TELL US HOW WE ENDED UP IN CUSTODY. ONE MINUTE WE'RE INSIDE THE STORE, THE NEXT WE'RE HAND-CUFFED AND SITTING OUT FRONT.
FIVE MINUTES LATER I WAS ON MY WAY TO PRISON. WE HAD NEVER HEARD OF THE FLASH. IT WAS RIGHT WHEN HE STORMED ONTO THE SCENE. THE FLASH WAS BARRY ALLEN BACK THEN. FOUND OUT AFTER HIS DEATH, HE HAD A DAY JOB. WORKED ON THE POLICE FORCE AS A FORENSICS SCIENTIST.
IF I HAD KNOWN THE FLASH WAS REALLY A COP--
--I WOULD'VE HATED HIM EVEN MORE.
POLICE
TO PROTECT & SERVE
CENTRAL CITY
1956

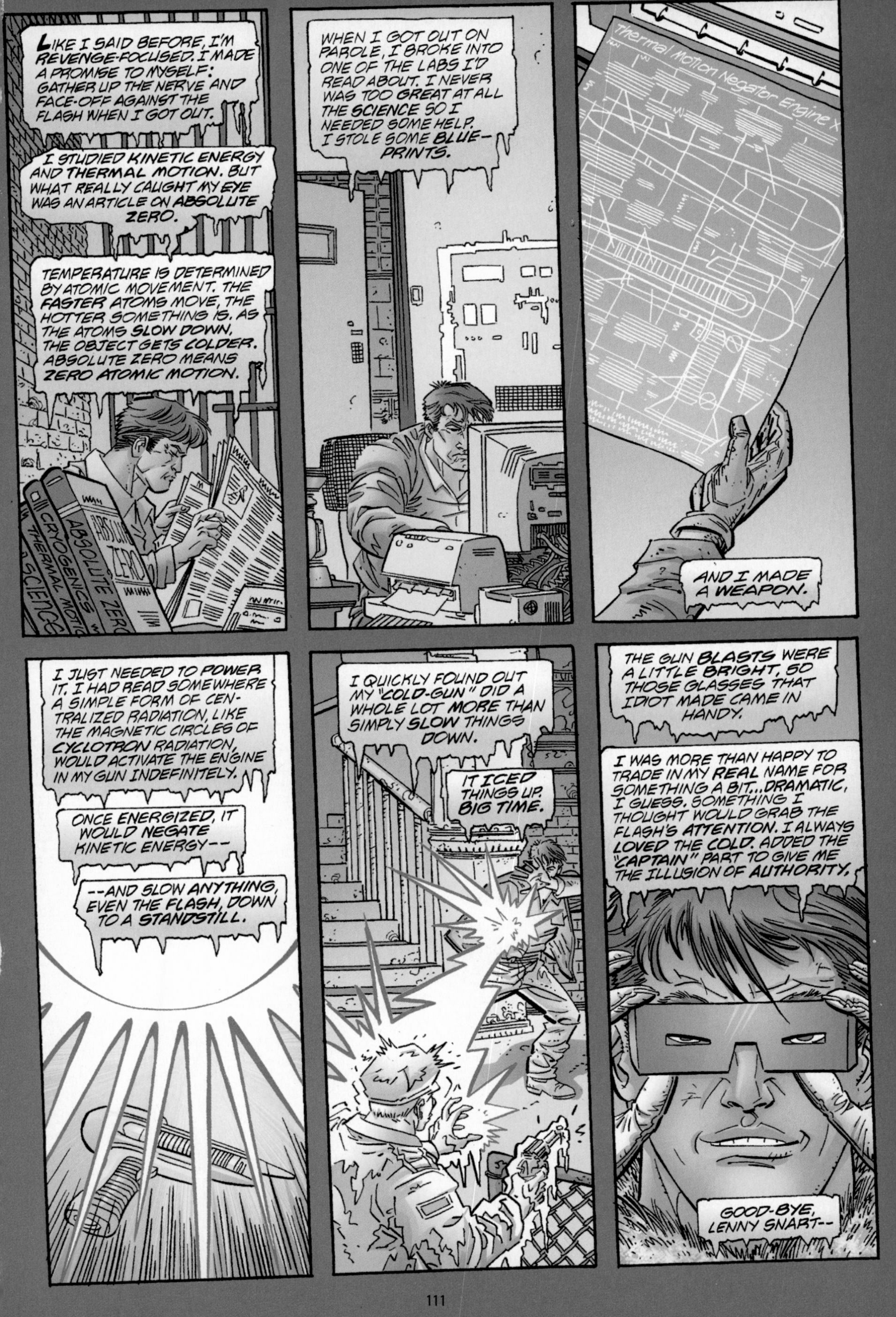
LIKE I SAID BEFORE, I'M REVENGE-FOCUSED. I MADE A PROMISE TO MYSELF: GATHER UP THE NERVE AND FACE-OFF AGAINST THE FLASH WHEN I GOT OUT.
I STUDIED KINETIC ENERGY AND THERMAL MOTION. BUT WHAT REALLY CAUGHT MY EYE WAS AN ARTICLE ON ABSOLUTE ZERO.
TEMPERATURE IS DETERMINED BY ATOMIC MOVEMENT. THE FASTER ATOMS MOVE, THE HOTTER SOMETHING IS. AS THE ATOMS SLOW DOWN, THE OBJECT GETS COLDER. ABSOLUTE ZERO MEANS ZERO ATOMIC MOTION.
CRYOGENICS
ABSOLUTE ZERO
WHEN I GOT OUT ON PAROLE, I BROKE INTO ONE OF THE LABS I'D READ ABOUT. I NEVER WAS TOO GREAT AT ALL THE SCIENCE SO I NEEDED SOME HELP. I STOLE SOME BLUE-PRINTS.
Thermal Motion Negator Engine X
AND I MADE A WEAPON.
I JUST NEEDED TO POWER IT. I HAD READ SOMEWHERE A SIMPLE FORM OF CEN-TRALIZED RADIATION, LIKE THE MAGNETIC CIRCLES OF CYCLOTRON RADIATION, WOULD ACTIVATE THE ENGINE IN MY GUN INDEFINITELY.
ONCE ENERGIZED, IT WOULD NEGATE KINETIC ENERGY--
--AND SLOW ANYTHING, EVEN THE FLASH, DOWN TO A STANDSTILL.
I QUICKLY FOUND OUT MY "COLD-GUN" DID A WHOLE LOT MORE THAN SIMPLY SLOW THINGS DOWN.
IT ICED THINGS UP. BIG TIME.
THE GUN BLASTS WERE A LITTLE BRIGHT, SO THOSE GLASSES THAT IDIOT MADE CAME IN HANDY.
I WAS MORE THAN HAPPY TO TRADE IN MY REAL NAME FOR SOMETHING A BIT...DRAMATIC, I GUESS. SOMETHING I THOUGHT WOULD GRAB THE FLASH'S ATTENTION. I ALWAYS LOVED THE COLD. ADDED THE "CAPTAIN" PART TO GIVE ME THE ILLUSION OF AUTHORITY.
GOOD-BYE, LENNY SNART--

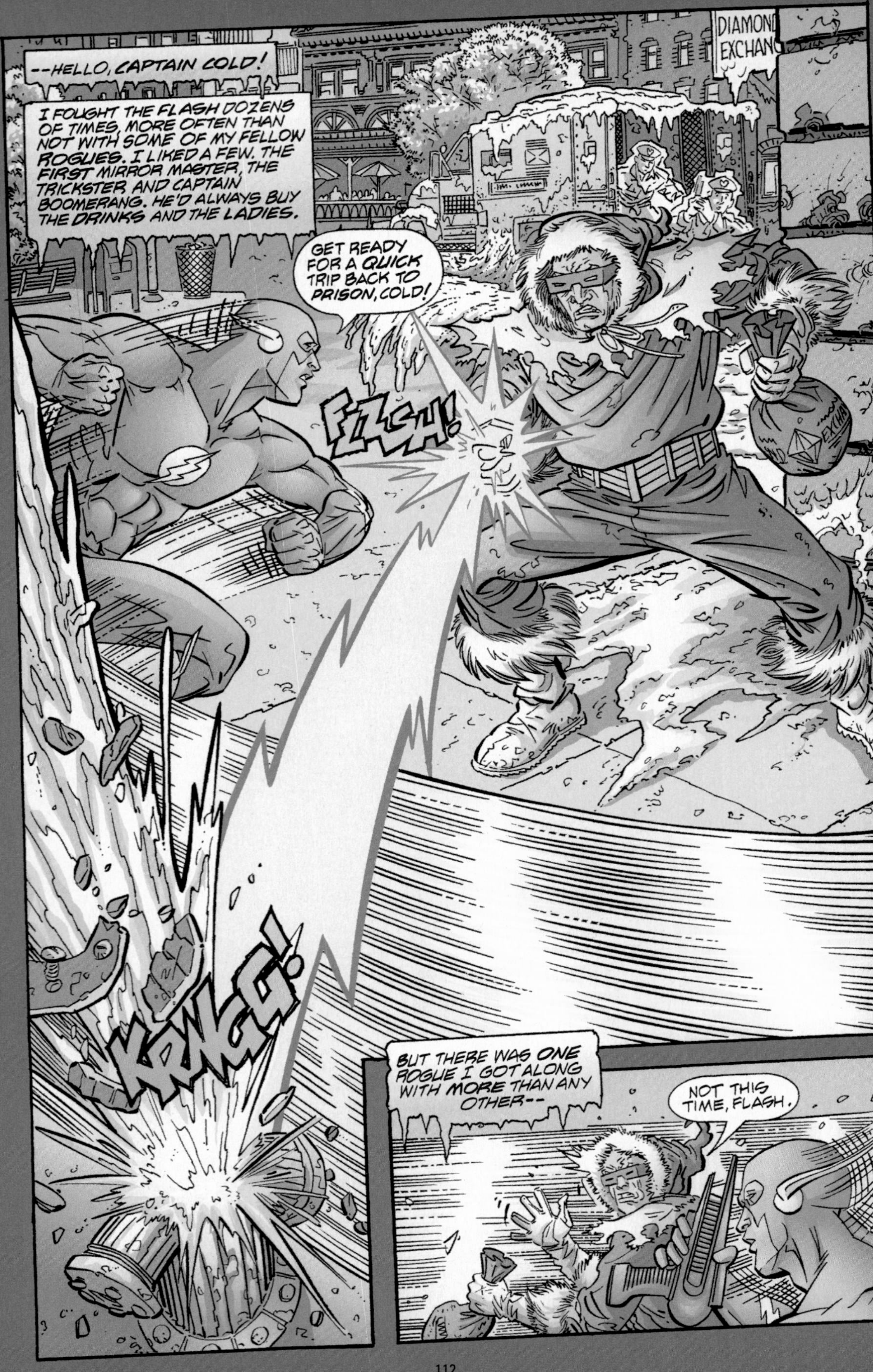
--HELLO, CAPTAIN COLD!
I FOUGHT THE FLASH DOZENS OF TIMES, MORE OFTEN THAN NOT WITH SOME OF MY FELLOW ROGUES. I LIKED A FEW. THE FIRST MIRROR MASTER, THE TRICKSTER AND CAPTAIN BOOMERANG. HE'D ALWAYS BUY THE DRINKS AND THE LADIES.
DIAMOND EXCHAN
GET READY FOR A QUICK TRIP BACK TO PRISON, COLD!
FZZSH!
KRAGG!
BUT THERE WAS ONE ROGUE I GOT ALONG WITH MORE THAN ANY OTHER--
NOT THIS TIME, FLASH.

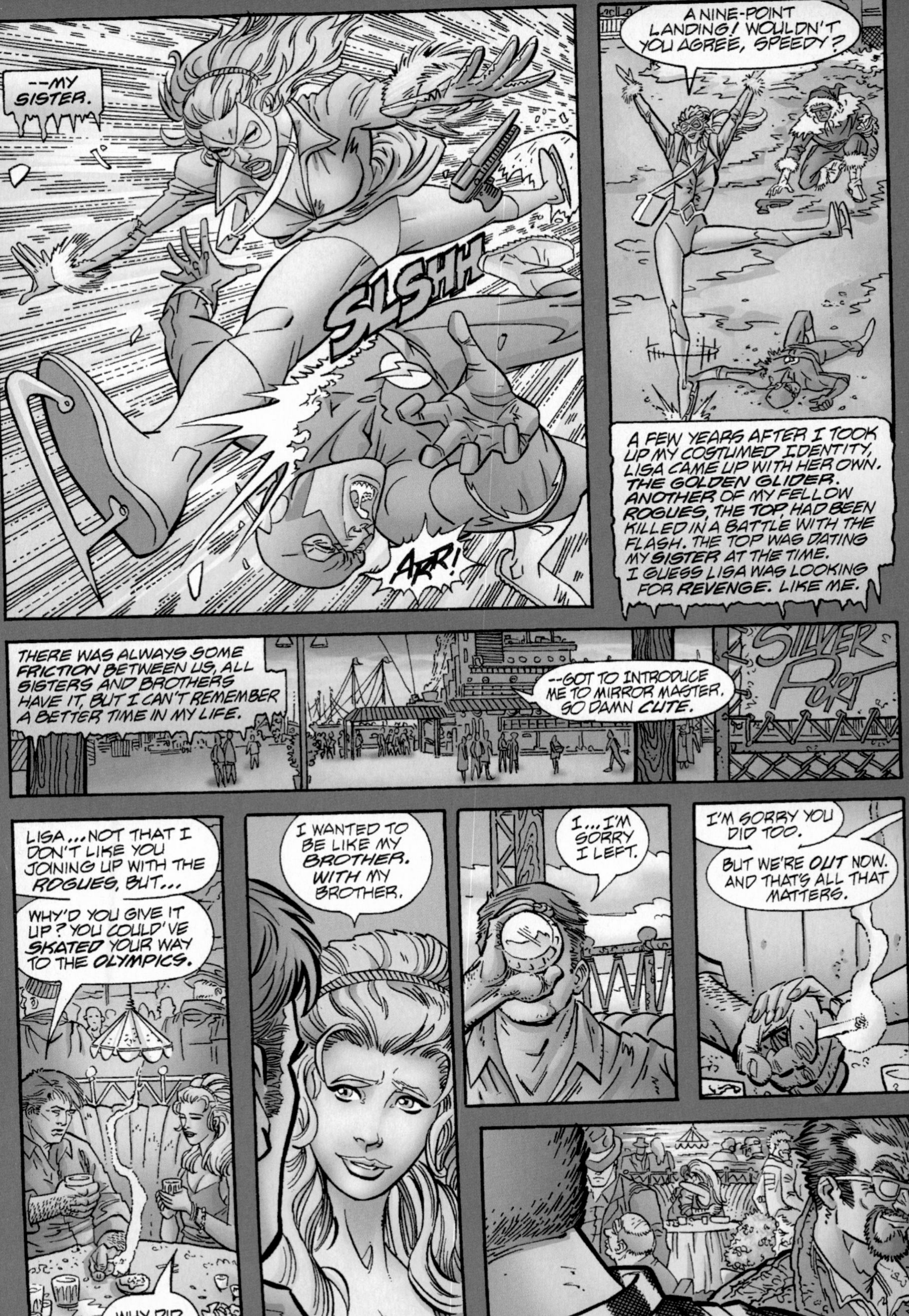
--MY SISTER.
SLSHH
ARR!
A NINE-POINT LANDING! WOULDN'T YOU AGREE, SPEEDY?
A FEW YEARS AFTER I TOOK UP MY COSTUMED IDENTITY, LISA CAME UP WITH HER OWN. THE GOLDEN GLIDER. ANOTHER OF MY FELLOW ROGUES, THE TOP, HAD BEEN KILLED IN A BATTLE WITH THE FLASH. THE TOP WAS DATING MY SISTER AT THE TIME. I GUESS LISA WAS LOOKING FOR REVENGE. LIKE ME.
THERE WAS ALWAYS SOME FRICTION BETWEEN US, ALL SISTERS AND BROTHERS HAVE IT, BUT I CAN'T REMEMBER A BETTER TIME IN MY LIFE.
--GOT TO INTRODUCE ME TO MIRROR MASTER. SO DAMN CUTE.
SILVER PORT
LISA... NOT THAT I DON'T LIKE YOU JOINING UP WITH THE ROGUES, BUT...
WHY'D YOU GIVE IT UP? YOU COULD'VE SKATED YOUR WAY TO THE OLYMPICS.
WHY DID I GIVE IT UP?
I WANTED TO BE LIKE MY BROTHER. WITH MY BROTHER.
I... I'M SORRY I LEFT.
I'M SORRY YOU DID TOO.
BUT WE'RE OUT NOW. AND THAT'S ALL THAT MATTERS.

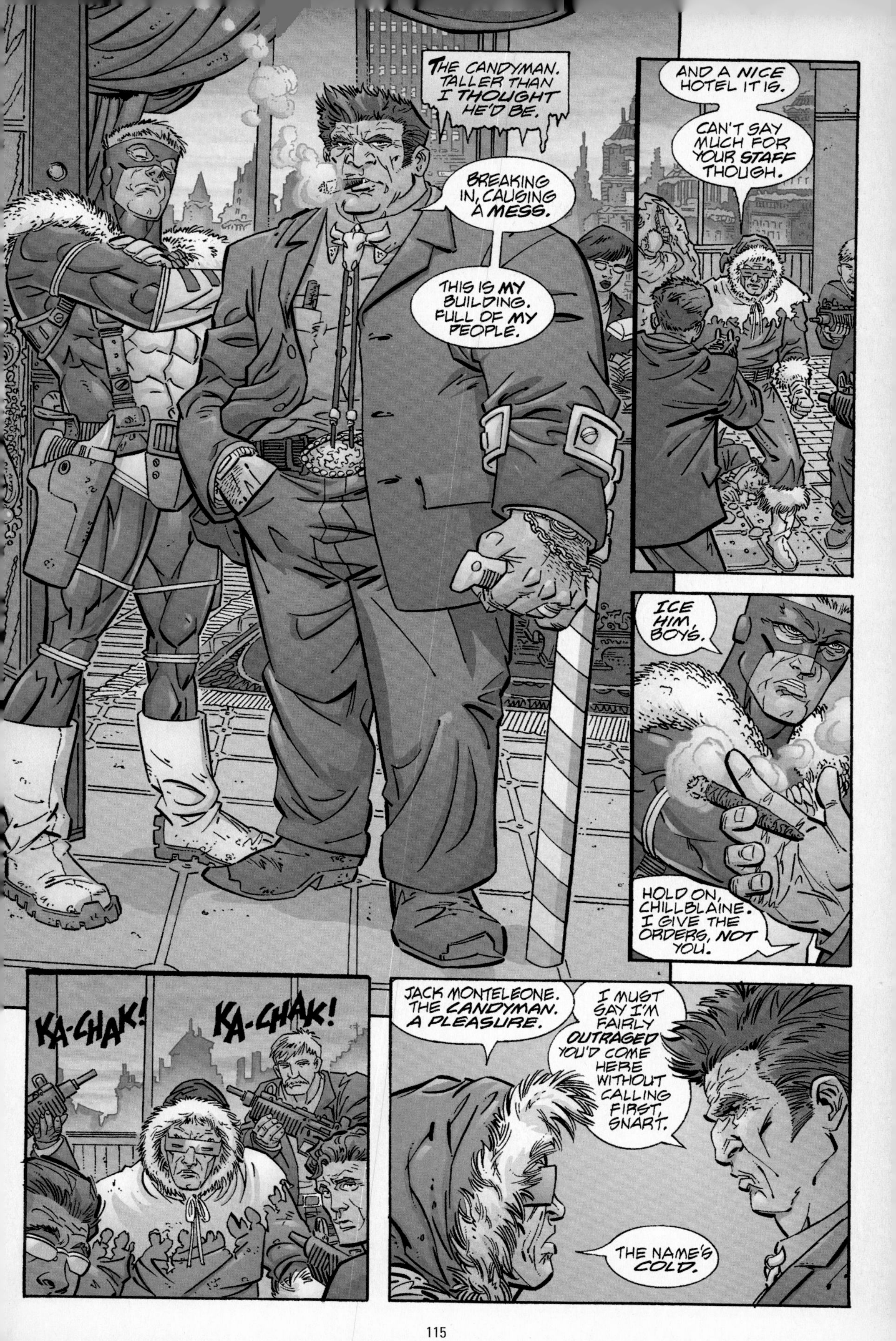
THE CANDYMAN. TALLER THAN I THOUGHT HE'D BE.
BREAKING IN, CAUSING A MESS.
THIS IS MY BUILDING. FULL OF MY PEOPLE.
AND A NICE HOTEL IT IS.
CAN'T SAY MUCH FOR YOUR STAFF THOUGH.
ICE HIM, BOYS.
HOLD ON, CHILLBLAINE. I GIVE THE ORDERS, NOT YOU.
KA-CHAK!
KA-CHAK!
JACK MONTELEONE. THE CANDYMAN. A PLEASURE.
I MUST SAY I'M FAIRLY OUTRAGED YOU'D COME HERE WITHOUT CALLING FIRST, SNART.
THE NAME'S COLD.

I KNOW WHAT YOUR *HANDLE* IS, FRIEND.

YOUR REPUTATION PRECEDES YOU, "CAPTAIN COLD."

YOU'VE CAUSED ME QUITE A BIT OF *TROUBLE* TODAY. NOT TO MENTION YOUR LITTLE *SCUFFLE* WITH MY BROTHER, JOEY, A FEW WEEKS BACK.*

THE *TWERP!*

EDITOR'S NOTE: * JOEY MONTELEONE A.K.A. TAR PIT! SEE THE FLASH #174.

KID'S GOT A LITTLE *WEIGHT* PROBLEM.

YOU LISTEN TO *ME,* COLD. YOU *DO* REALIZE THAT MY ENTIRE *ORGANIZATION* IS UNDER THE PROTECTION OF THE *NETWORK!* THAT *INCLUDES* YOU ROGUES.

BLACKSMITH GAVE ME HER *WORD.*

THE *ROGUES* DON'T *INTER-FERE* WITH ME OR MY PEOPLE.

I DON'T TAKE ORDERS FROM *ANYBODY,* PAL. I'M THE ROGUE AMONG ROGUES--

--SO DON'T *THINK* YOU'RE *SAFE* FROM ME BECAUSE OF A *HANDSHAKE* WITH THAT *WITCH.* THE *NETWORK* IS GOOD FOR *BUSINESS,* BUT I'M NOT HERE *ON* BUSINESS.

THIS IS *PERSONAL.*

DO I NEED TO *REMIND* YOU, YOU'RE IN A HOTEL FILLED WITH OVER *TWO HUNDRED* ARMED MEN. MY ARMY. YOU'VE GOT A *DOZEN* AUTOMATICS STARING AT YOU.

YOU'RE IN NO POSITION TO *THREATEN* ANYONE.

IT MIGHT *LOOK* THAT WAY, "JACK," BUT I *PROMISE* YOU... I'LL TAKE THESE *IDIOTS* OUT BEFORE THEY CAN *BLINK.* DID YOU FORGET I'M USED TO TANGLING WITH SOMEONE THAT MOVES AT THE SPEED OF *LIGHT?*

THEN I'LL COME AFTER *YOU.* SHOVE THIS GUN DOWN YOUR *THROAT* AND *FREEZE* YOU FROM THE *INSIDE* OUT.

IT CAN TAKE UP TO FIFTEEN MINUTES TO FINISH YOU OFF, BUT I'VE GOT THE TIME.

THINK I'M *BLUFFING?* TELL THEM TO *SHOOT.*

WHAT DO YOU *WANT?*

HIM.

JUST *HIM.*

116

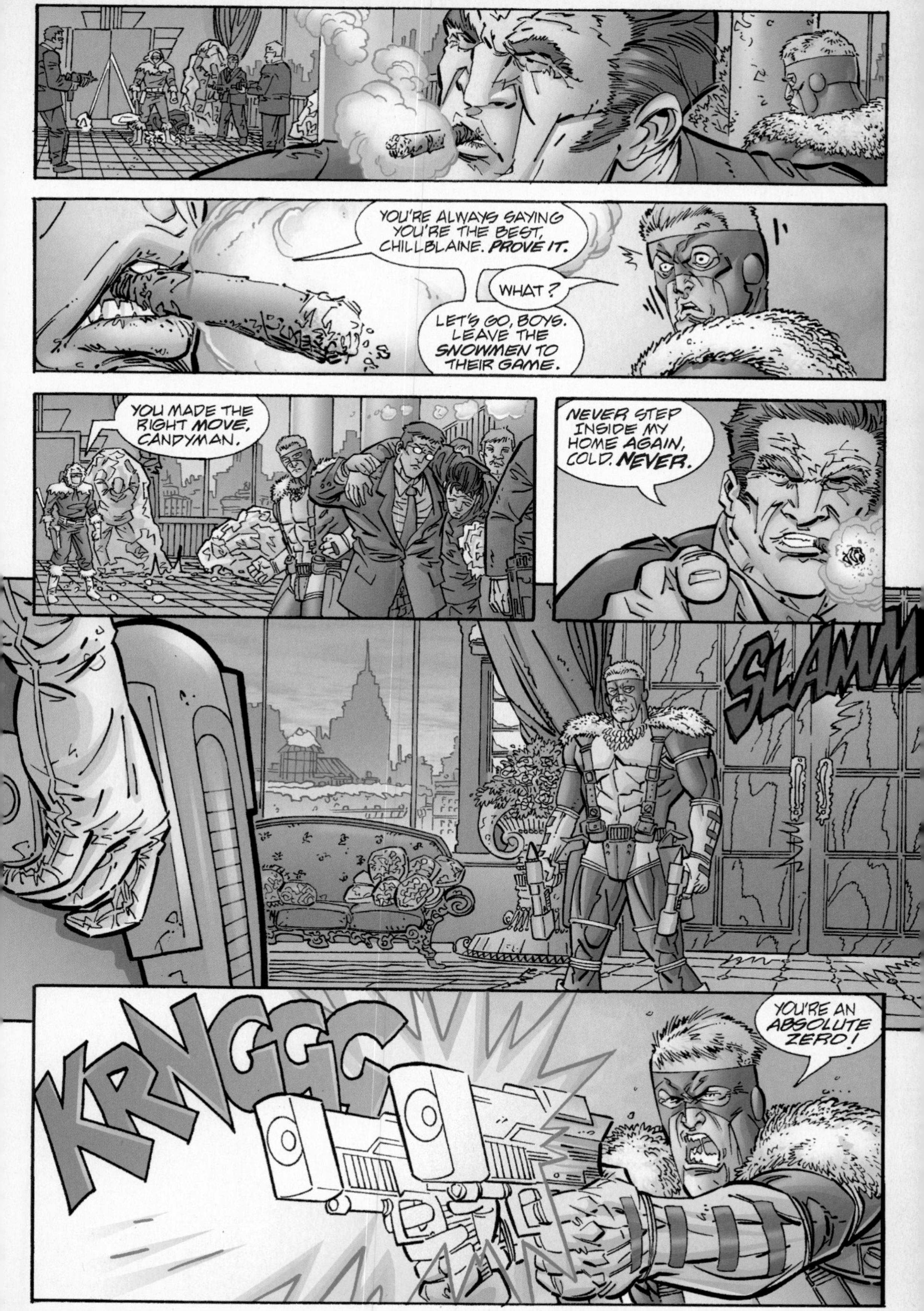
YOU'RE ALWAYS SAYING YOU'RE THE BEST, CHILLBLAINE. PROVE IT.
WHAT?
LET'S GO, BOYS. LEAVE THE SNOWMEN TO THEIR GAME.
YOU MADE THE RIGHT MOVE, CANDYMAN.
NEVER STEP INSIDE MY HOME AGAIN, COLD. NEVER.
SLAMM
KRNGGC
YOU'RE AN ABSOLUTE ZERO!

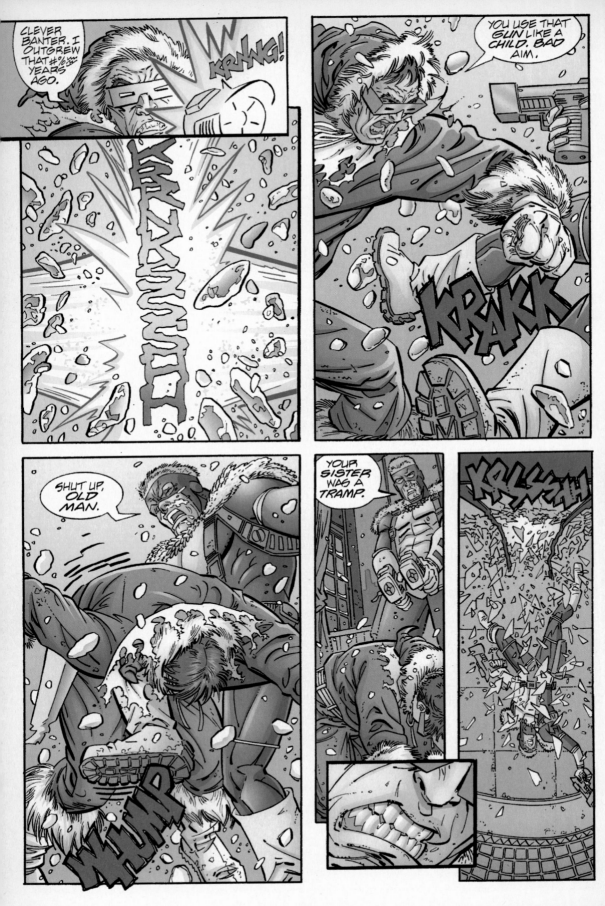

CLEVER BANTER. I OUTGREW THAT #%&=× YEARS AGO.

KRUNG!

YOU USE THAT GUN LIKE A CHILD. BAD AIM.

KRAKK

SHUT UP, OLD MAN.

WHUMP

YOUR SISTER WAS A TRAMP.

KRSSSH

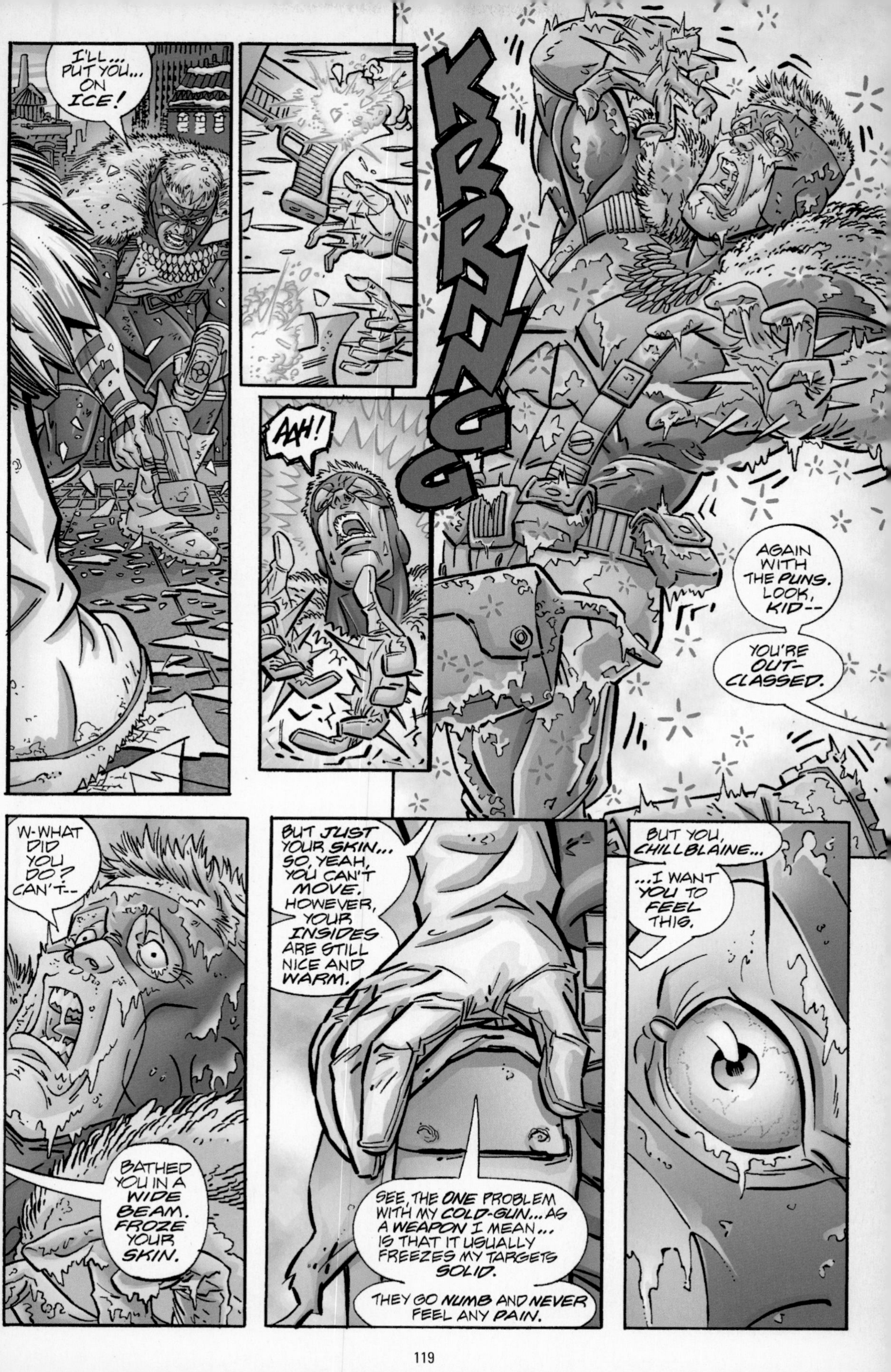

I'LL... PUT YOU... ON ICE!
KRRANG
AAH!
AGAIN WITH THE PUNS. LOOK, KID--
YOU'RE OUT-CLASSED.
W-WHAT DID YOU DO? CAN'T--
BATHED YOU IN A WIDE BEAM. FROZE YOUR SKIN.
BUT JUST YOUR SKIN... SO, YEAH, YOU CAN'T MOVE. HOWEVER, YOUR INSIDES ARE STILL NICE AND WARM.
SEE, THE ONE PROBLEM WITH MY COLD-GUN... AS A WEAPON I MEAN... IS THAT IT USUALLY FREEZES MY TARGETS SOLID.
THEY GO NUMB AND NEVER FEEL ANY PAIN.
BUT YOU, CHILLBLAINE...
...I WANT YOU TO FEEL THIS.

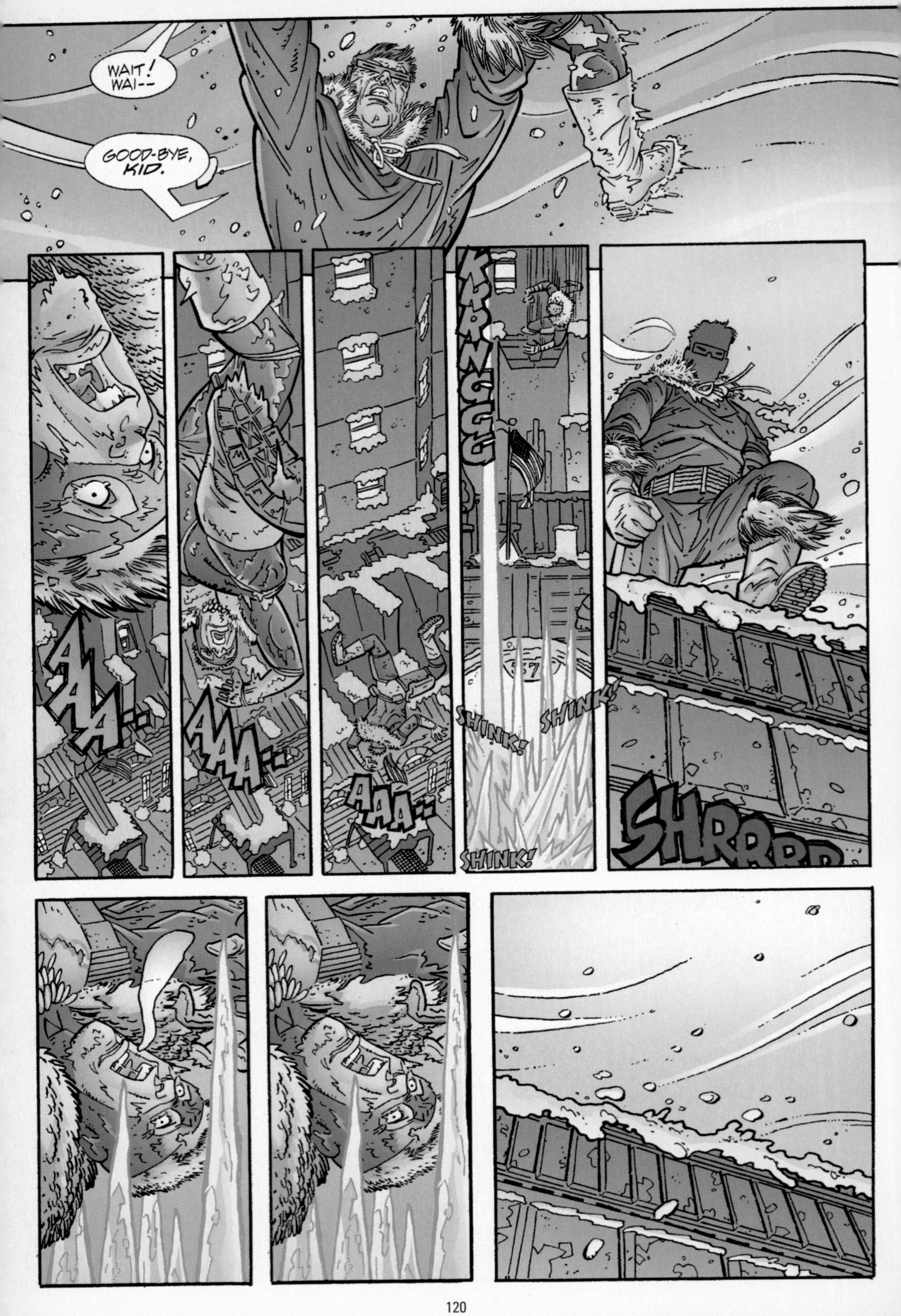
WAIT! WAI--
GOOD-BYE, KID.
AAA--
AAA--
AAA--
KKRNGGG
SHINK!
SHINK!
SHINK!
SHRRRR

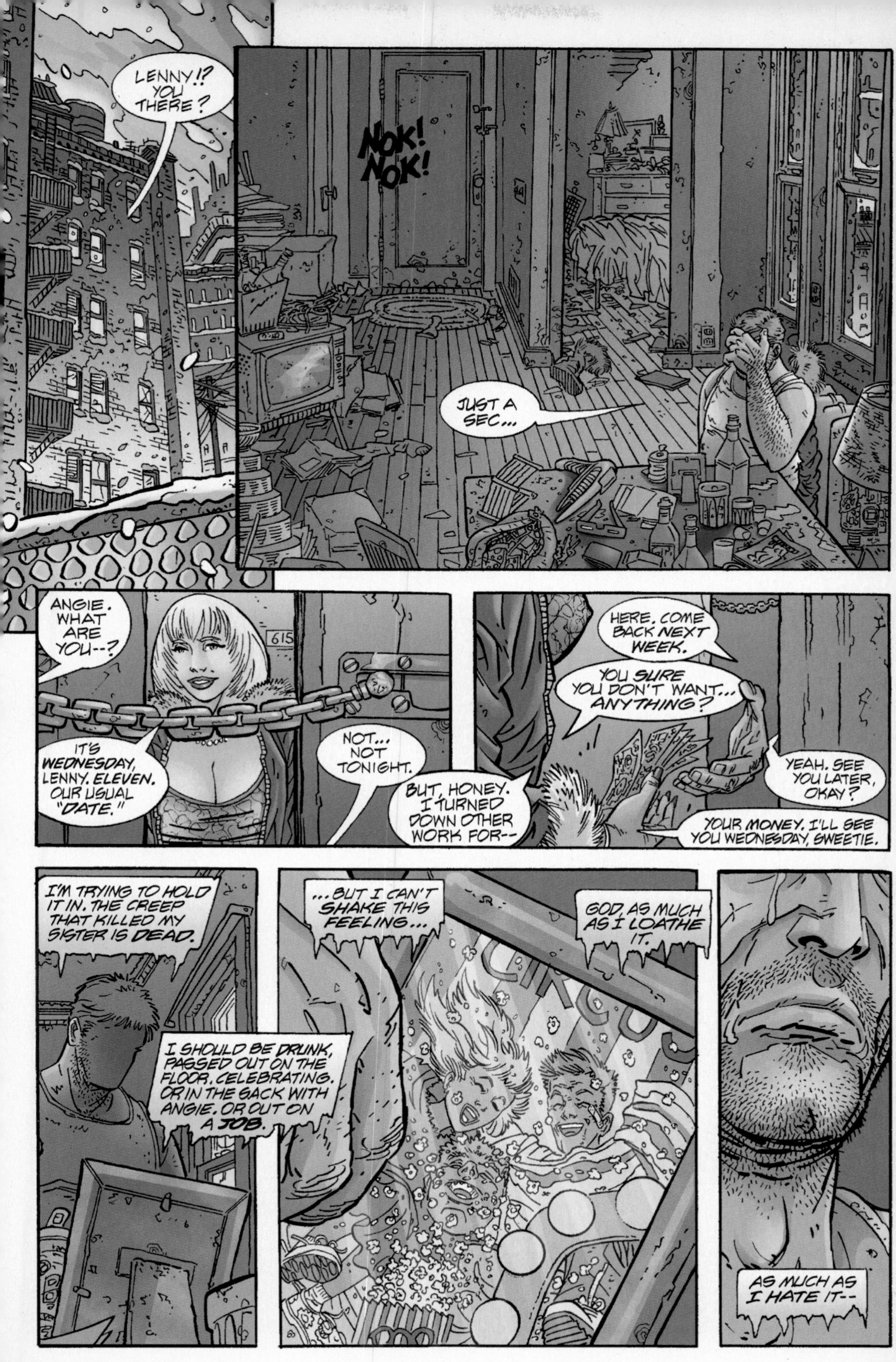
LENNY!? YOU THERE?
NOK! NOK!
JUST A SEC...
ANGIE. WHAT ARE YOU--?
615
IT'S WEDNESDAY, LENNY. ELEVEN. OUR USUAL "DATE."
NOT... NOT TONIGHT.
BUT, HONEY. I TURNED DOWN OTHER WORK FOR--
HERE. COME BACK NEXT WEEK.
YOU SURE YOU DON'T WANT... ANYTHING?
YEAH. SEE YOU LATER, OKAY?
YOUR MONEY. I'LL SEE YOU WEDNESDAY, SWEETIE.
I'M TRYING TO HOLD IT IN. THE CREEP THAT KILLED MY SISTER IS DEAD.
I SHOULD BE DRUNK, PASSED OUT ON THE FLOOR. CELEBRATING. OR IN THE SACK WITH ANGIE. OR OUT ON A JOB.
...BUT I CAN'T SHAKE THIS FEELING...
GOD, AS MUCH AS I LOATHE IT.
AS MUCH AS I HATE IT--

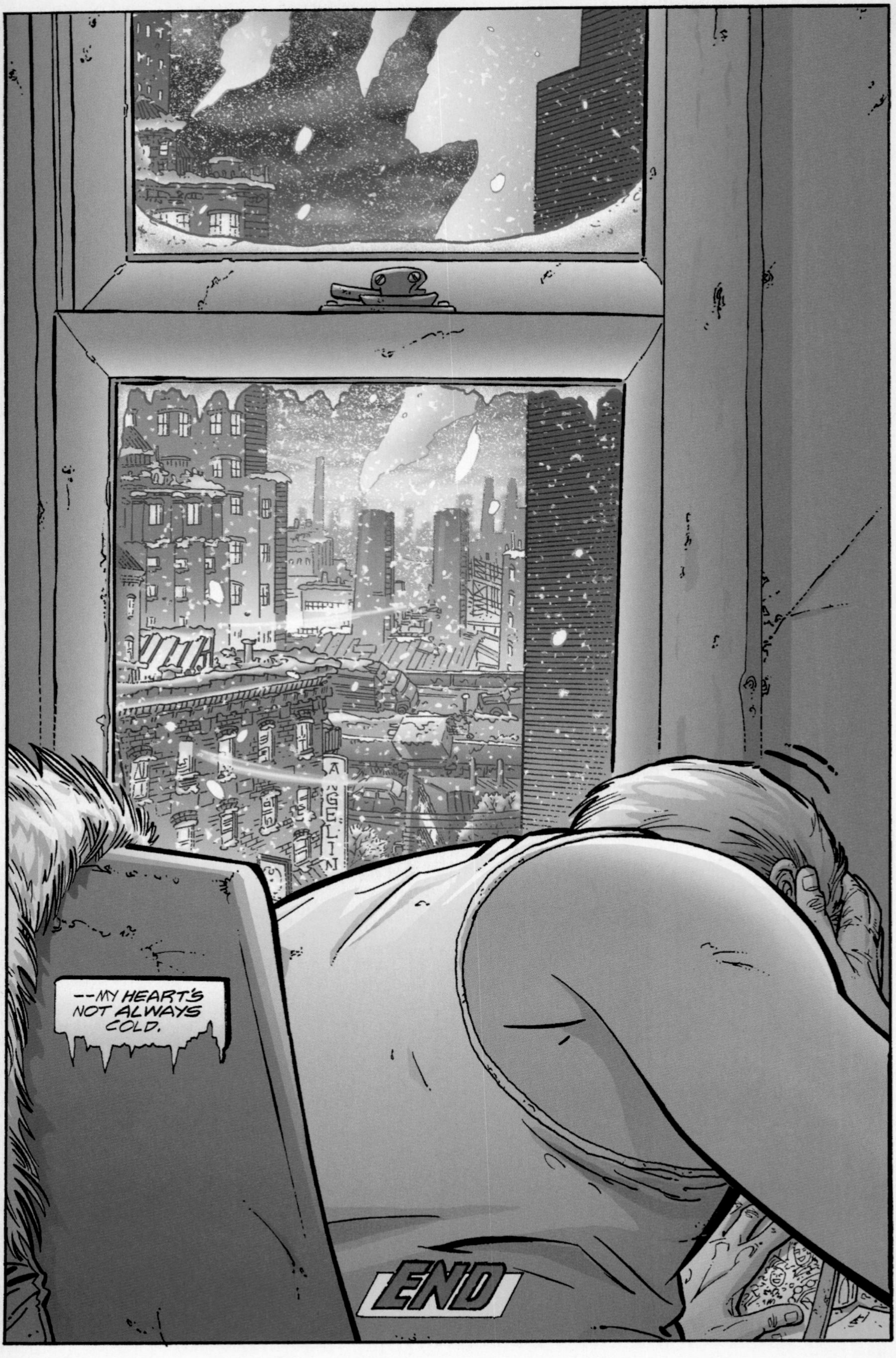

--MY HEART'S NOT ALWAYS COLD.
ANGELLINI
END

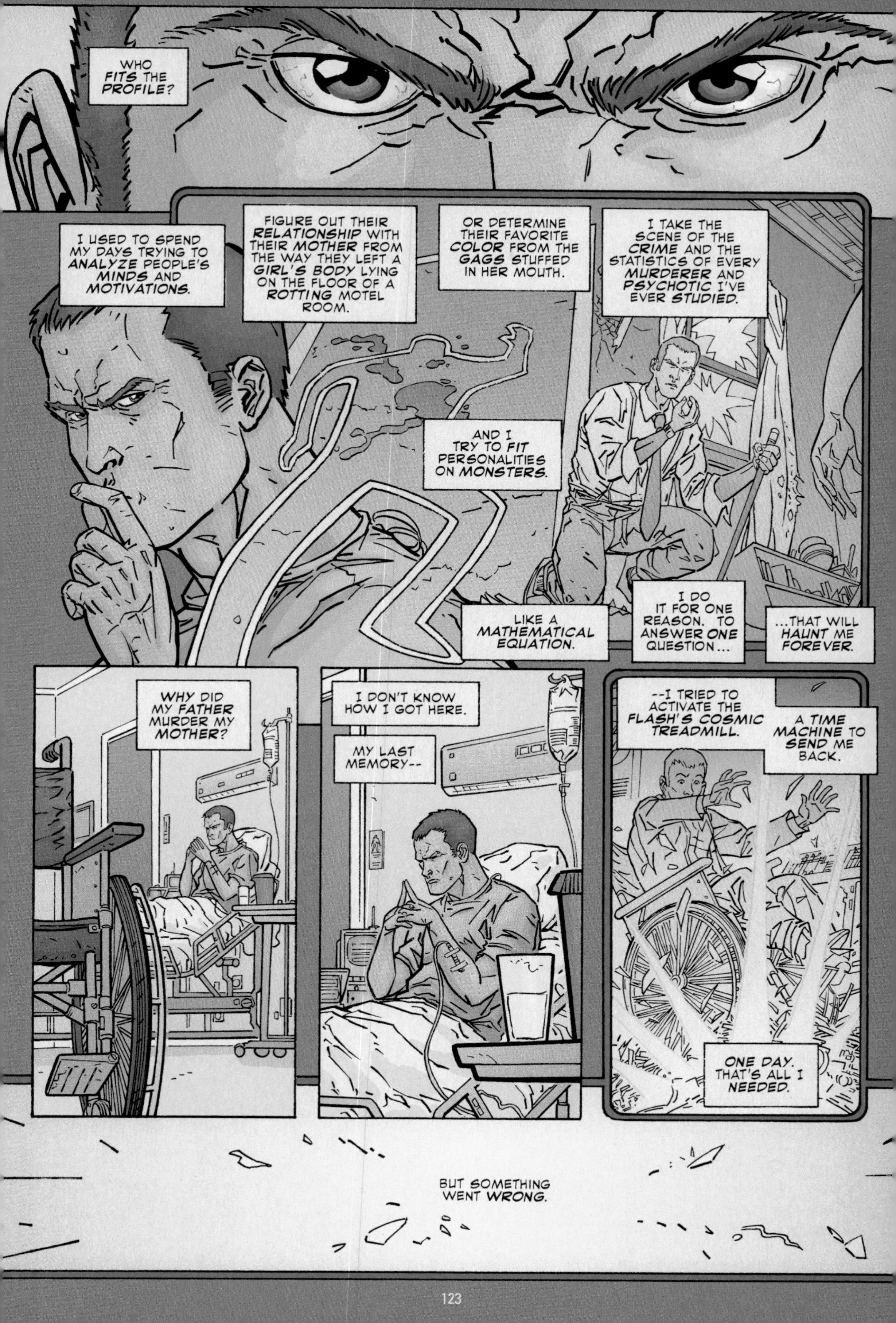
WHO FITS THE PROFILE?
I USED TO SPEND MY DAYS TRYING TO ANALYZE PEOPLE'S MINDS AND MOTIVATIONS.
FIGURE OUT THEIR RELATIONSHIP WITH THEIR MOTHER FROM THE WAY THEY LEFT A GIRL'S BODY LYING ON THE FLOOR OF A ROTTING MOTEL ROOM.
OR DETERMINE THEIR FAVORITE COLOR FROM THE GAGS STUFFED IN HER MOUTH.
I TAKE THE SCENE OF THE CRIME AND THE STATISTICS OF EVERY MURDERER AND PSYCHOTIC I'VE EVER STUDIED.
AND I TRY TO FIT PERSONALITIES ON MONSTERS.
LIKE A MATHEMATICAL EQUATION.
I DO IT FOR ONE REASON. TO ANSWER ONE QUESTION...
...THAT WILL HAUNT ME FOREVER.
WHY DID MY FATHER MURDER MY MOTHER?
I DON'T KNOW HOW I GOT HERE.
MY LAST MEMORY--
--I TRIED TO ACTIVATE THE FLASH'S COSMIC TREADMILL.
A TIME MACHINE TO SEND ME BACK.
ONE DAY. THAT'S ALL I NEEDED.
BUT SOMETHING WENT WRONG.

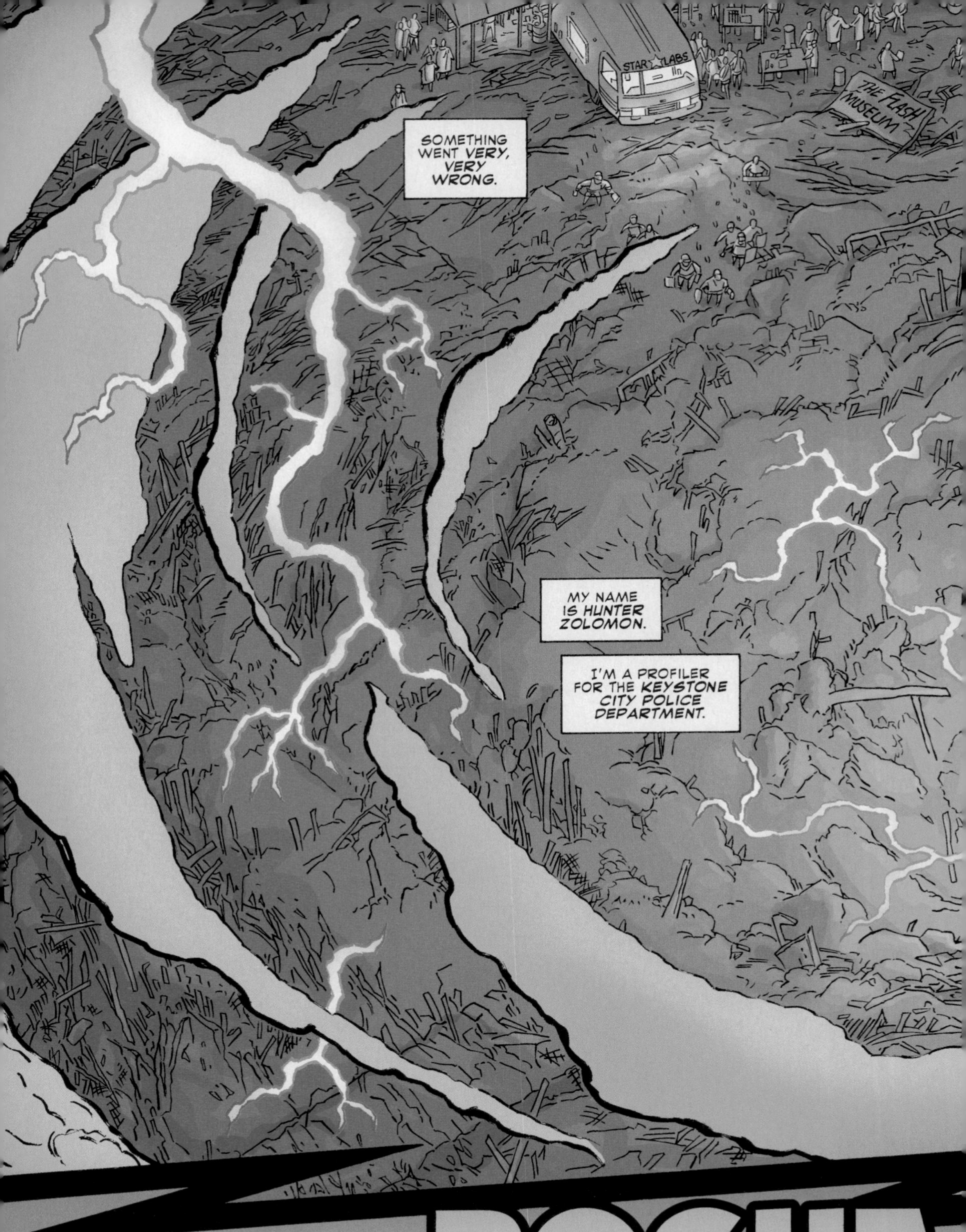
STAR LABS
THE FLASH MUSEUM
SOMETHING WENT VERY, VERY WRONG.
MY NAME IS HUNTER ZOLOMON.
I'M A PROFILER FOR THE KEYSTONE CITY POLICE DEPARTMENT.

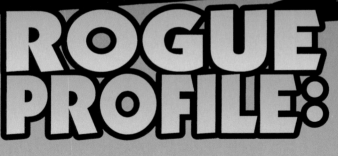

ROGUE PROFILE:

Geoff Johns writer
Scott Kolins penciller
Doug Hazlewood inker
Kurt Hathaway letterer
James Sinclair colorist & separator
Joey Cavalieri editor

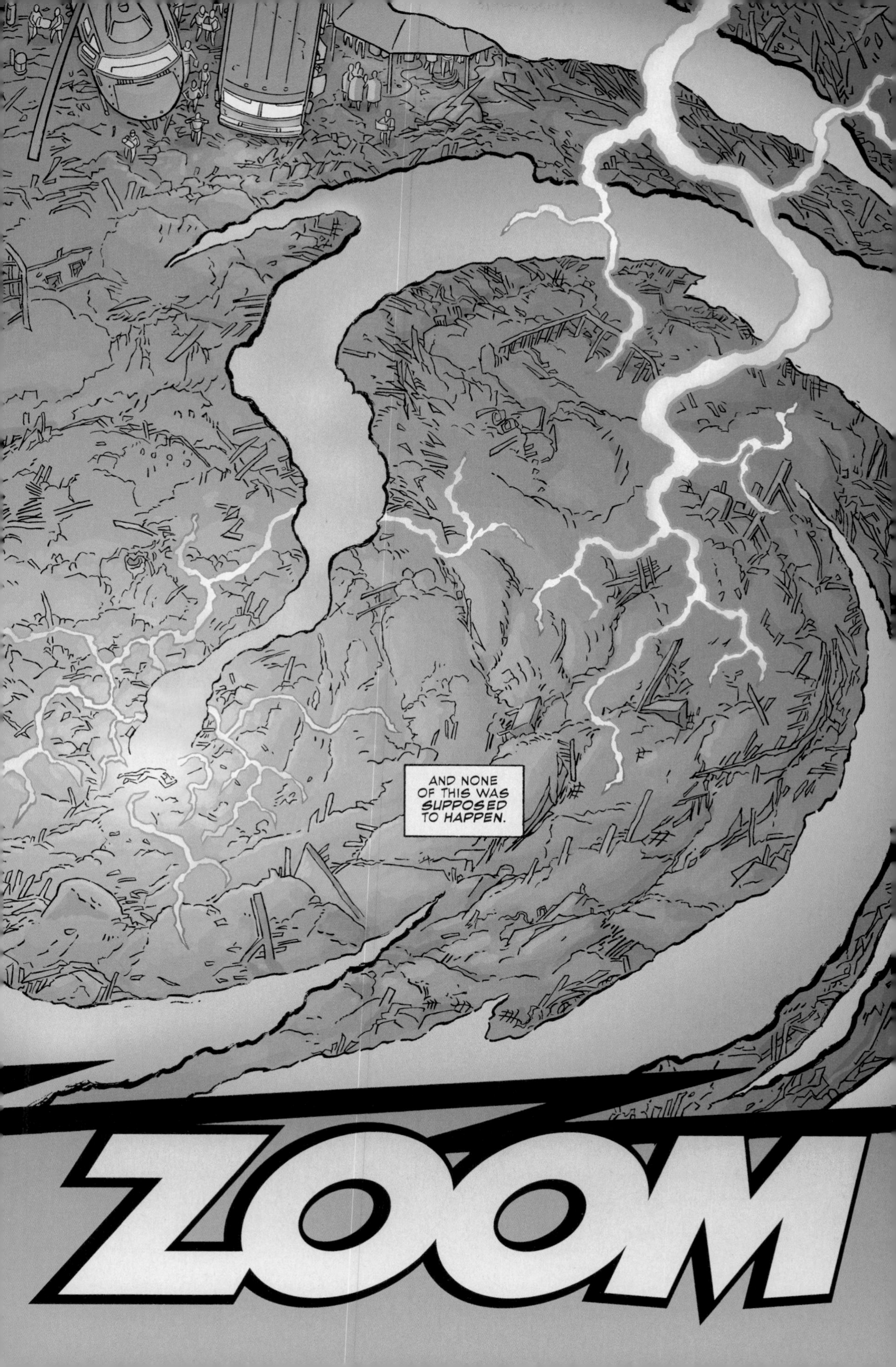
AND NONE OF THIS WAS SUPPOSED TO HAPPEN.
ZOOM

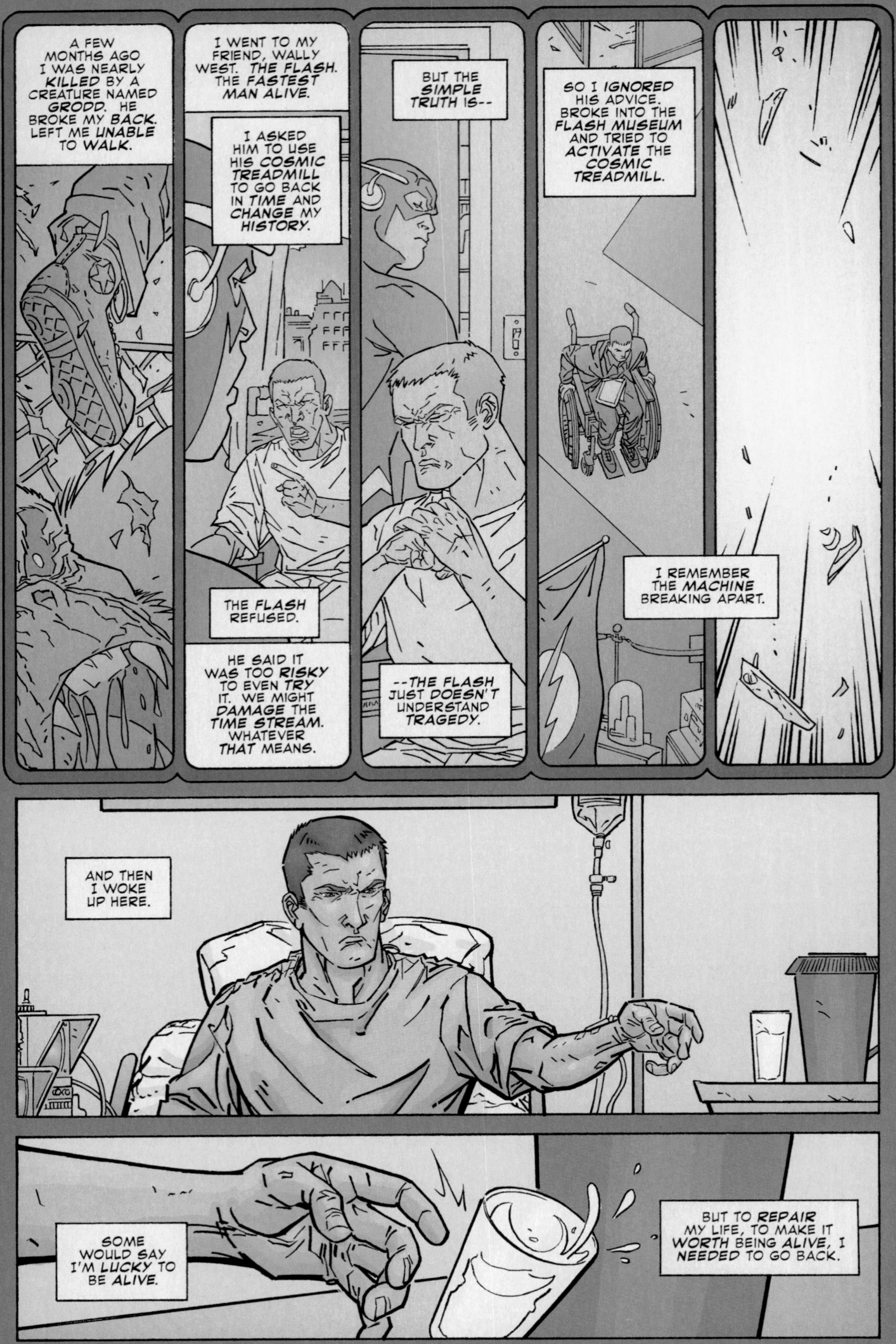
A FEW MONTHS AGO I WAS NEARLY KILLED BY A CREATURE NAMED GRODD. HE BROKE MY BACK. LEFT ME UNABLE TO WALK.
I WENT TO MY FRIEND, WALLY WEST. THE FLASH. THE FASTEST MAN ALIVE.
I ASKED HIM TO USE HIS COSMIC TREADMILL TO GO BACK IN TIME AND CHANGE MY HISTORY.
THE FLASH REFUSED.
HE SAID IT WAS TOO RISKY TO EVEN TRY IT. WE MIGHT DAMAGE THE TIME STREAM. WHATEVER THAT MEANS.
BUT THE SIMPLE TRUTH IS--
--THE FLASH JUST DOESN'T UNDERSTAND TRAGEDY.
SO I IGNORED HIS ADVICE. BROKE INTO THE FLASH MUSEUM AND TRIED TO ACTIVATE THE COSMIC TREADMILL.
I REMEMBER THE MACHINE BREAKING APART.
AND THEN I WOKE UP HERE.
SOME WOULD SAY I'M LUCKY TO BE ALIVE.
BUT TO REPAIR MY LIFE, TO MAKE IT WORTH BEING ALIVE, I NEEDED TO GO BACK.

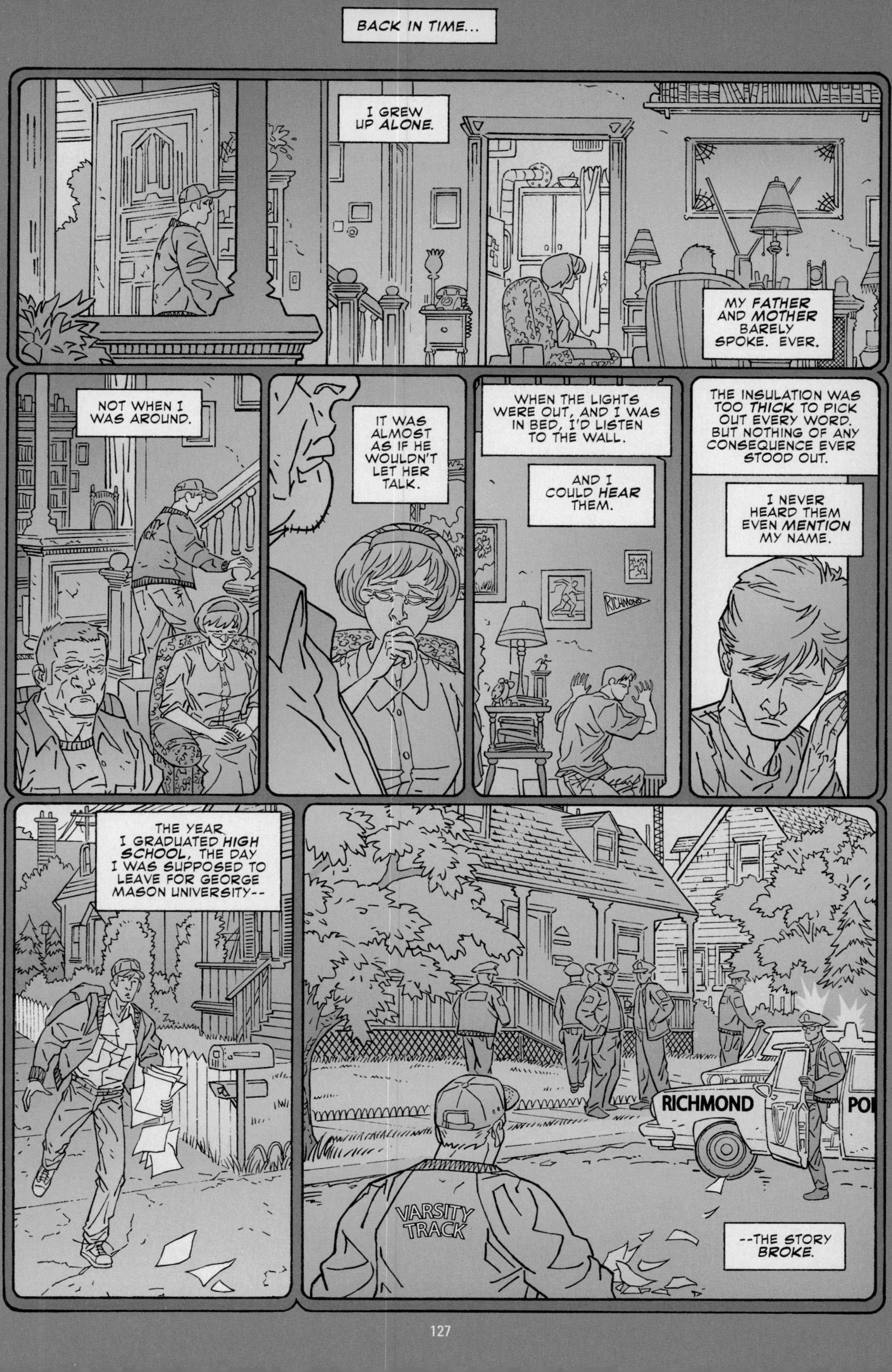
BACK IN TIME...
I GREW UP ALONE.
MY FATHER AND MOTHER BARELY SPOKE. EVER.
NOT WHEN I WAS AROUND.
IT WAS ALMOST AS IF HE WOULDN'T LET HER TALK.
WHEN THE LIGHTS WERE OUT, AND I WAS IN BED, I'D LISTEN TO THE WALL.
AND I COULD HEAR THEM.
RICHMOND
THE INSULATION WAS TOO THICK TO PICK OUT EVERY WORD. BUT NOTHING OF ANY CONSEQUENCE EVER STOOD OUT.
I NEVER HEARD THEM EVEN MENTION MY NAME.
THE YEAR I GRADUATED HIGH SCHOOL, THE DAY I WAS SUPPOSED TO LEAVE FOR GEORGE MASON UNIVERSITY--
RICHMOND
VARSITY TRACK
--THE STORY BROKE.

MY MOTHER HAD FINALLY **TALKED.**

SHE TOLD THE **POLICE** WHERE THE **FIVE MISSING** GIRLS FROM LAST **SUMMER** HAD GONE.

IN THE GROUND.

BEHIND OUR GARAGE.

BUT MY FATHER CAME HOME EARLY FROM THE LUMBERYARD--

--AND MY **MOTHER** WAS HIS **LAST** VICTIM.

THE POLICE SURROUNDED THE HOUSE. MY FATHER DIDN'T GIVE UP.

AND HE WAS **DEAD** AN HOUR AFTER MY **MOTHER** WAS.

FLOUR SUGAR

I DIDN'T KNOW HOW TO FEEL.

MY **PARENTS,** TWO PEOPLE WHO I HAD NEVER REALLY KNOWN, WERE GONE. ONE **KILLED** THE OTHER.

NO ONE KNEW **WHY** MY FATHER DID IT. THEY DIDN'T **CARE.** THEY WERE JUST **GLAD** THE **MONSTER** WAS GONE.

BUT I CARED.

I WANTED TO **KNOW** WHY HE DID IT.

I WANTED TO **UNDERSTAND** HIM IN ORDER TO **STOP** ANYONE ELSE **LIKE** HIM.

I LEFT FOR COLLEGE A WEEK LATER.

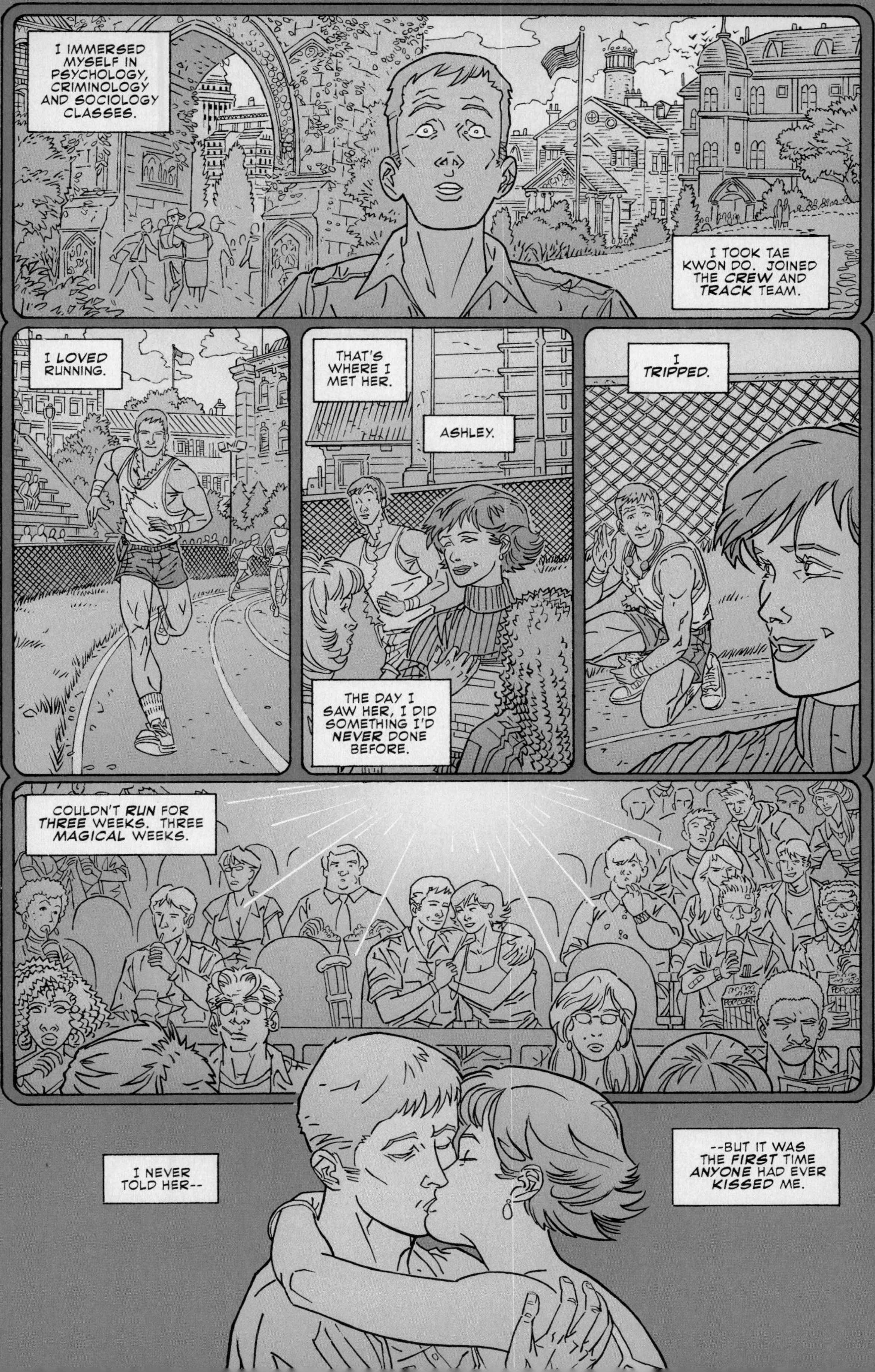
I IMMERSED MYSELF IN PSYCHOLOGY, CRIMINOLOGY AND SOCIOLOGY CLASSES.
I TOOK TAE KWON DO. JOINED THE CREW AND TRACK TEAM.
I LOVED RUNNING.
THAT'S WHERE I MET HER.
ASHLEY.
THE DAY I SAW HER, I DID SOMETHING I'D NEVER DONE BEFORE.
I TRIPPED.
COULDN'T RUN FOR THREE WEEKS. THREE MAGICAL WEEKS.
POPCORN
POPCORN
I NEVER TOLD HER--
--BUT IT WAS THE FIRST TIME ANYONE HAD EVER KISSED ME.

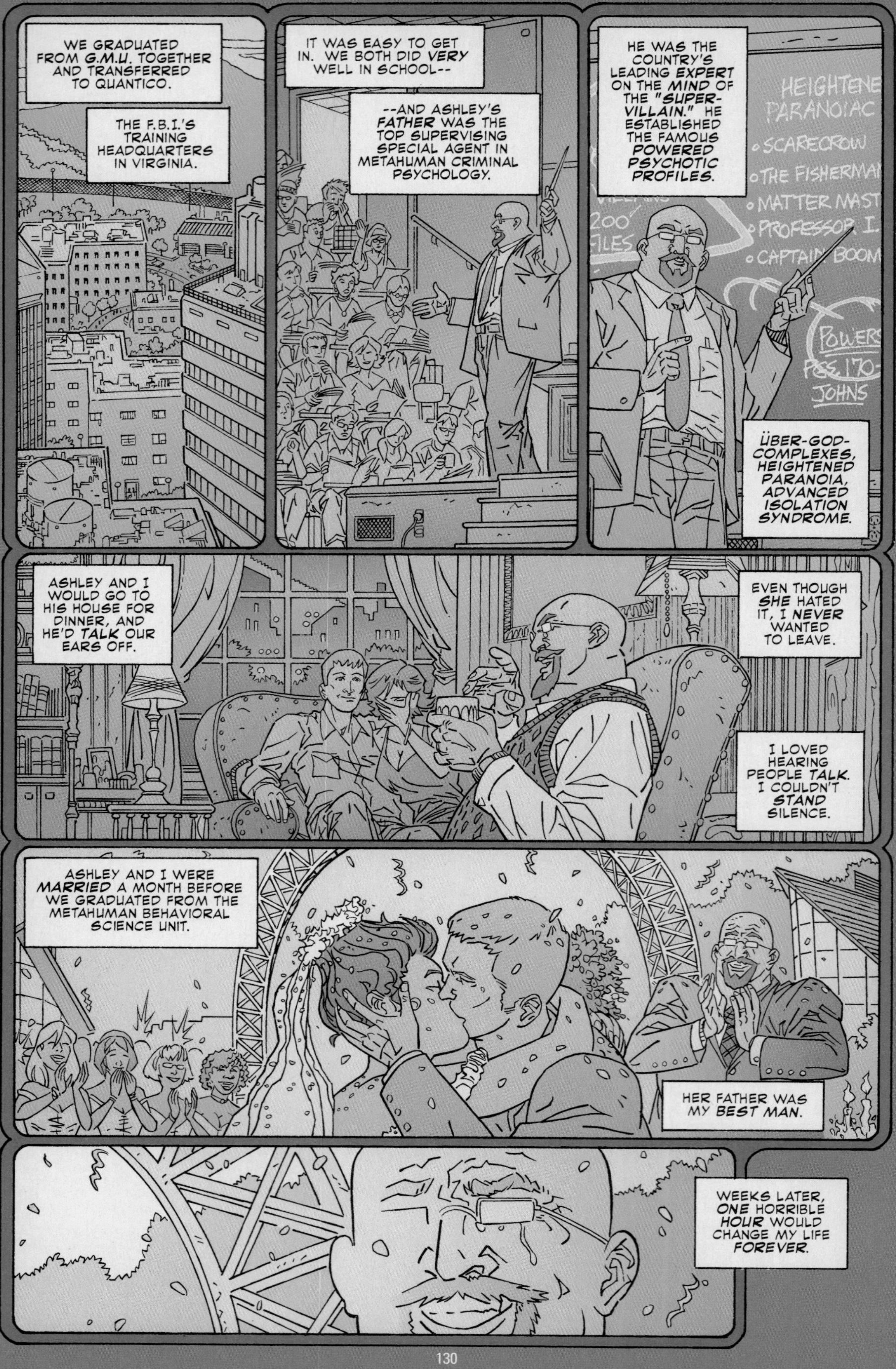
WE GRADUATED FROM G.M.U. TOGETHER AND TRANSFERRED TO QUANTICO.
THE F.B.I.'S TRAINING HEADQUARTERS IN VIRGINIA.
IT WAS EASY TO GET IN. WE BOTH DID VERY WELL IN SCHOOL--
--AND ASHLEY'S FATHER WAS THE TOP SUPERVISING SPECIAL AGENT IN METAHUMAN CRIMINAL PSYCHOLOGY.
HE WAS THE COUNTRY'S LEADING EXPERT ON THE MIND OF THE "SUPER-VILLAIN." HE ESTABLISHED THE FAMOUS POWERED PSYCHOTIC PROFILES.
HEIGHTENE
PARANOIAC
SCARECROW
THE FISHERMAN
MATTER MAST
PROFESSOR I.
CAPTAIN BOOM
200
FILES
POWERS
PGS. 170-
JOHNS
ÜBER-GOD-COMPLEXES, HEIGHTENED PARANOIA, ADVANCED ISOLATION SYNDROME.
ASHLEY AND I WOULD GO TO HIS HOUSE FOR DINNER, AND HE'D TALK OUR EARS OFF.
EVEN THOUGH SHE HATED IT, I NEVER WANTED TO LEAVE.
I LOVED HEARING PEOPLE TALK. I COULDN'T STAND SILENCE.
ASHLEY AND I WERE MARRIED A MONTH BEFORE WE GRADUATED FROM THE METAHUMAN BEHAVIORAL SCIENCE UNIT.
HER FATHER WAS MY BEST MAN.
WEEKS LATER, ONE HORRIBLE HOUR WOULD CHANGE MY LIFE FOREVER.

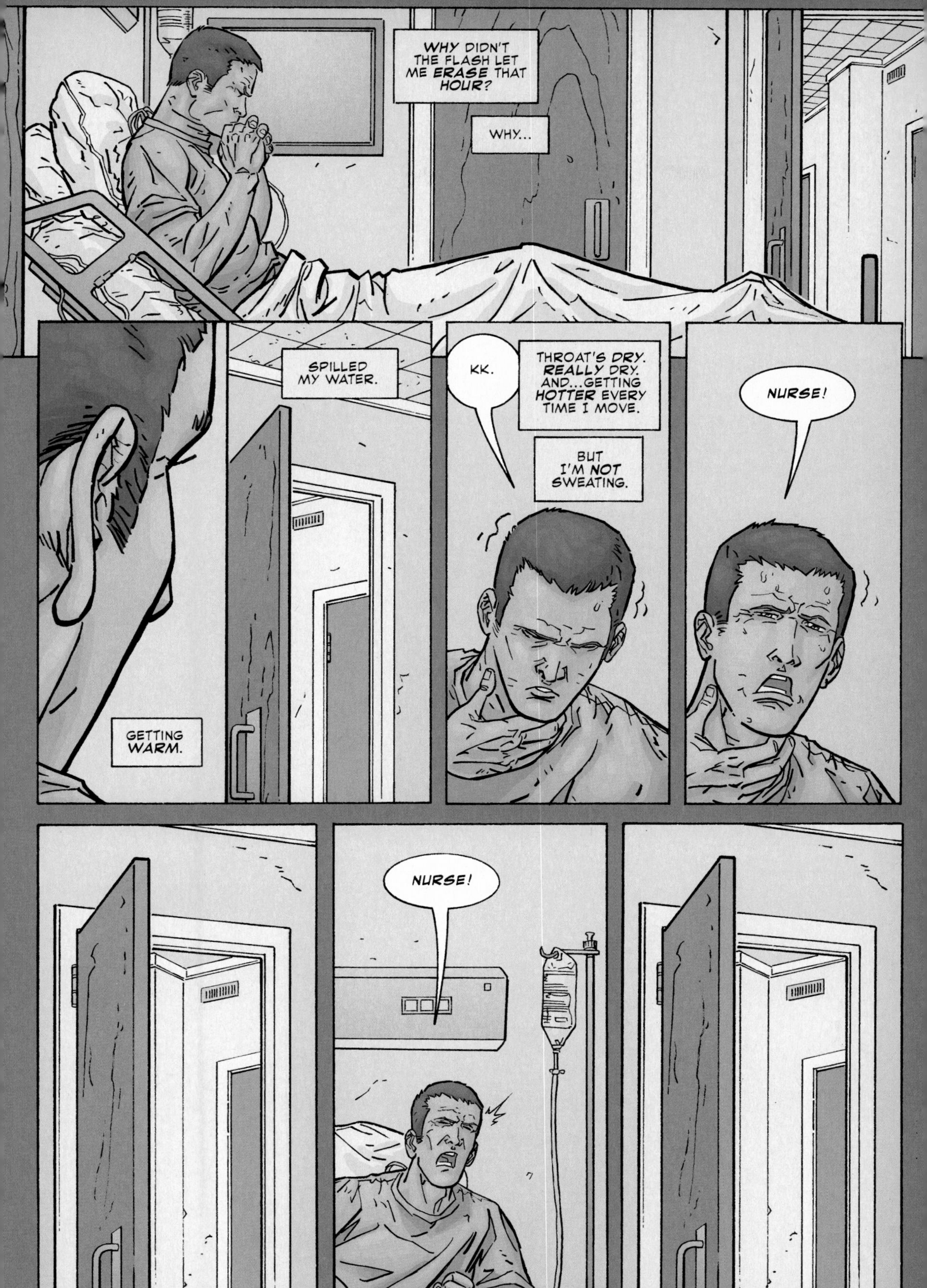

WHY DIDN'T THE FLASH LET ME ERASE THAT HOUR?
WHY...
SPILLED MY WATER.
GETTING WARM.
KK.
THROAT'S DRY. REALLY DRY. AND...GETTING HOTTER EVERY TIME I MOVE.
BUT I'M NOT SWEATING.
NURSE!
NURSE!

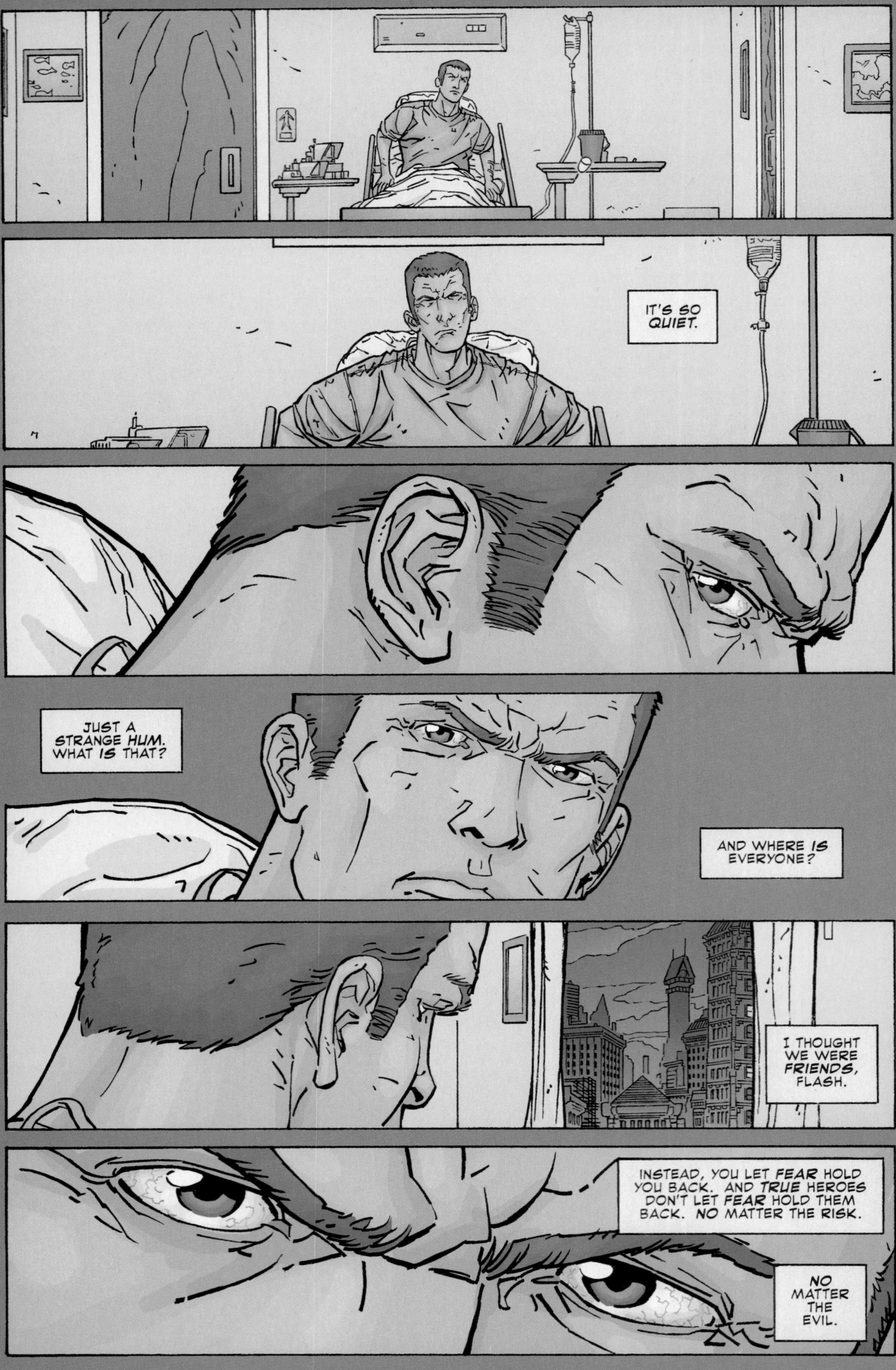
IT'S SO QUIET.
JUST A STRANGE HUM. WHAT IS THAT?
AND WHERE IS EVERYONE?
I THOUGHT WE WERE FRIENDS, FLASH.
INSTEAD, YOU LET FEAR HOLD YOU BACK. AND TRUE HEROES DON'T LET FEAR HOLD THEM BACK. NO MATTER THE RISK.
NO MATTER THE EVIL.

EOBARD THAWNE.
THE REVERSE-FLASH.

PROFESSOR ZOOM.

WHITE OUT

② REVERSE-FLASH/PRO
(EOBARD THAWNE ZOOM
TIME TRAVELER w/SUPER-S
"THE SLAYER & THE SLAIN"
1983 C. BATES
REATEST ARCHEO
IXATION
TO K!
· CAPTA
· GORILLA
· WEATHER
· MIRROR ME
· CAPTAIN BO
· THE T
READ:

THAWNE WAS THE
GREATEST ENEMY
OF BARRY ALLEN.
THE FLASH
BEFORE WEST.

HE WAS LET LOOSE
BECAUSE OF TIME
TRAVEL. A MANIAC
FROM THE FAR FUTURE.

THAWNE WAS
OBSESSED WITH
ALLEN. WANTED TO
TAKE HIS PLACE IN THIS
TIME PERIOD AS THE
FASTEST MAN ALIVE.

REVERSE FLASH = REVERSE THINKING
SUPER SPEED TIME TRAVELER
☆ SEEK TO FIT IN
LOOKING FOR:
—MONEY
2 FAME
LOVE

TYPICAL WEAK
SELF-IMAGE AND
NON-IDENTITY. MIXED
WITH DELUSIONS OF
SELF-IMPORTANCE AND
LACK OF RECOGNITION
BY SOCIETY.

A CLASSIC
STALKER.

WHEN IS IT RIGHT TO KILL?

EVENTUALLY
THAWNE CROSSED
THE LINE.
NEARLY KILLED
FIONA WEBB.

ALLEN'S
FIANCÉE AT THE
TIME.

SO ALLEN
CROSSED THE
LINE HIMSELF.

00:14:06

NEWS
DC DIRECT 5

THE FLASH CHARGED WITH MURDER...

HE BROKE
THAWNE'S
NECK.

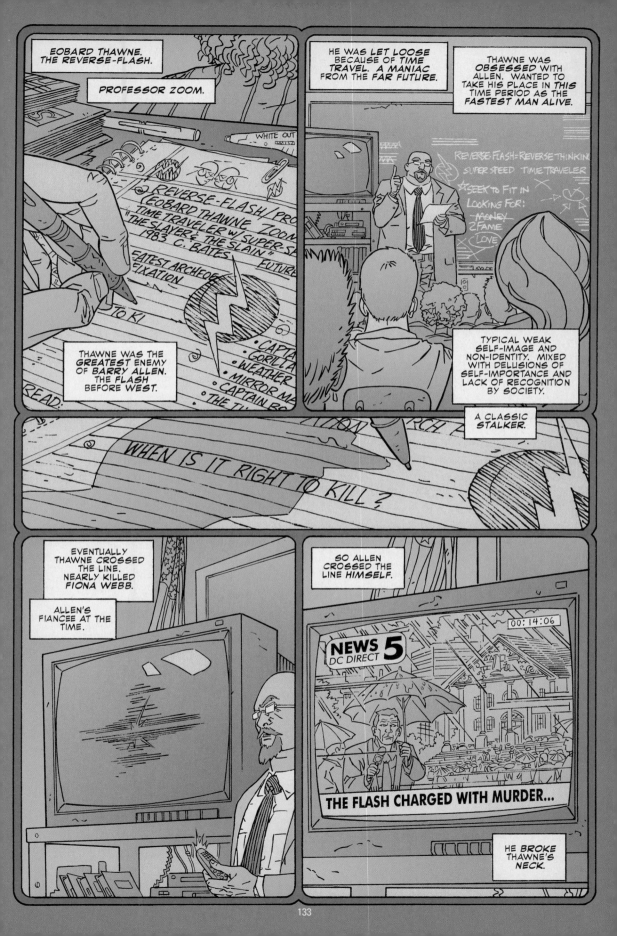

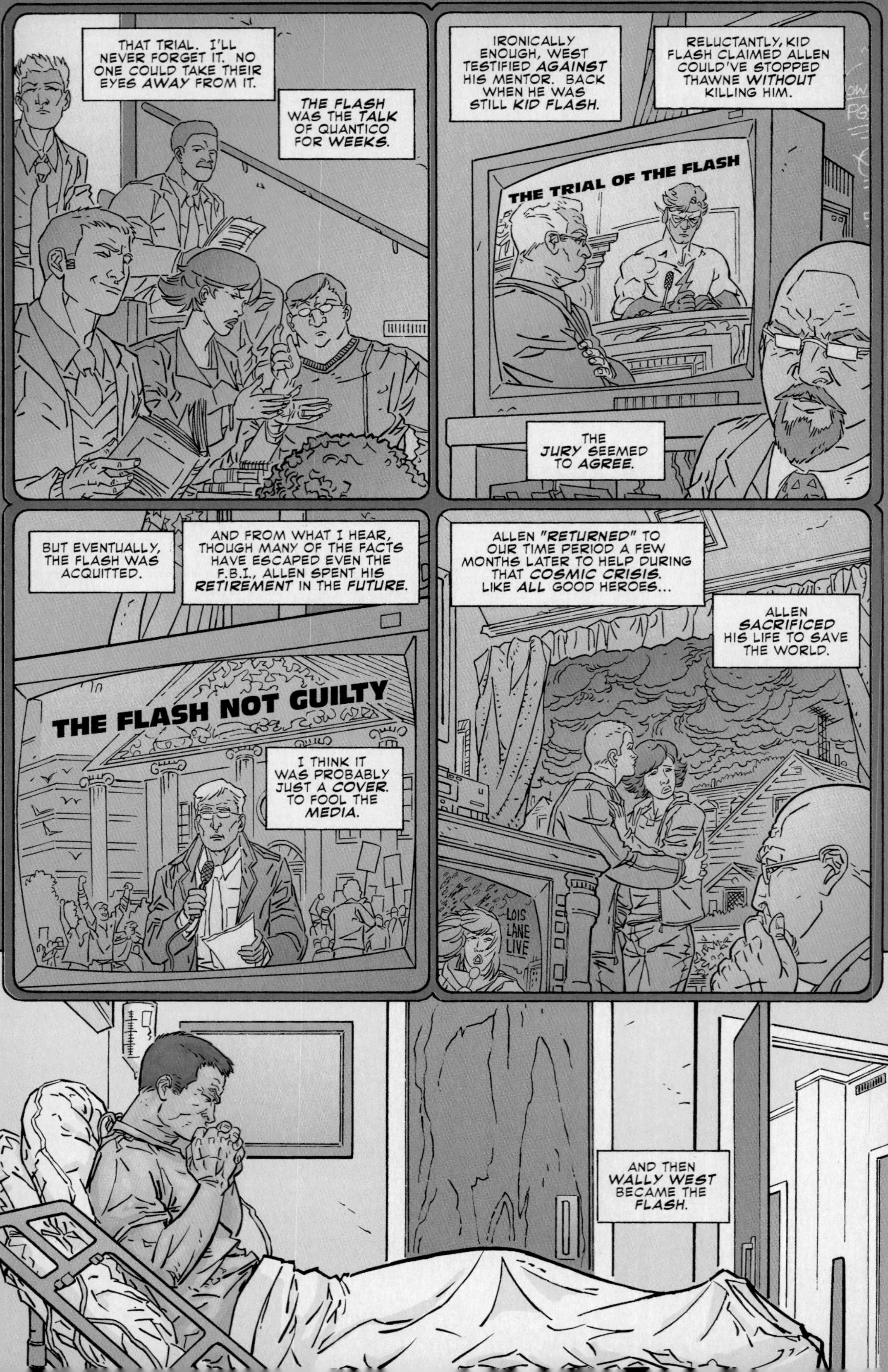
THAT TRIAL. I'LL NEVER FORGET IT. NO ONE COULD TAKE THEIR EYES AWAY FROM IT.
THE FLASH WAS THE TALK OF QUANTICO FOR WEEKS.
IRONICALLY ENOUGH, WEST TESTIFIED AGAINST HIS MENTOR. BACK WHEN HE WAS STILL KID FLASH.
RELUCTANTLY, KID FLASH CLAIMED ALLEN COULD'VE STOPPED THAWNE WITHOUT KILLING HIM.
THE TRIAL OF THE FLASH
THE JURY SEEMED TO AGREE.
BUT EVENTUALLY, THE FLASH WAS ACQUITTED.
AND FROM WHAT I HEAR, THOUGH MANY OF THE FACTS HAVE ESCAPED EVEN THE F.B.I., ALLEN SPENT HIS RETIREMENT IN THE FUTURE.
THE FLASH NOT GUILTY
I THINK IT WAS PROBABLY JUST A COVER. TO FOOL THE MEDIA.
ALLEN "RETURNED" TO OUR TIME PERIOD A FEW MONTHS LATER TO HELP DURING THAT COSMIC CRISIS. LIKE ALL GOOD HEROES...
ALLEN SACRIFICED HIS LIFE TO SAVE THE WORLD.
LOIS LANE LIVE
AND THEN WALLY WEST BECAME THE FLASH.

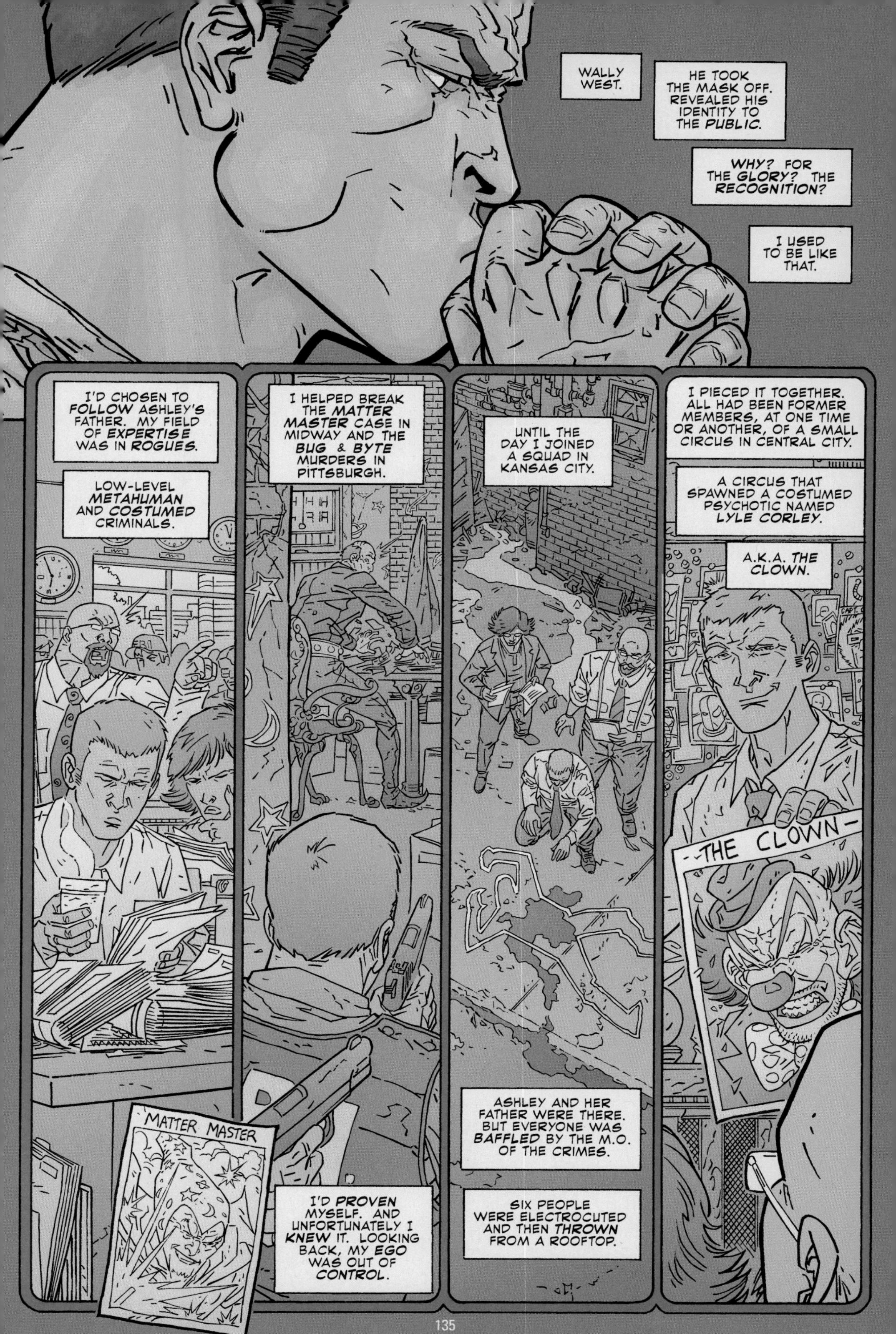
WALLY WEST.
HE TOOK THE MASK OFF. REVEALED HIS IDENTITY TO THE PUBLIC.
WHY? FOR THE GLORY? THE RECOGNITION?
I USED TO BE LIKE THAT.
I'D CHOSEN TO FOLLOW ASHLEY'S FATHER. MY FIELD OF EXPERTISE WAS IN ROGUES.
LOW-LEVEL METAHUMAN AND COSTUMED CRIMINALS.
MATTER MASTER
I HELPED BREAK THE MATTER MASTER CASE IN MIDWAY AND THE BUG & BYTE MURDERS IN PITTSBURGH.
I'D PROVEN MYSELF. AND UNFORTUNATELY I KNEW IT. LOOKING BACK, MY EGO WAS OUT OF CONTROL.
UNTIL THE DAY I JOINED A SQUAD IN KANSAS CITY.
ASHLEY AND HER FATHER WERE THERE. BUT EVERYONE WAS BAFFLED BY THE M.O. OF THE CRIMES.
SIX PEOPLE WERE ELECTROCUTED AND THEN THROWN FROM A ROOFTOP.
I PIECED IT TOGETHER. ALL HAD BEEN FORMER MEMBERS, AT ONE TIME OR ANOTHER, OF A SMALL CIRCUS IN CENTRAL CITY.
A CIRCUS THAT SPAWNED A COSTUMED PSYCHOTIC NAMED LYLE CORLEY.
A.K.A. THE CLOWN.
THE CLOWN

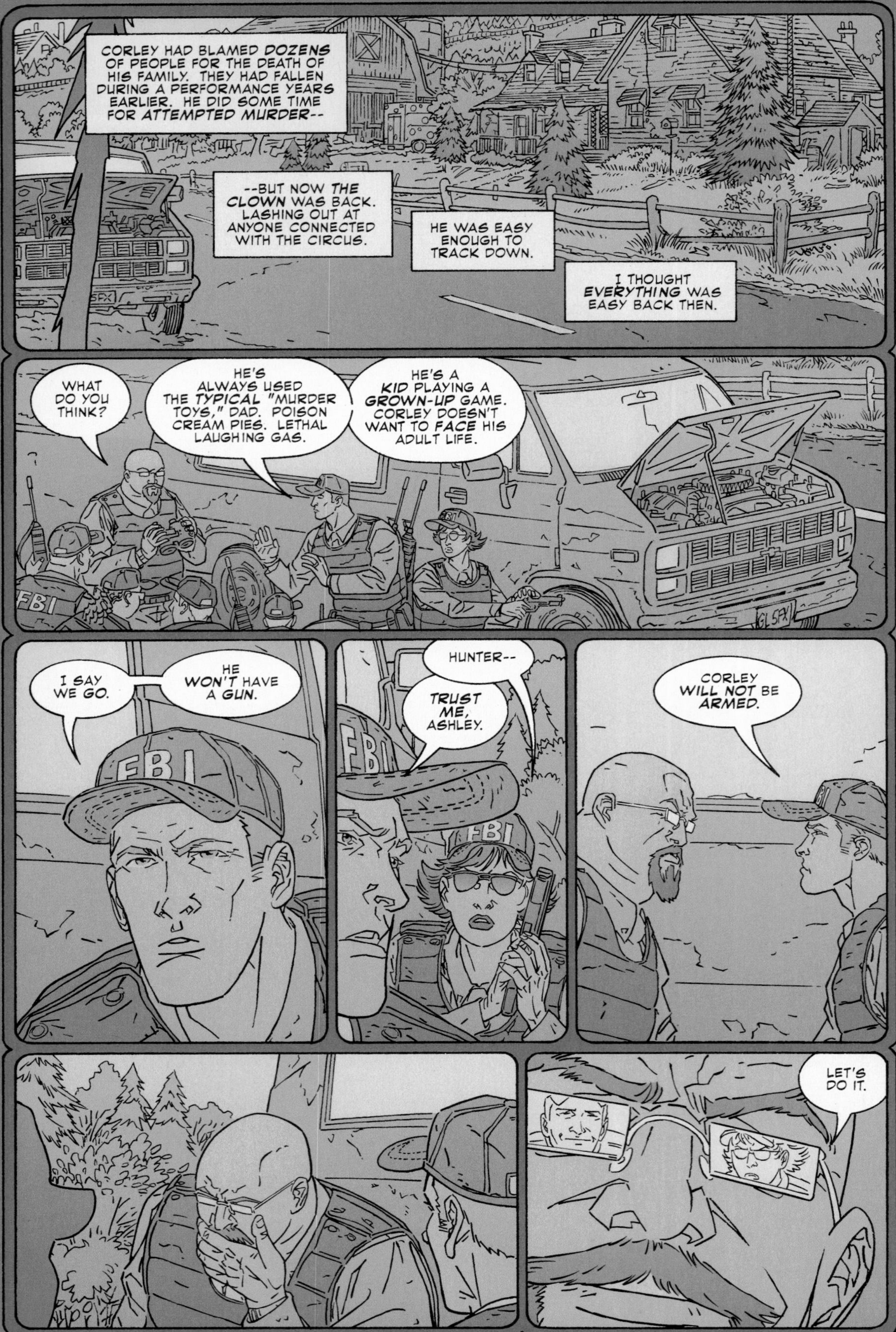
CORLEY HAD BLAMED DOZENS OF PEOPLE FOR THE DEATH OF HIS FAMILY. THEY HAD FALLEN DURING A PERFORMANCE YEARS EARLIER. HE DID SOME TIME FOR ATTEMPTED MURDER--
--BUT NOW THE CLOWN WAS BACK. LASHING OUT AT ANYONE CONNECTED WITH THE CIRCUS.
HE WAS EASY ENOUGH TO TRACK DOWN.
I THOUGHT EVERYTHING WAS EASY BACK THEN.
WHAT DO YOU THINK?
HE'S ALWAYS USED THE TYPICAL "MURDER TOYS," DAD. POISON CREAM PIES. LETHAL LAUGHING GAS.
HE'S A KID PLAYING A GROWN-UP GAME. CORLEY DOESN'T WANT TO FACE HIS ADULT LIFE.
I SAY WE GO.
HE WON'T HAVE A GUN.
HUNTER--
TRUST ME, ASHLEY.
CORLEY WILL NOT BE ARMED.
LET'S DO IT.

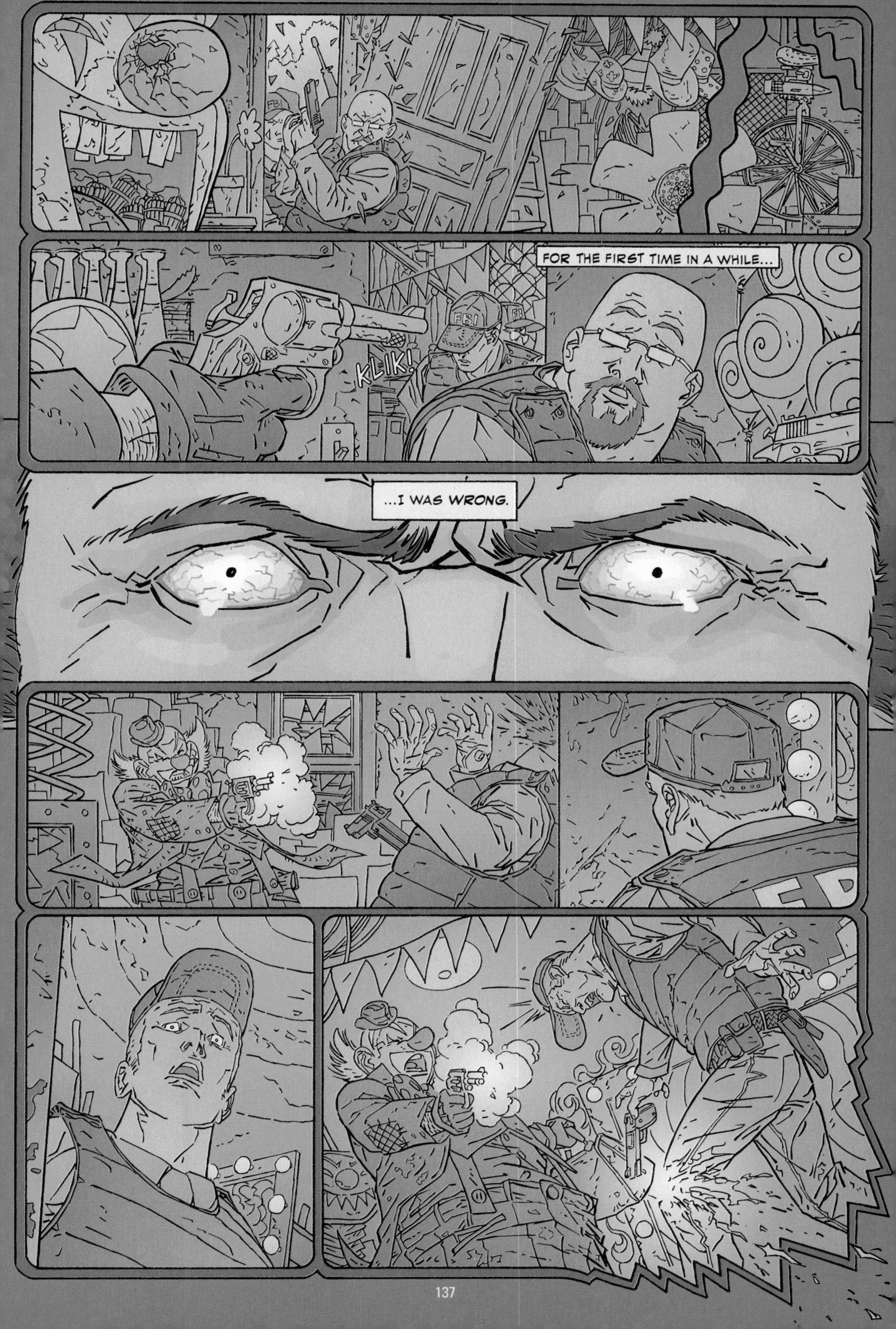
FOR THE FIRST TIME IN A WHILE...
KLIK!
...I WAS WRONG.

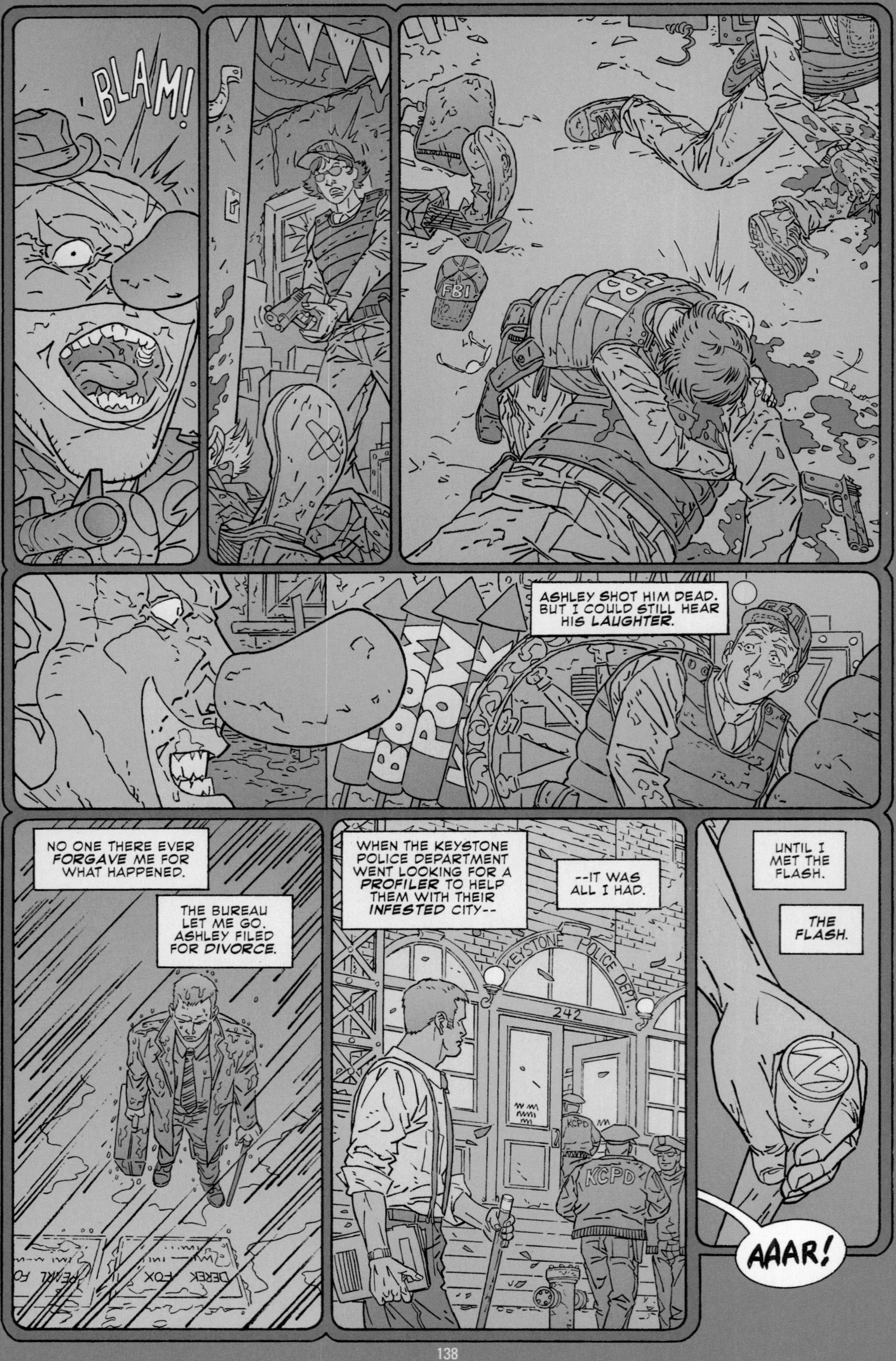
BLAM!
FBI
ASHLEY SHOT HIM DEAD. BUT I COULD STILL HEAR HIS *LAUGHTER*.
NO ONE THERE EVER *FORGAVE* ME FOR WHAT HAPPENED.
THE BUREAU LET ME GO. ASHLEY FILED FOR *DIVORCE*.
WHEN THE KEYSTONE POLICE DEPARTMENT WENT LOOKING FOR A *PROFILER* TO HELP THEM WITH THEIR *INFESTED* CITY--
--IT WAS ALL I HAD.
KEYSTONE POLICE DEPT.
242
KCPD
KCPD
UNTIL I MET THE FLASH.
THE FLASH.
AAAR!

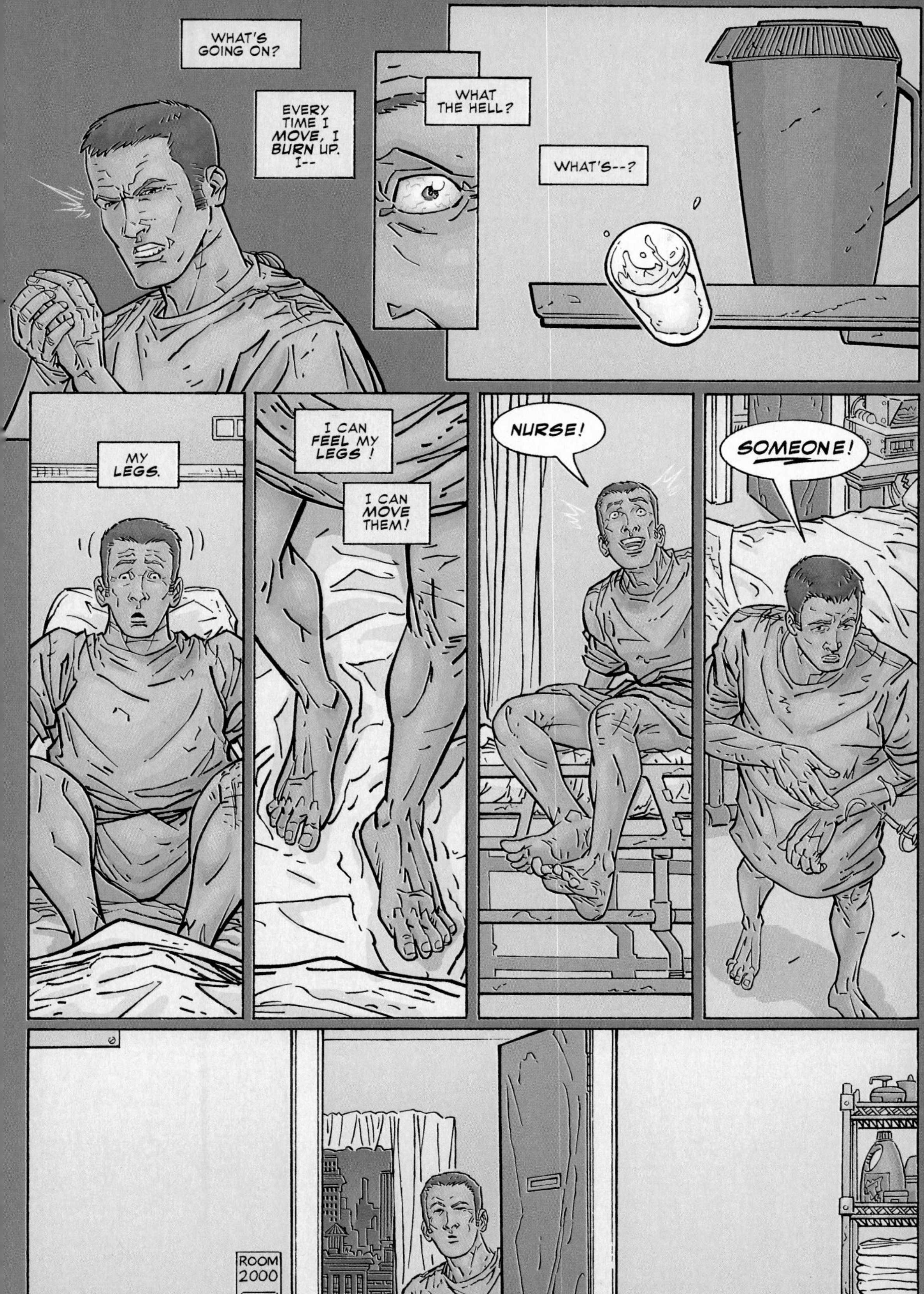

WHAT'S GOING ON?
EVERY TIME I MOVE, I BURN UP. I--
WHAT THE HELL?
WHAT'S--?
MY LEGS.
I CAN FEEL MY LEGS!
I CAN MOVE THEM!
NURSE!
SOMEONE!
ROOM 2000

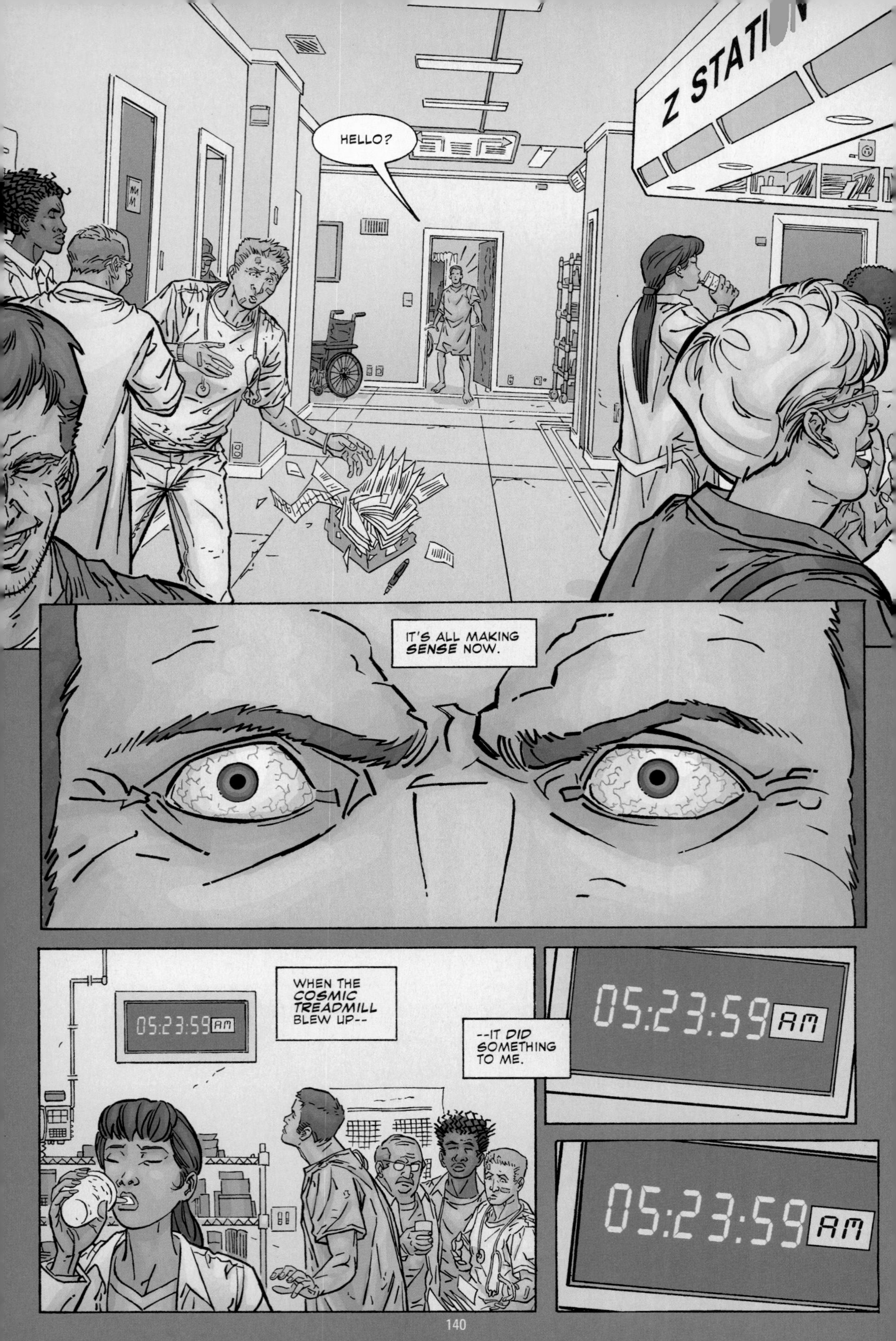
Z STATI
HELLO?
IT'S ALL MAKING SENSE NOW.
05:23:59 AM
WHEN THE COSMIC TREADMILL BLEW UP--
--IT DID SOMETHING TO ME.
05:23:59 AM
05:23:59 AM

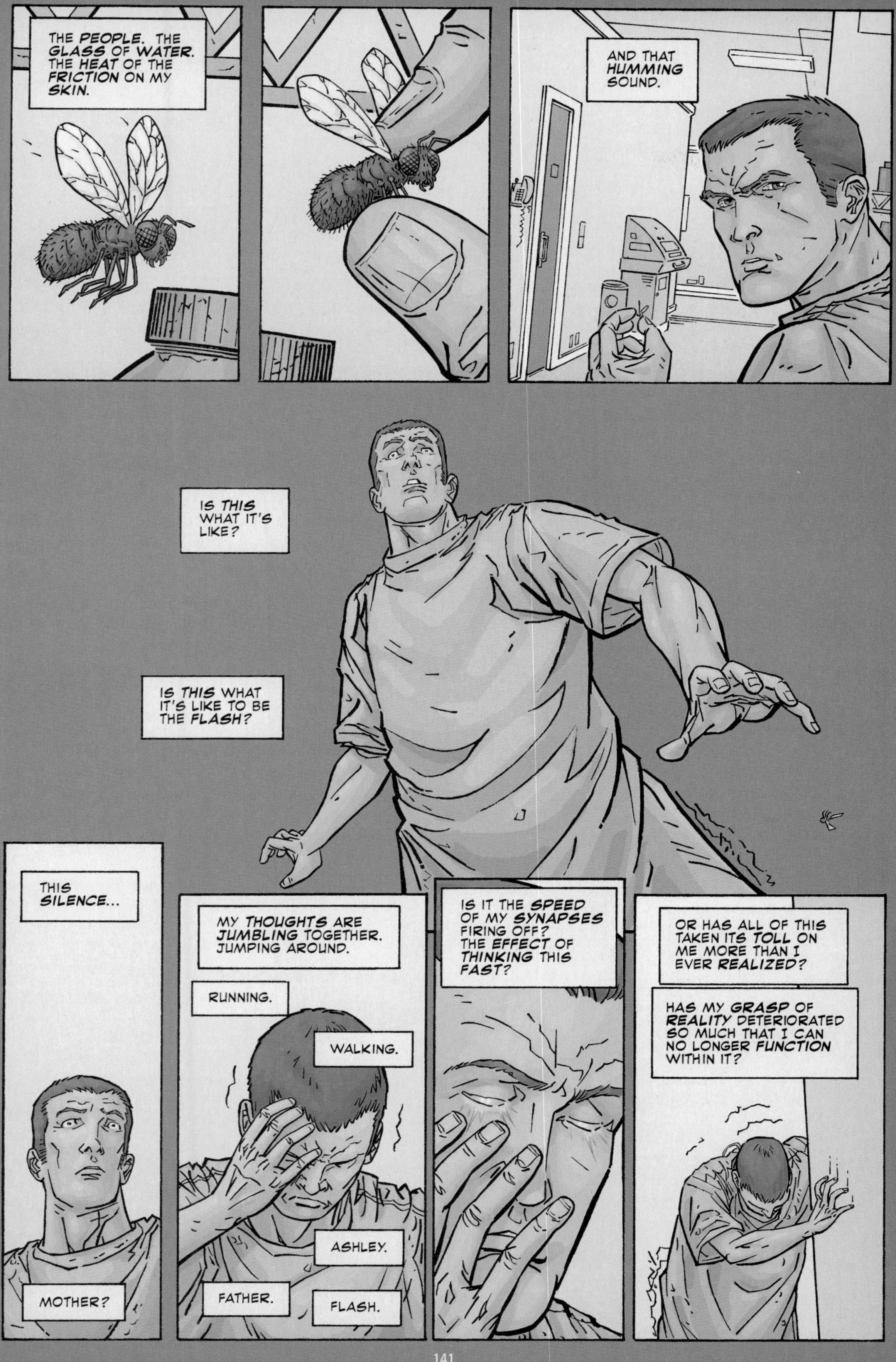
THE PEOPLE. THE GLASS OF WATER. THE HEAT OF THE FRICTION ON MY SKIN.
AND THAT HUMMING SOUND.
IS THIS WHAT IT'S LIKE?
IS THIS WHAT IT'S LIKE TO BE THE FLASH?
THIS SILENCE...
MOTHER?
MY THOUGHTS ARE JUMBLING TOGETHER. JUMPING AROUND.
RUNNING.
WALKING.
ASHLEY.
FATHER.
FLASH.
IS IT THE SPEED OF MY SYNAPSES FIRING OFF? THE EFFECT OF THINKING THIS FAST?
OR HAS ALL OF THIS TAKEN ITS TOLL ON ME MORE THAN I EVER REALIZED?
HAS MY GRASP OF REALITY DETERIORATED SO MUCH THAT I CAN NO LONGER FUNCTION WITHIN IT?

IS IT THE *COSMIC TREADMILL* THAT'S DONE THIS TO ME--

Z STATION

--OR JUST MY MIND?

MY PSYCHIC COHESION IS *BREAKING* DOWN, ISN'T IT?

THE *THOUGHTS* IN MY HEAD AREN'T *RATIONAL*. THEY'RE *EMOTIONAL*.

IS THAT *RIGHT?* WHAT *MOTIVATES* THESE THOUGHTS? WHAT...

IF THIS REALLY *IS* HAPPENING... IT'S A *SIGN*.

I TRIED TO TELL THE FLASH BEFORE. THE *BEST* HEROES ARE THE HEROES WHO WILL TAKE *RISKS* TO HELP PEOPLE.

WHO HAVE *FACED* UNBELIEVABLE *TRAGEDY* AND *UNDERSTAND* WHY IT *MUST* BE PREVENTED.

AT *ANY* COST.

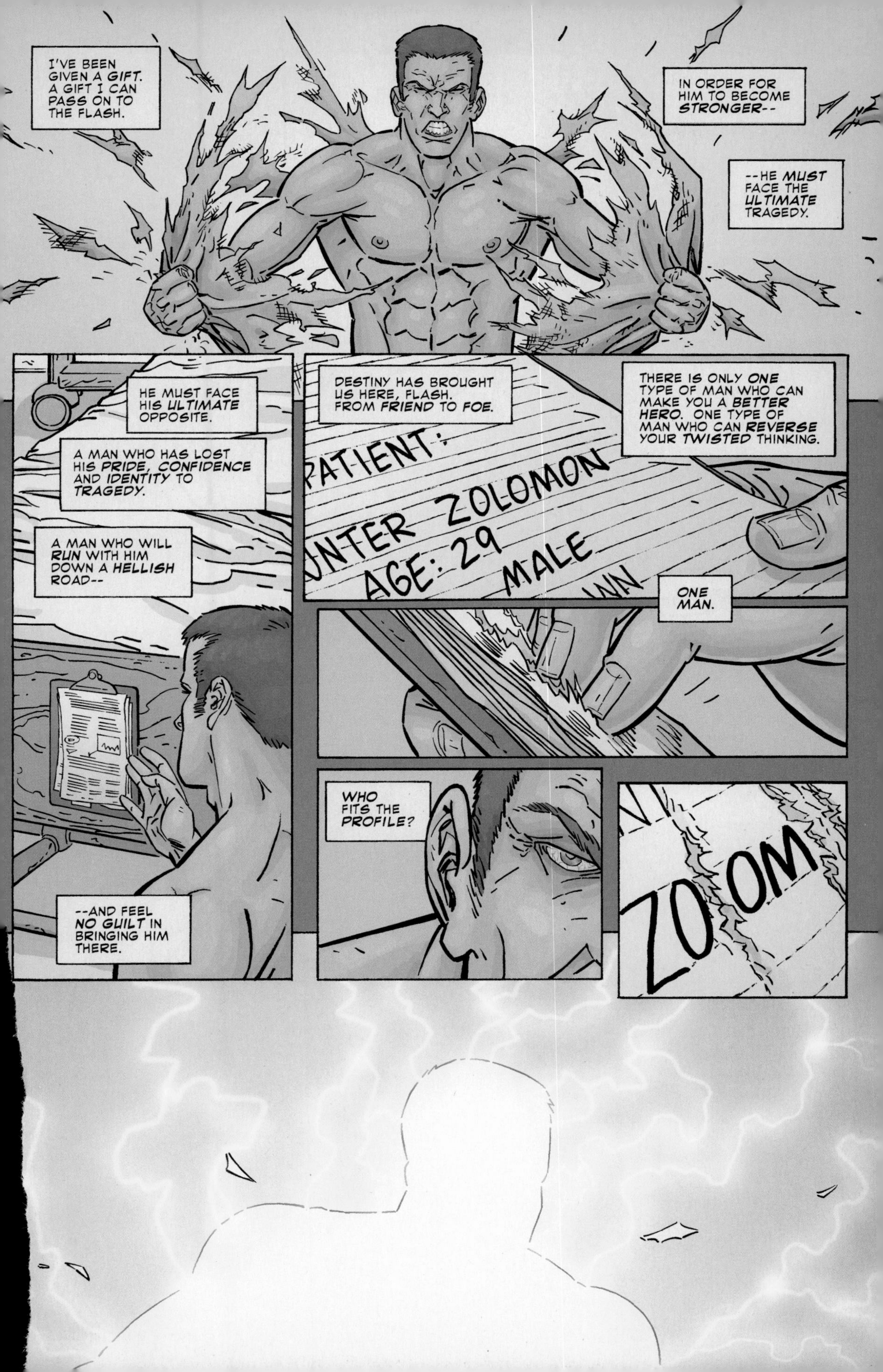
I'VE BEEN GIVEN A GIFT. A GIFT I CAN PASS ON TO THE FLASH.
IN ORDER FOR HIM TO BECOME STRONGER--
--HE MUST FACE THE ULTIMATE TRAGEDY.
HE MUST FACE HIS ULTIMATE OPPOSITE.
A MAN WHO HAS LOST HIS PRIDE, CONFIDENCE AND IDENTITY TO TRAGEDY.
A MAN WHO WILL RUN WITH HIM DOWN A HELLISH ROAD--
--AND FEEL NO GUILT IN BRINGING HIM THERE.
DESTINY HAS BROUGHT US HERE, FLASH. FROM FRIEND TO FOE.
THERE IS ONLY ONE TYPE OF MAN WHO CAN MAKE YOU A BETTER HERO. ONE TYPE OF MAN WHO CAN REVERSE YOUR TWISTED THINKING.
PATIENT:
UNTER ZOLOMON
AGE: 29
MALE
ONE MAN.
WHO FITS THE PROFILE?
ZOOM

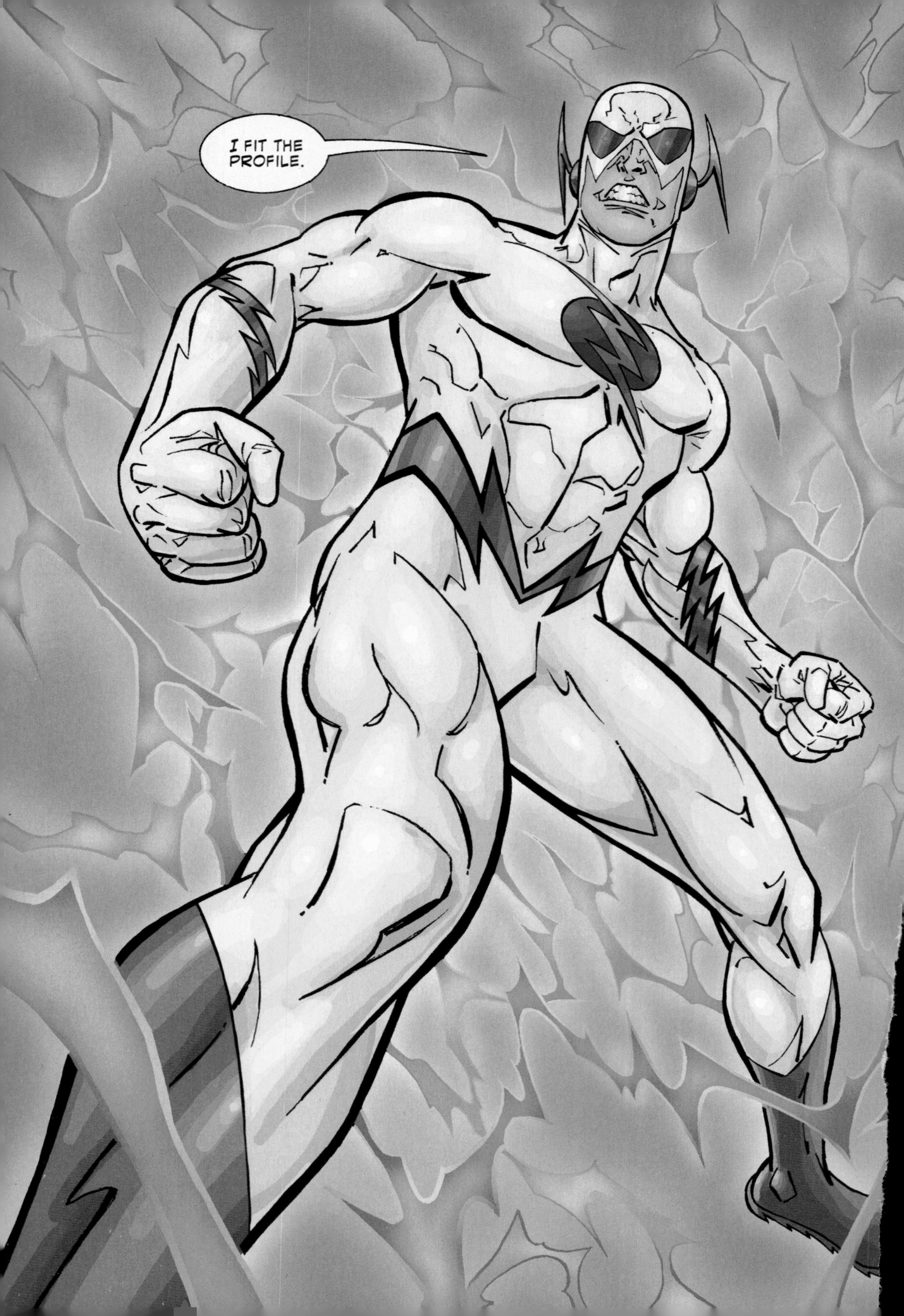
I FIT THE PROFILE.